Eritrea, the newest nation-state in Africa, gained independence from the Ethiopian state after a prolonged and bitter conflict. This book is the first comprehensive analysis of the country's political history over the past three decades. It examines the origins of Eritrean nationalism, and charts the development of its various nationalist movements, assessing the programmes and capabilities of the parties contending for power. It also analyses the regional and international context within which the battles for independence were fought.

'... an extremely useful and ... balanced account of the history of the Eritrean liberation movement', *African Affairs*

The Eritrean struggle for independence

African studies series 82

A list of books in the series will be found at the end of the volume

The Eritrean struggle for independence

Domination, resistance, nationalism, 1941–1993

Ruth Iyob

University of Missouri – St Louis

CAMBRIDGE
UNIVERSITY PRESS

Published by the Press Syndicate of the University of Cambridge
The Pitt Building, Trumpington Street, Cambridge CB2 1RP
40 West 20th Street, New York, NY 10011-4211, USA
10 Stamford Road, Oakleigh, Melbourne 3166, Australia

First published 1995
First paperback edition published 1997

Printed in Great Britain at the University Press, Cambridge

A catalogue record for this book is available from the British Library

Library of Congress cataloguing in publication data

Iyob, Ruth, 1957–
The Eritrean struggle for independence : domination, resistence,
nationalism, 1941–1993 / Ruth Iyob.
      p.   cm. – (African studies series : 82)
Includes bibliographical references.
ISBN 0 521 47327 6
1. Eritrea (Ethiopia) – History – Autonomy and Independence
movements.   2. Eritrea (Ethiopia) – Politics and
government – 1941–1952.   3. Eritrea (Ethiopia) – Politics and
government – 1952–1962.   4. Eritrea (Ethiopia) – Politics and
government – 1962–1991.   5. Eritrea (Ethiopia) – Politics and
government – 1991– I. Title.   II. Series.
DT397.I96   1995
963.505 – dc20   94-12845–CIP

ISBN 0 521 47327 6 hardback
ISBN 0 521 59591 6 paperback

SE

This book is dedicated to the memory of

Dr. Iyob Teklu
1926–1977

A gentle father, a loyal friend, and an intellectual of his time who did not live long enough to witness the *dénouement* of contemporary Eritrea's narrative.

Contents

Acknowledgements   *page* xi
List of abbreviations   xiii
Map 1 The principal towns of Eritrea   xv
Map 2 The boundaries of Eritrea   xvi

Introduction   1

Part I

1   The Eritrean question in perspective   11

2   Regional hegemony in the post-World War II order   29

3   Eritrea and the African order   47

Part II

4   The origins of the Eritrean conflict   61

5   The federation years: 1952–1962   82

6   Secular nationalism: the creative radicalism of the ELM   98

7   Defiant nationalism: the ELF and the EPLF, 1961–1981   108

8   The EPLF's quest for legitimacy   123

9   Building the Eritrean polity   136

Notes   149
Bibliography   180
Index   193

Acknowledgements

Many people have contributed in the making of this book. I owe a special debt to Victor T. Le Vine who read and commented on the multiple versions of the draft and provided me with constant encouragement and support. He has been a wonderful friend, colleague and mentor. Special thanks are due to Edmond J. Keller for help and encouragement through difficult times. His comments were incisive and right on target. I am also very grateful to René Lemarchand for inspiration and support. I learned a great deal and benefited enormously from all these contributions but any errors or misinterpretations are mine.

I would also like to thank Dr. Richard Joseph at the Institute of African Studies and the Department of Political Science at Emory University for providing me with a postdoctoral fellowship which enabled me to complete this work. I am indebted to Dean Eleanor Main, who facilitated two field trips to Eritrea and Ethiopia to bring my research to date. I would like to express my appreciation to Harvey Klehr who allowed me a great deal of flexibility in my teaching schedule and to Cornell Hooten and David Davis for giving me much-needed computer assistance in the preparation of the final draft.

I would like to acknowledge the various people, institutions and organizations who assisted me in my archival research abroad. Special thanks are due to the FORD Foundation, the Graduate Division of the University of California at Santa Barbara; to Memher Alemseged of the Research and Information Center on Eritrea (RICE), Dr. Carla Ghezzi of the Istituto Italo-Africano, Dr. Fessehatzion Petros of the EPLF office, and the representatives of the ELF and ELF-UO in Rome for allowing me access to their archives. Dr. Alexander Naty took time out from his research to familiarize me with the Institute's holdings and Solomon Abraha and Michael Ghezzhei provided me with the logistical support which made my stay in Rome productive.

I would also like to express my gratitude to those people who shared their ideas, experiences and materials with me. Special thanks are due to Woizero Zewdi Gebremeskel Woldu who made her father's papers available to me and Dr. Tekie Fessehatzion and Roy Pateman who generously shared their collections. Special thanks are due to Sewit Bocresion who came to the rescue with her computer and printer for the final printout. Time and space do not permit me to thank all those who enriched my work in one way or another. Their contributions are appreciated. A final word of thanks to Jessica Kuper of Cambridge University Press who was encouraging and supportive during the evolution of the manuscript to its present form.

Friends and colleagues eased the burden of the long hours of research and re-writing. I owe special debts to Dr. Belai Ghiorghis for his constant support that never failed to spur me on; Menbere and Mekbib Surafiel who opened up their minds and homes to me; Mengesha Yohannes for his unfailing friendship and sense of humour and Charlene N. Kass for sharing my moments of sorrow and triumph. I am grateful to William Hughes for his critical comments and editorial help; to Boris Young for widening my horizons and introducing me to the vast literature on resistance and nationalism; to Kelly Hwang for initiating me into the art and technology of computer-based research; to Zion Yohannes, Almaz G. Dh-ar and Semai G. Berhe who were always there when needed. I would also like to thank Haruhiro Fukui who always made time to hear my ideas and encourage me to pursue my research further and Fernando Lopez-Alves, who kept my flair for the melodramatic in check. Without their friendship and support the arduous task of completing this work would have been a lonely and alienating endeavor.

My deepest gratitude goes to my extended family – Mehret, Ararat, Senait, Salome, Hendekye, Aradom, Hannibal, Simon and Biniam Iyob; Lul Ghiorghis; Bev, Selwyn, Brad and Kirby Hotchner; Dianne, Byron, Sally and Eric Samuelson; Habitit Beyene and Kuflom Ghiorghis; Mildred and William Gellerman; Joe and Belle Innis; James, Anita and David DeClue – for their unwavering faith in me.

Finally, I gratefully acknowledge Oxford University Press for permission to use extracts from G. K. N. Trevaskis, *Eritrea: A Colony in Transition 1941–52*, London: Oxford University Press, 1960.

Abbreviations

ALF	Afar Liberation Front
ANC	African National Congress
BMA	British Military Administration
CFM	Council of Foreign Ministers
EDF	Eritrean Democratic Front
EDM	Eritrean Democratic Movement
EDMLE	Eritrean Democratic Movement for the Liberation of Eritrea
EFLNA	Eritreans for Liberation in North America
ELF	Eritrean Liberation Front
ELF–PLF	Eritrean Liberation Front–People's Liberation Front
ELM	Eritrean Liberation Movement
EPDM	Ethiopian People's Democratic Movement
EPRDF	Ethiopian People's Revolutionary Democratic Front
EPLA	Eritrean People's Liberation Army
EPLF	Eritrean People's Liberation Front
EPRP	Ethiopian People's Revolutionary Party
ETEL	Eritrean Toilers' Emancipation League
EWVA	Eritrean War Veterans Association
FPC	Four Powers Commission
FPLC	First Panel of Legal Consultants
FRELIMO	Frente de Libertação de Mozambique
IAE	Intellectual Association of Eritreans
IEA	Italo-Eritrean Association
IEP	Independent Eritrea Party
IEUP	Independent Eritrea United with Ethiopia Party
IML	Independent Moslem League
LPP	Liberal Progressive Party
LUP	Liberal Unionist Party
MFHE	Mahber Fikri Hager Ertra
ML	Moslem League
MLWP	Moslem League of Western Province

MPLA	Movimiento Popular de Libertação de Angola
MTA	Mahber Teatre Asmara
NDP	National Democratic Program
NEP	New Eritrea Party
NEPIP	New Eritrea Pro-Italia Party
NGO	Non-governmental organization
NMPM	National Moslem Party of Massawa
NPM	National Party of Massawa
OAU	Organization of African Unity
OLF	Oromo Liberation Front
PAFMECA	Pan-African Freedom Movement of East and Central Africa
PDRY	People's Democratic Republic of Yemen
PGE	Provisional Government of Eritrea
PLO	Palestine Liberation Organization
POLISARIO	Frente Popular para la Liberación de Saguia el-Hamra y Rio de Oro
RICE	Research and Information Center on Eritrea
SCP	Sudanese Communist Party
SLF	Sidama Liberation Front
SNM	Somali National Movement
SPLC	Second Panel of Legal Consultants
SSF	Somali Salvation Front
SWAPO	South-West Africa People's Organization
TGE	Transitional Government of Ethiopia
TPLF	Tigrayan People's Liberation Front
UN	United Nations
UNOVER	United Nations Observer Mission to Verify the Referendum in Eritrea
UP	Unionist Party
WSLF	Western Somali Liberation Front
ZANU	Zimbabwe African National Union

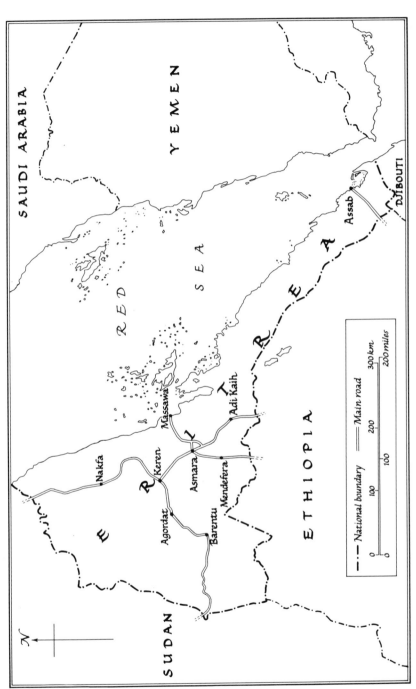

Map 1 The principal towns of Eritrea

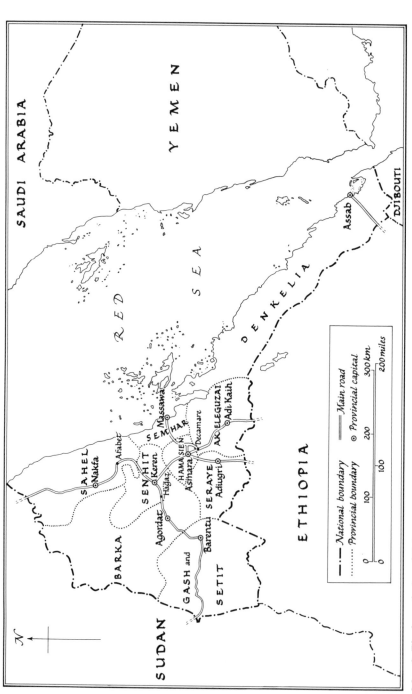

Map 2 The boundaries of Eritrea

Note: These boundaries were correct at the time of going to press.

Introduction

> The capricious manner of Eritrea's creation, its long history of immigrations, invasions, and partition between alien rulers, and the physical diversity of its terrain have left their stamp on the inhabitants. They are not in any accepted sense a single people but a conglomerate of different communities which are themselves in most cases akin by culture and blood to their neighbors in Ethiopia, the Sudan and French Somaliland.
>
> G.K.N. Trevaskis, *Eritrea: A Colony in Transition, 1941–1952,* London: Oxford University Press, 1960, p. 11

On May 24, 1993, Eritrea declared its independence. It was a time of great celebration as Eritrea emerged as Africa's fifty-second nation-state and ended its exclusion from the international and African political arena. In the words of President Issaias Afeworki, speaking on Independence Day: "Let us rejoice that our dream and aspirations of attaining national sovereignty and dignity have been realized." The "conglomerate of different communities" who had been strangers to each other in the 1940s and 1950s had developed an all-encompasing national identity during the long years of armed struggle. In response to continuous efforts by the Ethiopian state to impose a single Ethiopian identity, the Eritrean nationalists had emphasized the diversity of its people. The Ethiopian regimes' habitual resort to coercion and the continued resistance to Ethiopian hegemony had fostered a sense of solidarity and a shared identity among the nine Eritrean ethnic groups. With the attainment of national sovereignty the long and painful chapter of nationalist resistance, civil war and armed struggle against Ethiopian hegemony was closed.

This characteristic of being an artificial construct of colonial empire-building is not unique to Eritrea or its people. What distinguishes Eritrea from the other former colonies in Africa is that this feature – the establishment of new boundaries and the creation of "a colonial construct" – was used to deny official recognition to Eritrea as a country and to its people as Eritreans.

The appeal for a "room ... a country of one's own"[1] characterizes

1

Eritrea's post-colonial history. The Eritrean saga began with the dream of "a country of one's own," a dream, however, which was soon thereafter compromised into acceptance of a "federal" arrangement, which provided "a room of one's own" under the sovereignty of an absolutist empire.

Imperial control soon stifled all autonomy and the room's inhabitants rebelled, reviving the old dream in the process. Once incorporated within the vast imperial edifice they sought to change the rules of occupancy. Civil disobedience was followed by clandestine opposition and armed resistance. Before long, the inhabitants forged a common identity and devised creative strategies to escape from their status as unwilling guests.

This book focuses on the quest for an Eritrean nation, and why it took so long to achieve. It is a narrative told from within and from without; it describes the intricate skeins of competing visions, disparate dreams, wars, and destruction painfully woven into a new national tapestry. The main strands of the Eritrean narrative (common themes in the post-World War II era) are domination, resistance, liberation, and competing nationalisms.

What is so compelling in this particular narrative from the northeastern corner of the Horn of Africa is that in the Eritrean case, the dream of having one's own country was fulfilled after thirty years of armed struggle against the formidable military and diplomatic might of the Ethiopian state sanctioned and supported by both superpowers at different historical periods. That achievement is also significant because it was the first successful secession in post-colonial Africa.

The Eritrean dream came tantalizingly close to fulfillment on three occasions before it was finally realized. The first time was when Italian colonial rule ended in 1941, only to be replaced by a British caretaker administration until 1952. The second was in 1952, when the dream was compromised in order to appease Ethiopian claims, and the aspirations to a "country of one's own" were reduced to "a room of one's own" within the neighboring empire's larger and more powerful structure. The United Nations (UN) resolution to federate Eritrea under the Ethiopian Crown rode roughshod over a series of unaddressed Eritrean grievances and eliminated what little remained of the façade of Eritrean autonomy. In 1961 a new chapter began: one marked by open defiance leading to war. The dream was revived again by Eritrean guerrilla armies, and the demand for self-determination was invoked to echo the desire for a country of one's own. On November 14, 1962 even the illusion of a "room of one's own" was shattered by the annexation of the territory and its classification as Ethiopia's fourteenth province. The third time the dream almost came true was in 1974, when Emperor Haile Selassie's empire was replaced by a Marxist regime. The hope that the new Ethiopian revolutionary government might recognize Eritrean aspirations quickly proved to be a delusion.

Three times denied their dream, the Eritreans now had no other recourse than to take their destiny into their own hands.

This book began as an attempt to find an answer to what appears to be a simple question: Why did it take so long for Eritrea to emerge into nationhood? Again, that answer is neither simple nor easily expressed. To begin with, Eritrea is more than a land mass or territory. On the figurative level, it is an entity constructed from the encounters with Italian colonialism, Ethiopian hegemony, and the post-1945 international state system. Thus, for those who claim Eritrean identity, it is a space of their own – shared by different ethnic, linguistic and religious groups – but distinguishable nevertheless from the Ethiopian identity imposed upon them by a powerful neighbor and an indifferent world. For them, Eritrea signifies that bounded domain to which they can lay claim and within which they can validate their right of occupancy. The sense of nationhood achieved after three decades of struggle also transcends the legacy of fragmentation that characterized traditional Eritrean society. Those cleavages, religious and regional in character, had split the nationalists in the 1940s and persisted into the 1980s. It was only during the 1980s, when the single imperative of liberation from Ethiopian hegemonic control emerged to unite the Eritrean factions, that an all-encompassing nationalism was achieved. Eritrea thus ceased to be a mere dream and became a reality because those who shared in its construction attained the capabilities needed to counter those of its main opponent, Ethiopia.

Viewed from the perspective of the Ethiopian state, Eritrea meant possession of a prized corridor to the Red Sea. Emperor Haile Selassie's diplomacy and shrewd manipulation of Eritrean rivalries during the 1940s succeeded in gaining him imperial control over this geostrategic terrain. It was a dream come true for the shrewd and ambitious emperor. However, although the initial acquisition of the territory was relatively cost-effective for Haile Selassie, it eventually turned into the nightmare that ultimately destroyed his empire.

The military regime that succeeded Haile Selassie, the *Dergue*, continued the imperial tradition of combining clever diplomacy with military campaigns but justified its methods by new ideological symbols (Ethiopian Socialism, Marxism–Leninism). Earlier, the acquisition of the former Italian colony had become a source of diplomatic leverage in the Cold War, which translated into millions of dollars in economic and military aid. The astute manipulation of regional and international interests by both the imperial and Afro-Marxist regimes legitimated and buttressed Ethiopia's thirty-year war to contain the "secessionist threat" from Eritrea. Thus, for Ethiopia's immediate neighbors the war became a hotbed of conflict whose spill-over of refugees and guerrillas either forced them into confrontation with Addis Ababa or pressured them into acquiescence with Ethiopian policies.

Eritrea, however, is more than a corridor to the Red Sea, more than an artificial colonial creation carved by the Italians from the eastern Horn of Africa in the late 1880s. It first came into being as part of Italian aspirations to colonial grandeur which were later dashed by the reality of defeat in World War II. What remained was an unfinished script to an uncompleted play, and a stage on which the ill-prepared Eritrean actors were left to devise their own lines and action. Suddenly freed from colonial direction, they moved about the stage in confusion, animated by largely inchoate, contradictory, and competing nationalist agendas. Most painful, however, was the realization that within the new borders of what had been hailed in 1890 as Italy's "first-born colony" (*la colonia primogenita*), its different communities were in fact strangers to one another. With the end of Italian rule and the arrival of a British caretaker military administration "Eritreans" were forced to interact with each other on a stage not of their own making. More important, they were now being asked to act as a self-conscious unit at a time when the majority of the inhabitants had not yet come to see themselves as part of a nation.

Until the establishment of Italian centralized colonial administration the ties that bound the various peoples of Eritrea had been based on kinship, lineage, culture, and region. The establishment of Italy's colonial rule enclosed these disparate communities within a single administrative system. Between 1890 and 1941 Eritrea came into existence and a narrative of "Eritrean" experience began to unfold. As in the rest of colonized Africa, political, economic, and social transformations in varying degrees began to take place in Eritrea. The demographics of the territory changed as cities were built and groups migrated (voluntarily and involuntarily) to new areas. Eritrean *askaris* fought Italy's wars in Libya, Somalia, and Ethiopia. Rebellious chieftains were either coopted, coerced, or replaced in the new colony. The story of the Italian occupation is both long and complex; its details need not detain us at this point. What is important is that however the Italian period is judged, for good or for ill, what emerged from it were the outlines of an Eritrean consciousness, an awareness which the British, in their role as interim caretakers, were forced to cope with, and eventually to recognize, when they presided over the creation of the territory's first representative institutions in the late 1940s.

Then, in 1952, with the end of British rule, came the second opportunity to realize the Eritrean dream. This time, the dream was compromised by the absence of a common Eritrean vision and by Ethiopia's imperial ambitions which within nine years paved the way to the nightmare of war and devastation. Ethiopian hegemony over Eritrea was institutionalized in 1962 when the territory was proclaimed as the fourteenth province of Ethiopia.

Justified as "reunification," the demands for justice and self-determination of the Eritrean people were subordinated to the imperatives of maintaining Ethiopian unity and territorial integrity. From 1961 until 1991, Eritrean aspirations to nationhood were manifested through armed struggle.

On May 24, 1991 Eritrea's long struggle against Ethiopian hegemony ended. With the end of hostilities between Eritrean nationalists and the Ethiopian state the veil of silence that had shrouded modern Africa's longest war was lifted. Eritrea, long equated with the twin spectre of secessionism and continental balkanization, made the headlines. The armed struggle, which began in 1961, outlasted Haile Selassie's empire and continued on to challenge and finally to defeat the Afro-Marxist regime that replaced it.

This book is an attempt to explain why Eritrean resistance endured in the face of Ethiopia's diplomatic, military, and political prowess. The visibility of Ethiopian political leadership, the international support and legitimacy accorded to the costly maintenance of its most recent province, the regional consensus articulated by the Organization of African Unity (OAU) which denied legitimacy to the Eritrean demand for self-determination, and the UN's disregard for its historical responsibility, all contributed to the extraordinary length of the Eritrean–Ethiopian conflict. This book focuses on the vicissitudes of Eritrean nationalism, from its fragmented origins in 1941 to the complex process of its evolution to creative radicalism, from its defiant reaction in the 1960s until its emergence as a pragmatic and mature movement finally able to defeat Black Africa's most prestigious and well-equipped army.

Others who have written about the conflict have used the metaphor of an Eritrean David against the Ethiopian Goliath. However, in this modern version of the classic confrontation between a small territory and its giant neighbor, it appeared, until the very end, that God had favored Goliath and not David. This strange role of a divinely favored Goliath played by Ethiopia in the post-World War II period was inspired by the *realpolitik* of a bipolar international system and generously "blessed" by the super-powers. Thus, the David role of the Eritrean resistance left no room either for the glorification of noble resistance or the liberal romanticism reserved for the underdog.

What really happened to cause a people to fight so tenaciously for three decades? Why did it take the Eritreans so long to realize their dream of a nation of their own? In the effort to find answers to these questions the ugly and harsh realities of state rivalry, greed, and the corruption of power emerge with vivid clarity. At the same time, the images of the indomitable human will to survive as a collective entity, the painful articulation of shared ideals, and the gradual evolution of a common identity also emerge to balance the story.

It remains a fact that in the modern history of almost all nations, nationalism and the quest for one's own political space have caused untold misery and destruction. Eritrea, as a case in point, is not the exception but the norm. The special nature of the Eritrean case, its sustained resistance to Ethiopian hegemony, lies not in the uniqueness of its people (although none would deny them due credit), but in the particular convergence of socio-historical, economic, and political factors that shaped events in post-colonial Africa.

This book is divided into two parts. Part I introduces the concept of regional hegemony as a framework for understanding relations of domination and resistance in the post-colonial era and its application to the Eritrean–Ethiopian conflict. Part II provides a historical analysis of the conflict from its origins in 1941 until Eritrea's independence in 1993. It provides the reader with the background to the evolution of Eritrean nationalism, its development and maturation, and concludes with the establishment of an independent Eritrea in 1993.

Chapter 1 examines the various portrayals of the Eritrean–Ethiopian conflict in scholarly works and shows how these different perspectives reflect the ideological and philosophical underpinnings which served to legitimate Ethiopian claims over Eritrean demands for three decades. It introduces the concept of regional hegemony, the successor to colonial domination, which operates through the dissemination of a "regime of truth" that enables states with military, diplomatic, economic and/or geostrategic capabilities to dominate territories and inhabitants in violation of the international and regional laws of the post-colonial era.

Chapter 2 discusses the evolution of new international and regional norms, values and regulations within which the hegemon establishes the dominance of its interests. It examines the charters of the UN and the OAU and analyzes the contradictions between the ideals and the implementation of these laws. It is argued that membership of such regional and international institutions enhances a hegemon's capability to formulate and manipulate norms, values, and rules to achieve its goals even in violation of the stated goals of these organizations. This chapter provides an analysis of how Ethiopia's privileged position at both the UN and the OAU, its selective adaptation of Pan-Africanism, and its maintenance of Pan-Ethiopianism as a regime of truth constituted an exercise of hegemonic power in the post-colonial era.

Chapter 3 places the Eritrean conflict in the larger African arena. It focuses upon the transformation of anti-colonial sentiments in Eritrea into two currents of competing nationalisms: Pan-Ethiopianism and Pan-Eritreanism. This chapter examines the role of Pan-Africanism as a rationale for coercive unity which portrayed an independent Eritrea as a dual threat to the Pan-Ethiopianist and Pan-Africanist status quo, preying on fears of secession and balkanization. It addresses the philosophical, ideological, and institutional issues that led to the African consensus to deny access or support to the Eritrean liberation fronts in their struggle for self-determination.

Part II provides an analysis of the Eritrean–Ethiopian conflict and the emergence, development, fragmentation, and consolidation of Eritrean nationalism. Chapter 4 provides a historical account of the origins of the Eritrean conflict from 1941 to 1952. It chronicles the first decade of multi-party politics and introduces the reader to all political parties that emerged in Eritrea between 1946 and 1949. This chapter also discusses the absence of a common vision among Eritrean nationalists, Ethiopian imperial and ecclesiastical intervention, the politicization of religion, and the polarization of Eritrean society into two camps – pro-Ethiopian unionists and pro-independence – which led to the UN's decision to federate the territory with Ethiopia.

Chapter 5 demonstrates how Eritrea's autonomous status was gradually stripped away between 1952 and 1962 through violations of the Eritrean Constitution and an extensive network of patronage and coercion. This culminated in the abrogation of federal status in 1962 and the intensification of protest and armed struggle.

Chapter 6 introduces the Eritrean Liberation Movement (ELM), the first organization to establish the foundations of the Eritrean clandestine resistance network from 1958 to 1965. The ELM's politics of protest, its goals of secular nationalism and the formal and informal expression of popular opposition, and the replacement of the creative radicals of the ELM by those of another liberation front are discussed in detail.

Chapter 7 examines the emergence in 1961 of the second opposition group: the Eritrean Liberation Front (ELF). This involves a discussion of the challenges it faced from a splinter group, the Eritrean People's Liberation Front (EPLF), and the internal rivalry that led to fratricidal wars until its demise in 1981.

Chapter 8 analyzes the EPLF's quest for legitimacy by examining three key periods: 1969–1975, 1976–1981, and 1982–1991, culminating in the total liberation of Eritrea.

Chapter 9 provides an overview of key events in post-war Eritrea. It analyzes the demise of Ethiopian hegemony and the transformation of relations of hegemonic domination into cooperation and coexistence. It brings the reader up to date with the events leading to international and regional legitimation of the Eritrean demand for self-determination and the establishment of the first government of independent Eritrea in May 1993. This chapter concludes with a commentary on the challenges facing independent Eritrea.

Part I

1 The Eritrean question in perspective

The Eritrean question in perspective

Eritrea's war for national independence from Ethiopia was a highly debated and controversial issue for almost three decades. The predominant focus rested on the importance of retaining Ethiopia's boundaries and the preservation of the status quo. As a result, Eritrean resistance to Ethiopian hegemony was consistently misrepresented and, at times, distorted in literature dealing with the conflict prior to 1993. The academic and political discourse on the Eritrean quest for independence can be divided roughly into two approaches. The first regarded the problem of Eritrea as an "internal affair" of the Ethiopian state. This perspective characterized the Eritrean conflict as "secessionist insurgency" and/or "sectarian nationalism" directed against the historic unity of Greater Ethiopia. The second, a colonial thesis, viewed Eritrea as a colony of the Ethiopian state and characterized the Eritrean conflict as an anti-colonial revolutionary struggle.

The first perspective emphasized the pre-colonial links between the Ethiopian and Eritrean peoples. It minimized the development of a distinct Eritrean identity during the European colonial period and the crystallization of a defiant Eritrean nationalism during three decades of resistance to Ethiopian hegemony. The Eritrean–Ethiopian conflict was thus regarded as a legacy of centralization by a modernizing empire-state arising out of core–periphery tensions. A central assumption of this approach was that Eritrea constituted an integral part of modern Ethiopia, leading to the portrayal of the Eritrean armed struggle as a secessionist or civil war.

Ethiopia's long history and its recognition by classical Western writers led to a great deal of attention being paid to its historical development from antiquity to modern times. A crucial underpinning of modern scholarly works was the "Greater Ethiopia" thesis advanced by Donald N. Levine. Levine posited the existence of an organic unity of the peoples of Ethiopia by ascribing to modern Ethiopia "the image of a vast ecological area and historical arena in which kindred peoples have shared many traditions and interacted with one another for millenia."[1]

This invocation of a distant past to explain the centralized unity of modern Ethiopia was at the core of the academic debate about the Eritrean conflict. Eritrean opposition to centralized control of either the imperial or Afro-Marxist state was marginalized in this perspective, which subscribes to what Levine and others have espoused as the Greater Ethiopia framework:

(1) A continuous process of interaction of the differentiated Ethiopian peoples with one another; (2) the existence of a number of pan-Ethiopian cultural traits; and (3) a characteristic mode of response to the periodic intrusion of alien peoples.[2]

Ethiopianist literature, resting on the acceptance of the Greater Ethiopia thesis, was highly influenced by this outlook. It constrained any analysis of opposition movements which, like Eritrea's, had as their basis the rejection of the imposed unity of Greater Ethiopia. From this perspective, historic opposition to Ethiopia's coercive unity was not denied but marginalized as a phenomenon of the internal politics of Ethiopia. With particular regard to Eritrea, the Greater Ethiopia thesis led to the dichotomy between the "unified" nationalism epitomized by the Pan-Ethiopian state and the fragmented nature of Eritrean opposition.

Haggai Erlich's study of Ethiopia typified this focus. Erlich examined the socio-political factors that contributed to Ethiopia's capability to preserve its identity in the face of foreign invasions. The author's central thesis was that "Ethiopia's strength and survival stem[med] from its unique internal sociopolitical flexibility."[3] Opposition to assimilation to the Ethiopian fold was neglected except insofar as it contrasted with Ethiopian nationalism which resulted "from twenty centuries of flexible and pragmatic continuity."[4] Eritrean nationalism as a challenge to the Greater Ethiopia framework was prematurely dismissed as a:

by-product of recent history ... based essentially on the negation of Ethiopianism ... [It is] too shallow and rootless to help Eritreans overcome a historically rooted sectarianism and the temptations of destructive radicalism.[5]

Christopher Clapham, drawing on this tradition, portrayed the Eritrean–Ethiopian conflict as a result of core–periphery tension. Clapham argued that Eritrean attempts to secede from the Ethiopian state were due to the "marginalization of what had once been the core region of Ethiopia"[6] and the "political incapacity of the imperial system of government."[7] Clapham questioned the maturation of Eritrean nationalism and the capability of any of the liberation movements to transcend parochial rivalries or effectively challenge the authority of the Ethiopian state.

It is hard to suppose that despite the claims of opposition movements such a nationalism can have entirely displaced a deeply entrenched political culture, nurtured in the factionalism, conflict and warfare which have marked the area over many centuries.[8]

Like Erlich, Clapham viewed the development of the Eritrean resistance as a sectarian movement emerging out of

tensions between center and periphery ... coupled with the availability of military and diplomatic support from nearby Moslem states [which] made armed guerrilla opposition a much more viable option than in most [of] post-colonial Africa.[9]

Ethiopia's historic claims over Eritrea were reiterated in the "insider's" portrait offered by John H. Spencer. Spencer, advisor to the Ethiopian Crown from 1936 to 1974, provided a documented narrative of the imperial policies that facilitated the centralization of Ethiopian control after World War II. A careful reading of Spencer's account of Eritrea's incorporation into Ethiopia through the distortion of the federal framework yields rich information about the motives behind the centralization of Ethiopian rule over Eritrea and the origins of the ensuing conflict.

In modernizing the constitution and laws of Ethiopia to bring them in line with the innovations introduced into Eritrea by the UN Constitution for that territory, the Emperor was not acting out of liberal motives ... [Haile Selassie] was pursuing his longstanding policies of centralization and of constructing check-values against mounting pressures for liberalization.[10]

... The vote by the Assembly [in favor of federation] had certainly been engineered, and the union therefore violated the spirit of UN resolution 390V.[11]

Despite his assertion that Eritrean constitutional rights were violated by Ethiopia, the subsequent emergence of armed opposition was not seen as a conscious – or even logical – Eritrean response to Ethiopia's policies of coercive unity. Instead, the launching of armed struggle was attributed to neighboring Arab states.

The consequence of the re-integration of Eritrea was a redoubling of efforts by the Arab states, through propaganda, money and arms, to undermine the [Ethiopia–Eritrea] union.[12]

Paul B. Henze placed the Greater Ethiopia thesis within a larger geopolitical context. He did this not by emphasizing the socio-cultural dynamics of a 3,000-year historical continuum but by underscoring the crucial economic interdependence between Eritrea and Ethiopia as the primary legacy of that history. Henze's globalist interpretation of the Eritrean conflict invoked historic economic ties – Eritrea's economic non-viability and Ethiopia's dependence on Eritrean ports – which placed the conflict in the wider sphere of global competition for spheres of influence. Without regressing to economic determinism, Henze utilized the economic argument to demystify the Greater Ethiopia thesis by incorporating the language of modernization theory, Cold War ideological references, and neo-classical economics.

The Free World can help Ethiopia, including Eritrea, get free enterprise and a market economy operating again and lay the groundwork for creation of an open, pluralist society – a process well under way when the country fell into the hands of dogmatic military [Marxist-Leninist] revolutionaries.[13]

This recasting of the relations of dominance and resistance in the Horn integrated what was previously marginalized as either an "internal" Ethiopian problem or a regional phenomenon into the wider realm of global *realpolitik*.

Dissidence in the region was raised in the late 1960s to a level of insurgency by support, for reasons of great power politics, from radical Arab and distant Marxist governments for groups of predominantly conservative separatists.[14]

Thus, what was elsewhere described as "sectarian insurrection" or secession could – through Henze's eyes – best be understood as a manifestation of great power exercises with global, as well as regional and local, implications.

If Henze demystified Greater Ethiopia, he still utilized an essentially Pan-Ethiopian framework in his discussion of Eritrean self-determination. His analysis was couched in the vernacular of neo-classical liberalism, but his view of the Eritrean–Ethiopian conflict until 1991 remained constrained within the status quo of a disequilibrium favoring Ethiopian territorial integrity at the expense of Eritrean self-determination.

Eritrea's autonomy – its right to self-determination in the sense of self-rule – *is thus no longer at issue*.[15]

However, by 1992, Henze had visited Eritrea and accepted its *de facto* independence. Now "access to the Red Sea" was not merely a quarrelsome claim of the Ethiopian empire but an enormous economic incentive for Western powers to invest in Eritrea. Henze could now wax enthusiastic about the very "self-rule" which only recently he had dismissed as "no longer at issue."

As a group, these analyses suffered to varying degrees from the inability of each scholar to transcend the myth-cum-reality of "Greater Ethiopia." Levine's framework of Greater Ethiopia as a "regional network" was based on fragmentary evidence and sometimes dubious assumptions of "unity" spanning millenia. It imposed a 3,000-year historical continuum as the basis for inter-African and intra-African affairs. Levine used selective facts – ethnic, linguistic, and historical affinities – and blended them with legendary exotica to produce a doctrine – Greater Ethiopia – which obscured as much as it revealed.

Spencer subscribed to this doctrine even while condemning as "thoroughly deplorable"[16] Ethiopia's blatant disregard for international law and Eritrea's constitutionally guaranteed rights through the forcible annexation of Eritrea in 1962. Rather than place the onus on Ethiopia, Spencer conveniently redirected his major critique to the ineffectiveness of international law and authorizing bodies such as the UN in the implementation of equal and fair laws in the post-World War II era. More importantly, Spencer's work underscored, by default, the impressive capacity of the Ethiopian state to manipulate existing laws to fit its needs.

Clapham pointed out the negative consequences of both the imperial and Marxist regimes' policies of handling opposition, thus constraining his treatment of the conflict within the boundaries of internal core–periphery tension. His work, which focused on Ethiopia as the "core," did not permit a detailed analysis of the crucial dynamics fermenting in the "periphery."

Erlich so embraced the historical legitimacy of Greater Ethiopia – replete with legendary linkages to Biblical Israel – that the weight of history often pulled against the momentum of unfolding events. Erlich's insistence that Eritrean resistance was discretely linked to "an Arab movement"[17] denied the existence of both the early, secular politics of the Eritrean Liberation Movement (ELM) and the current nationalist consolidation under the EPLF. In other words, he drew upon one aspect of Eritrean resistance – Moslem separatism – and cast it as the fundamental basis of that resistance. In so doing, he either marginalized or ignored altogether the secular basis of Eritrean nationalism. This perspective likewise removed the conflict from its political, social, and economic moorings within the African community, ignoring the crucial exercise of Ethiopian diplomatic capability in the OAU and the larger issue of Ethiopia's prestige in international diplomatic circles. Nevertheless, Erlich's work effectively underscores the linkage between Ethiopia's institutional flexibility, its leadership and its maintenance of sovereignty.[18]

Henze's pre-liberation analysis offered a re-tooled Greater Ethiopia without transcending the perceptual limitations of such a view. Whether described as a centuries-long historical continuum or an integrated component of the international state system, this essentially Ethio-centric perspective negated the fundamental nature of the Eritrean demand for self-determination. Henze's *realpolitik* approach to geopolitical imperatives, although superficially acknowledging past Eritrean grievances, left no room for redress or significant reconfiguration of the status quo.

The second school of thought moved out of the shadow cast by Greater Ethiopia to examine the structure and function of the Ethiopian state and its exercise of colonial domination over occupied territories such as Eritrea.[19] Bereket Habteselassie identifed the Eritrean resistance to Ethiopian rule as essentially an anti-colonial movement. He argued that Eritrea was a case of "unconsummated decolonization" which involved two crucial elements: (1) the flawed and unequal federal relations imposed upon Eritrea as the conditions of formal decolonization; and (2) the Ethiopian violation of even this flawed arrangement and the illegal annexation of Eritrea in 1962 as a *de facto* colony.

After the Ethiopian imperial regime had by its own acts become an illegal occupationist colonial regime, the duty of the UN was to sanction the illegal acts and apply the principles of self-determination. [Failure to do so returned] the Eritrean people to the status quo ante (to pre-September 1950) in which the Eritrean people were once more a people struggling against colonial rule and/or alien occupation. That is why the Eritrean question is a colonial question, and not one of secession.[20]

Bereket Habteselassie's legal analysis countered the Greater Ethiopia thesis by characterizing the Ethiopian state as a colonizer and the Eritrean nationalist resistance as a bona fide anti-colonial struggle for self-determination.

Roy Pateman echoed Habteselassie's legal argument for Eritrean self-determination, asserting that the Ethiopia–Eritrea federation was "an imposition of Ethiopian direct rule."[21] Pateman dismissed the notion of an organic unity of Eritrean and Ethiopian peoples as "illusory" and characterized Ethiopia as "a colonial occupying power – an empire akin to the British, French, German and Italian empires."[22]

Pateman argued that despite pre-colonial linkages and a shared geographical habitat, Eritrea's formation and existence as a nation were validated not only by its historic past but through its struggle for national self-determination against Ethiopian rule.

The development of the Eritrean nation was accelerated by the imposition of Italian colonization, Ethiopian occupation and prolonged armed and political resistance to external intervention in Eritrean affairs. A nation has been formed which is a far cry from its ancient roots as a battleground for invaders and migrants.[23]

Arguing for the legitimation of Eritrean self-determination, Pateman claimed that the maturation of a distinct Eritrean national identity and the development of Eritrean military power were sufficient to challenge Ethiopia's control over Eritrea.

A. M. Babu suggested that the Eritrean conflict was deliberately portrayed as a war of secession in order to camouflage Ethiopia's expansionist policies and the justification of those policies within the OAU. Babu indicted Ethiopian coercive control over Eritrea as "the predatory nationalism of an occupying power"[24] and its annexation and attempts to dominate Eritrea as "black-on-black colonialism."[25] He argued that the Eritrean case was

a colonial question, not a secessionist one. Eritrea was colonized by Ethiopia by means of annexation.[26]

Babu drew a telling analogy between Ethiopia and South Africa, highlighting the pervasive power of Ethiopia's diplomatic effectiveness in the African arena, through which it effectively blunted or deflected opposition to its policies. He criticized the moral relativity that characterized post-colonial African institutions and which effectively insulated the Ethiopian state – whether imperial or Afro-Marxist – from the kinds of sanctions imposed on South Africa. Moreover, Babu questioned the validity of the Pan-Africanist tenets that legitimated Ethiopia's coercive unity as a norm in post-colonial Africa.

You do not exonerate colonialism because it is a black-on-black colonialism. And if the right to self-determination can be sacrificed for a higher cause of Pan-Africanism, then no African country has the right to independence.[27]

By characterizing Ethiopian violations of Eritrea's right to self-determination as "a colonialism which discredits the entire continent,"[28] Babu not only challenged Ethiopian claims over Eritrea but indicted the African order's acquiescence to this selective legitimation of relations of dominance and subordination in the continent.

Edmond J. Keller examines the historical and political development of Ethiopia, from a bureaucratic empire into a multi-ethnic nation-state. In so doing, he underscores the expansionist policies of nineteenth-century Ethiopia as encompassing various ethnic groups within its expanded boundaries. Keller referred to the incorporation of Eritrea into modern Ethiopia as "late colonialism."[29] He argued that Ethiopia's "bureaucratic empire" embarked on its own course of colonial expansion in the period of time roughly corresponding to the era of European colonization in Africa. Thus incorporation, whether by conquest (as in the Ogaden) or through violation of international law (as with Eritrea), was not differentiated in character or procedure.[30]

Lionel Cliffe compared the EPLF with other liberation movements in Africa, Asia, and Latin America. Cliffe argued that the acquiescence of the international and African regional organizations to Ethiopia's claims over Eritrea – particularly through the invocation of non-intervention in internal matters of nation-states – effectively isolated Eritrea, leaving it "cut off from [external] material and political support."[31]

This isolation had benefits as well as costs for Eritrean nationalists. One benefit was Eritrea's "emphasis on self-reliance and popular mobilization"[32] which was necessitated by its relative marginalization in international and regional communities; the primary cost was the subsequent absence of regional and international legitimacy, exacerbated by Ethiopia's diplomatic effectiveness in isolating the conflict.

This last point – Ethiopia's diplomatic capability – was an important element in Cliffe's analysis.

[A] crucial determinant [in the development of the conflict] has been the character of the Ethiopian coloniser ... [T]he strong position of the Ethiopian state ... in diplomatic circles in Africa and globally, together with the OAU countries' collective nervousness in the face of anything that smacked to them of "secession," deprived the Eritrean cause of any influential voice of support in international circles.[33]

Cliffe brought to light the fundamental, and often underplayed, role of the exercise of diplomatic capabilities in the legitimation or delegitimation of conflicts. Although his work was limited to the development and achievements of the Eritrean liberation movements, he raised very important questions about the mechanisms through which Ethiopia's hegemonic claims were consolidated in the post-colonial era.

The principal weakness of the colonial thesis is that it failed fully to appreciate the inherent contradiction between the two dominant principles of the post-colonial African order: territorial integrity and self-determination. The pre-World War II colonial order was characterized by a clear distinction between the "civilizing" rulers and the "natives," a demarcation that politically and legally separated the so-called "natives" from the colonialists. By contrast, the post-colonial order emphasized the organic unity of both the ruler and the ruled, a unity that was justified by the advent of the nation-state which purported to encompass the various societal elements within the ambit of its legitimate exercise of coercion. By failing to analyze adequately the contradictions of territorial integrity and self-determination, the colonial thesis constrained analysis to a framework within which post-colonial relations of dominance and resistance could not be fully understood.

In the Eritrean case, the primacy accorded to the principle of territorial integrity of sovereign nations over that of self-determination of peoples led to the launching of a nationalist struggle against the hegemonic dominance by a neighboring African state. The uniqueness of Eritrea's struggle for national liberation lay not in its colonial past, which it shares with most of Africa, but in its long and successful challenge to Ethiopia's hegemonic domination despite the lack of significant support from either the regional or international orders. Thus, an approach that limited the conflict to the status of a colonial residual obscured the process by which Ethiopia's access to regional and international diplomatic channels, as well as external (military and economic) support, contributed to the political isolation of the conflict.

Although the debate over the nature of the Eritrean conflict and the Ethiopian state was examined at length by scholars representing the two schools discussed above, there was also a growing number of works that focused on the development of Eritrean nationalism, the revolutionary achievements and transformation of Eritrean society, and the nature and dynamics of the post-colonial African regional order. This third perspective included scholars like John Markakis who viewed the Eritrean conflict as a "revolution [which] epitomizes the rise of dissident nationalism in contemporary African history."[34] Richard Leonard focused on the development of effective organizational infrastructures and the achievements of the EPLF.[35] He traced the development of the EPLF from its early years as a splinter guerrilla organization to its emergence as an effective popular liberation movement. Both Markakis and Leonard provided rich empirical details for future studies of liberation politics in the Horn and elsewhere.

Nzongola-Ntalaja and Michael Chege presented excellent examples of African scholarship on the impact of the post-colonial conflicts in the African and international arena. Both authors projected the conflict into a much wider regional and international realm rather than obscuring it as merely an "internal problem" of Greater Ethiopia or observing it as a vestige of colonialism. Chege was careful to point out the crucial "dialectic of internal causes and international intervention in which alterations in one induce changes in the other."[36] Nzongola-Ntalaja drew a revealing comparison between the Namibian and South African liberation struggles and resistance movements in Western Sahara and Eritrea. He noted that,

whereas the liberation of South Africa and Namibia evokes unanimous support among Africans, the questions of Eritrea and Western Sahara are more controversial since they involve the interests of two major African states and their strategic alliances in the world ... In the case of Ethiopia, few people seem to notice the paradox that a state that seems comfortable with the OAU principle of maintaining colonial frontiers with respect to the Somali claim on the Ogaden is content to invoke similar reasons for its claim on Eritrea. The majority of African states have rejected all of Morocco's claims but *remain conspicuously silent on the question of Eritrea.*[37]

The point, as Nzongola-Ntalaja aptly observed, was that all liberation movements are not the same, either in their origins, capabilities, legitimacy or opposition. Hence,

not all movements seeking self-determination in Africa should be automatically dismissed as separatist or secessionist movements which are detrimental to Africa, or the lawless activities of bandits. Each movement ought to be examined on its own merits.[38]

This last observation was especially relevant since it emphasized the significance of regional and international prestige. An important element in Ethiopia's hegemonic capability was its systematic development of regional consensus of its legitimacy. Menelik's victory over Italian colonial forces at Adowa in 1896 enhanced Ethiopia's regional prestige, which in turn became a building block upon which modern Ethiopia's status as the leading African nation-state was based.[39] This assumption of regional leadership, plus manipulation of the interests of the more fragile new African nation-states, allowed the Haile Selassie and Menghistu regimes to consolidate Ethiopian hegemony over the Horn.

International legitimacy was likewise an indispensable component of Ethiopia's regional hegemony. Although the Eritrean–Ethiopian conflict cannot be described merely as an arena for superpower rivalry fought through surrogates, its political fate was influenced by the alliances that the opponent – Ethiopia – forged with those major international actors. These patron–client relationships strengthened Ethiopia's traditional position of prominence in the Horn and provided it with a well-trained army, an impressive arsenal, and crucial diplomatic leverage in the international community.

Comparative definitions of hegemonic relations

In this study the term *hegemony* is used to encompass three different but interrelated conceptualizations of power relations: realism, world systems, and Gramscian hegemony. The concept of hegemony has been applied by scholars to explain different relationships of military, economic, political, and cultural dominance. These three schools of thought have dominated studies of hegemonic relations.

The realist school of international relations, epitomized by Hedley Bull, focuses on superpower hegemonic relationships of the United States and the Soviet Union. Bull defines hegemony as a relationship in which "there is resort to force and the use of force, but this is not habitual and uninhibited but occasional and reluctant." The United States' relations with Central America and the Soviet Union's relations with Eastern Europe were analyzed as hegemonic because each superpower was

ready to violate the rights of sovereignty, equality and independence enjoyed by the lesser states, but it does not disregard them; it recognizes that these rights might exist, and justifies violations of them by appeals to some specific *overriding principle.*[40]

The second school, represented by world-systems theorists such as Immanuel Wallerstein, links hegemony to economic expansion. Hegemonic status viewed through the analytical lens of the world-systems theorists is typically limited to the most industrialized states. For example, Wallerstein asserts that:

hegemony in the interstate system refers to that situation in which the ongoing rivalry between the so-called "great powers" is so unbalanced that one power is truly *primus inter pares*; that is, one power can largely impose its rules and wishes . . . in the economic, political, military, diplomatic and even cultural arenas.[41]

This focus on the core and periphery of the global economic system limits the hegemonic analysis to North–South relations. South–South relations of dominance and subordination, categorized as the "periphery," are glossed over due to the focus on economic superiority which at times manifests itself in military hegemony.

The third school of thought, represented by Antonio Gramsci's articulation of cultural hegemony, encompasses relations of dominance and resistance in cultural, economic, and political spheres. Gramsci focuses mainly on state–society relations, the acquisition of power, and the construction of a political discourse by elites and intellectuals which undergirds the exercise of power. In examining the relations of dominance, Gramsci differentiates between the coercive power of the state and the response of various elements within civil society. Gramsci's concept of hegemony takes into account the role of intellectuals and the dissemination of knowledge in the mobilization and organization of the people. Gramsci links the production of knowledge and the legitimation of certain versions of history over others to the struggle for power.

The "power" includes cultural as well as economic and political power – the power to define the boundaries of common-sense "reality" either by ignoring views outside those boundaries or by labelling deviant opinions "tasteless" or "impossible."[42]

Although Gramsci's concept of hegemony focuses on the mechanisms of consensus-building within a given state, his significant contribution is the link between power, language, and the socialization of peoples, classes, and states to a specific interpretation of history and ideas. Gramsci seems to have anticipated Michel Foucault's later emphasis on the political significance of discourses in the legitimation of ideologies of domination.[43] Power is linked with the interpretation and dissemination of the history of nations, providing the foundations of what we could regard as hegemonic ideologies.

The Gramscian concept of hegemony differs from the first two in its integration of the economic and political spheres.[44] Although shaped by Gramsci's own Marxist orientation, his conceptualization reflects a significant departure from the mechanistic Marxist view of the dominance of the state. The orthodox perception of state power does not explain the relative autonomy of the state which is evident in its ability to form coalitions of various classes.[45]

Gramsci's conceptualization applied the concept of hegemony as the consensual basis for the organization and legitimation of power within civil society.[46] The focus on civil society, class relations, nationalism, and specific historical changes broadened the application of hegemonic relations. This included the wider impacts of historical timing, cultural factors, philosophical underpinnings, and ideology. The coalition of various forces that shape hegemonic relations between state and society as well as interstate interactions are the crucial contributions of the Gramscian conceptualization of hegemony.

An interesting and provocative application of hegemonic power relations in "subregional power relations in the [African] continent" is presented by René Lemarchand.[47] Using Libya and South Africa as comparative regional hegemons, Lemarchand examines the emergence of regional hegemony in post-colonial Africa. In applying the concept of hegemony to the African context he underscores the importance of the driving logic and the diplomatic dimension that undergirds the quest for regional hegemony. In his comparison of Libya and South Africa as regional hegemons, Lemarchand applies the realist conceptualization of international or superpower hegemony to the particular context of regional power relations. Hegemony, for Lemarchand, "does not imply a static relationship ... [but] allows for varying degrees of control and forms of influence."[48] Initially, the hegemon will exercise diplomacy and respect for existing norms. Should reliance on diplomacy prove "unavailing, resource to force loom[s] increasingly large in their foreign policy arsenal."[49]

The concept of regional hegemony is especially useful in understanding the role of institutionalized legitimacy accorded or denied to certain states. The importance of the exercise of diplomatic capability and the degree of legitimacy of a hegemon become crucial in regional conflicts that threaten the terms of order envisioned by any regional hegemon. In the case of both Libya and South Africa, hegemonic claims were impeded, if not prevented, due to the absence of regional legitimacy and the contradictions between hegemonic interests and regional norms. By contrast, Ethiopia was able to sustain thirty years of armed conflict with virtually no sanction from either international or regional channels primarily because it possessed the diplomatic capability and legitimacy essential to hegemonic dominance.

As applied in this study, the concept of regional hegemony most resembles that advanced by Lemarchand, but differs from it in the extraction of an operational definition of the component parts of regional hegemony and a focus on resistance to hegemonic domination. My application of the concept of regional hegemony is based on the following central assumptions:

1 All hegemonic relations are based on domination and consensus. The development of consensus through the formulation and manipulation of existing rules and the invocation of Bull's "overriding principles" differentiates hegemony from colonial domination, which is character-

ized by the habitual resort to force in the absence of constraining norms
and rules.

2 The legitimation of domination and delegitimation of any opposition to
the terms of order envisioned by the hegemon is a crucial component of a
hegemonic power base. This capability is manifested primarily in the
exercise of effective diplomacy. Its most profound manifestation is the
construction of a legitimating regime of truth.[50]

3 Opposition to hegemonic domination that threatens the hegemonic
status quo is militarily contained or diplomatically isolated from regional
and international institutions which are authorized to address violations
or redress grievances.

Regional hegemony, I argue, is a phenomenon of the post-colonial era.
This perspective focuses on post-colonial relations of domination and the
legitimation of hegemonic violations of rules institutionalized in the post-
World War II regional and international orders. This is achieved through
the building of consensus on "overriding principles" that legitimate
hegemonic violations. I use elements of Gramscian cultural hegemony to
examine the mobilization of consensus among disparate segments, in this
case regional and international rather than domestic. I argue that the
regional consensus on the principles of "unity" and "balkanization" was
effectively used by Ethiopia to delay Eritrean self-determination by strip-
ping Eritrean demands of any regional and international legitimation and
support.

Given the relatively underdeveloped nature of Ethiopia's economy, the
application of the world-systems theory's conceptualization of economic
hegemony is admittedly problematic. In this case, it is not economic but
diplomatic capability that is emphasized most strongly. I assert that
significant geostrategic resources can be translated into economic capability through the effective exercise of diplomacy by a non-industrial nation-
state. Moreover, existing military capabilities can be augmented through a
trade-off of geostrategic resources – an essentially diplomatic exercise – and
utilized to strengthen a regional hegemon's power base. The case of
Ethiopia, an underdeveloped country with a high degree of regional and
international legitimacy, is used to illustrate this point.

Regional hegemony refers to the dominant position of specific states by
virtue of their military, diplomatic, economic, and/or geostrategic capabilities. This dominance manifests itself in at least three ways: (1) these states'
ability and willingness to formulate and implement basic rules governing
interstate relations that are legitimated as rights and obligations; (2) their
ability to transgress these very norms and maintain their dominance by
invoking specific overriding principles sanctioned by international and
regional norms; and (3) the production of a "regime of truth" and a

hegemonic ideology that delegitimates opposition to the status quo.

A regional hegemon can be differentiated from other regional powers by its capacity to establish and maintain the norms and rules of a political order that maximizes its own interests (domestic, regional, and international) while neutralizing opposition and minimizing the capabilities of other actors to respond independently. Based on regionally and internationally accepted or condoned norms and rules, the hegemon justifies its use of military and economic capabilities to maintain its position as a dominant power in the region. Military force is used to counter armed opposition. Economic capability and/or geostrategic resources are used to sustain the hegemon's arms supply and domestic needs in the pursuit of its policies. The invocation of an overriding principle shared by the international and regional orders becomes the basis for the diplomatic capabilities exerted to fulfill the pursuit of goals that may violate other equally important norms and rules, such as self-determination.

The mere existence of a powerful state is not sufficient to ensure hegemony unless it combines considerable military strength and diplomatic effectiveness in the regional and international arena. Diplomatically, a hegemon's power can be differentiated by its access to key positions in regional and international organizations. Its dominance is at times reflected in blatant disregard for established laws and norms that prove to be incongruent with its proclaimed "national interests." This is facilitated by fostering an ideological consensus on commonly held values such as "regional stability," or a perceived threat such as "balkanization," "arabization," or "communist penetration."

Development of or access to sophisticated military hardware and training often dovetails with the capacity of the hegemon to develop and sustain regional and international legitimacy. This is especially true when superpower support is solicited. In most cases, the hegemon can boast externally validated legitimacy. In cases where legitimacy is questionable or does not exist overtly, sophisticated military capabilities, an advanced economy, and a well-developed technological and industrial infrastructure can shield a hegemon from quick demise. The relationship between regional hegemons and their transnational patrons, although far from equal, can facilitate the development of a degree of autarky which allows hegemonic deviation from regional and international norms.[51]

Differences in military capability, diplomatic effectiveness, economic and geostrategic assets, and the degree of regional and international legitimacy alter and shape the scope of hegemonic exercises in a region. Military might alone cannot create or sustain regional hegemony, although relative military superiority is necessary for the maintenance of hegemonic power.[52] Lemarchand points out that "symmetry, of course does not imply perfect identity [and that] the theme of regional hegemony admits of many variations."[53]

Hegemonic advantage can also be exercised through a successful deployment of economic and/or geostrategic resources. Both international and regional prestige and power are often linked to economic capacity or geostrategically significant position. This is conspicuous where superpower support is concerned but can also be manifested in specifically regional terms. For example, South Africa maintained a viscerally repugnant political regime, with a regionally and internationally unfavorable agenda, largely through its economic domination of the region and its relative independence in the world capitalist system.[54] Similarly, Israel's peculiar ability to obtain international support for regionally unpopular policies and actions (at least until relatively recent times) relates in part to its geostrategic disposition in the Middle East *vis-à-vis* the United States and the Western world.[55]

Finally, regional hegemony can be acquired and sustained through a dextrous manipulation of prevailing imagery and historical circumstance in both the regional and international arena. Pre-existing notions of the uniqueness of a historical experience are transformed into prevailing and supranational symbols which can legitimate hegemonic aspirations. The congruence of visions, goals, and mechanisms of a hegemon with those of the regional and international orders determines the degree of legitimacy for hegemonic power relations. This symmetry between hegemonic aspirations and regional imperatives, in turn, shapes the nature of political discourse as well as containing or attenuating any conflicts arising from challenges to hegemony. Ethiopia's hegemonic claims to ex-colonial territories such as Eritrea were aimed at fulfilling its vision of a Greater Ethiopia. These territorial expansions were justified through the regional imperative for stability and unity legitimated through the invocation of the right of sovereign states to territorial integrity and the fears of "arabization" and "balkanization."

Ethiopian hegemony in the Horn was facilitated by its concurrent rise to leadership in the new African order. Established historical legitimacy, a strong modernized military, and an effective diplomacy using the newly established norms and symbols served to override any claims that countered Ethiopian interests. In the post-colonial era Ethiopia emerged as the symbol of African nationalism and independence. The empire-state utilized its prestige to further enhance its military capability by entering into agreements with various Western powers and the USA. Post-World War II Ethiopia expanded its boundaries and legitimated its vision of a Greater Ethiopia by effective military occupation and astute diplomatic moves in the UN and the OAU. The image management of the Ethiopian empire-state consisted of myth interwoven with historically drawn justification for the expansion of rule. The end result was a particular "regime of truth" based on modern Ethiopia's vision of a Greater Ethiopia which incorporated the former Italian colony of Eritrea.

The Ethiopian "regime of truth"

Ethiopia's ability to establish and maintain its diplomatic capability and legitimacy emanates from its successful development of a hegemonic "regime of truth." The concept of a regime of truth derives from the focus on the relationship between power and knowledge found in the works of Michel Foucault. Foucault's major premise is that:

> every society has its "regime of truth," its "general politic of truth" . . . and the role it plays in the socio-economic and political order of things . . . which is central to the structure and functioning of society. The disqualification and prohibition of local forms of knowledge has been achieved not through the implementation of a legal authority of censorship but principally by the "ensemble of rules according to which the true and false are separated and specific effects of power attached to the true," in short through the existence of a particular politico-economic regime of the production of truth.[56]

This socio-political approach can shed light on the broader analysis of the function of norms and values in the study of conflicts that challenge hegemonic powers and their versions of the regime of truth. The contribution of this approach is in the examination of the international and regional consensus within which institutions legitimate certain views while delegitimating others. The realist, world-systems, and Gramscian theories of hegemonic relationships are based on the exercise of military, economic, political, and organizational capabilities. The Foucauldian approach provides a framework for disaggregating the foundations of hegemonic discourse and the exercise of diplomatic capabilities in legitimating claims in the international and regional arena.

Within a regime of truth the decoding of history and the encoding of contemporary "reality" are linked by invoking a superficially "logical" (if ultimately specious) continuum from what is to what was. The driving "logic" is derived from the prevailing regime, that is, from the prevailing norms and values and the sustaining apparatus of those norms and values. Indeed, the only definite and consistent purpose of such "logic" is, in all cases, the maintenance of the regime.[57]

The degree to which norms and values prevail is in turn a product of the relative strength and weakness of the corresponding institutions and processes; that is, the rules of the game are either enforced or overruled, depending upon the strength of the apparatus of enforcement. In Ethiopia's case, by 1964 the OAU had become sufficiently dominated by Ethiopia to function as little more than a rubber stamp for the hegemon's claims. Ethiopia's role in the drafting of the OAU Charter and the emphasis on non-intervention and the safeguarding of existing boundaries legitimated its claims and delegitimated any claims which countered the prevailing consensus.

As an analytical device the regime of truth is an organization of knowledge in justification of a given distribution of power, defining what is and what is not legitimate discourse. The very pervasiveness of the Ethiopian regime of truth is the foundation of its hegemonic dominance in the political and diplomatic consensus that sustained its interests.

In the case of Ethiopia, the regime of truth is conditioned by a number of prevailing norms, values, institutions, and processes within Ethiopia, throughout the regional (African) order, and even at the level of the international arena. The mythic image of Ethiopia as a quintessential nation of liberated Africa is skillfully woven into a complex fabric of regional territorial integrity and international sovereignty. The biblical reference to Ethiopia has acquired through the years the status of a "nation" which does not equate with the actual boundaries of the modern Ethiopian nation-state. Despite the difficulty of proving the existence of such a nation or a proto-nation, the "ideal" of such an entity in antiquity has served as the reference point for modern Ethiopian politics. In the international arena, references to Ethiopia in classical Greek and Roman texts have endowed it with a unique status and exposure.[58]

In the early 1960s the Ethiopian empire-state emphasized its role as an anti-colonial crusader in order to gain leadership in the formulation of rules to pre-empt any challenges to its vision of a Greater Ethiopia. The political imperatives of maintaining its newly extended boundaries, which included Eritrea, were articulated in terms consonant with the prevailing African consensus of "unity" and the "restoration" of areas usurped by European colonialists.

The rise of Pan-Africanist leaders who regarded Ethiopia as the "Black Zion" reinforced Ethiopia's invented mythical and historical claims over other territories such as Eritrea. Scholarly publications extolling the Ethiopian version of unity contributed to the academic legitimation of Ethiopia's hegemonic aspirations in the Horn.[59]

By the end of the 1970s, when the successor to the imperial regime switched superpower patrons in order to counter increasing armed challenge from the Eritrean liberation fronts, Ethiopian "unity" served as the overriding principle that delegitimated Eritrean and Somali challenges. The Ethiopian regime of truth was accepted as the only "true" version in the bloody struggles of the Horn.

With the attenuation of Cold War hostilities by the late 1980s, the international alliances that had fostered Ethiopian hegemony began to unravel. In the early 1990s the hegemonic "truth" faced a crucial test when the policy of a Greater Ethiopia was successfully challenged by a cohesive Eritrean armed resistance, in coordination with a coalition of Ethiopian opposition groups. The combined challenges taxed Ethiopia's military capability. More importantly, it exposed the fallacy of Ethiopia's mythical unity – the very underpinning of its regime of truth and its source of regional and international legitimacy.

2 Regional hegemony in the post-World War II order

Introduction

An important premise of this work is that regional hegemony is a creature of the post-colonial regional and international orders. The constraints placed on a regional hegemony by its predecessor (colonialism) prohibit the exercise of naked aggression and the subjugation of peoples, which were the dominant characteristics of colonial policies. The willingness to resort to brute force in colonialism is captured satirically in Hilaire Belloc's much-quoted couplet on the technology of violence:

> Whatever happens, we have got
> The Maxim Gun, and they have not.[1]

However, the demise of colonialism did not signal the end of domination of "weaker" peoples by "stronger." The new norms and values that characterize the post-colonial international and regional environments require an adaptation to – and, where possible, the exploitation of – a consensus based upon the formal rejection of violent aggression. The ability to exercise expansive regional power within such a consensus is the most striking feature of regional hegemony.

This chapter is designed to introduce regional hegemony as a logical outgrowth of the consolidation and codification of regional and international norms and values. More specifically, the formation of the United Nations (UN) and, later, the Organization of African Unity (OAU) formalized a consensus around overriding principles of non-aggression, sovereignty, and security of nation-states, and the right of peoples to choose their own political destiny. In order to maintain and even expand its hegemonic dominance, Ethiopia had to legitimate its aspirations by integrating them into this post-colonial rubric. As we shall see, Ethiopia succeeded in exercising hegemonic domination not by blatantly thwarting the new norms but by exploiting a peculiar contradiction that lay at the heart of the post-colonial consensus: the fragile balance of state sovereignty (territorial integrity) and the right of peoples to self-determination.

Delegitimating the colonial international order

WE THE PEOPLES OF THE UNITED NATIONS determined to save succeeding generations from the scourge of war, which twice in our lifetime has brought untold sorrow to mankind ... have resolved to combine our efforts to accomplish these aims.

Chapter I

Article 1: The purposes of the United Nations are:
1 To maintain international peace and security, and to that end: to take effective collective measures for the prevention and removal of threats to the peace, and for the suppression of acts of aggression or other breaches of peace, and to bring about by peaceful means, and in conformity with the principles of justice and international law, adjustment or settlement of international disputes or situations which might lead to a breach of that peace ...

Chapter II Membership ...

Article 6:
A member of the United Nations which has persistently violated the Principles contained in the present Charter may be expelled from the Organization by the General Assembly upon the recommendation of the Security Council. (Charter of the United Nations, June 26, 1945)[2]

The Charter of the United Nations was signed on June 26, 1945. Under the Charter's terms, the United Nations was established as the guardian of the new international order of the post-World War II era. Despite juridical equality accorded to its members under the Charter, the UN did not (and could not) equalize the power relations between strong and weak nations. In fact, the UN's structure reinforced a stratified international system and provided a new format of control by granting veto rights to the principal, old, but now weakened, rulers of colonial empires as well as to the emergent global actors, the United States and the Soviet Union.[3]

A major change of this new international order was embodied in the legal sanctions against the acquisition of territories by brute force, which had characterized the colonial order. Invasions, purchases of territories, and gunboat diplomacy had once been fully legitimate norms of conduct, justified by the need to "expand empires" and "civilize" the natives during the colonial era. The demise of colonialism was marked not only by the exodus of the foreign colonial administrative, but also by a growing body of norms and regulations that emphasized the new anti-colonial consensus.[4]

The statutes of the UN revolve around the concepts of peace and equality, both to be attained through negotiation. Negotiations through the UN are not limited to formal channels, but where they do occur formally they determine access and a degree of participation through which national interests and needs are addressed. Informal negotiations are held away from official forums but are nevertheless just as influential in determining outcomes of disputes. In cases involving conflicts between sovereign states and non-state actors (such as national liberation movements), tacit or informal understandings between powerful states may facilitate or block access to fulfillment of the goals of disputants. Since membership of the UN is based on sovereign statehood, access to or participation in this international forum by non-state actors requires sponsorship by member states directly or indirectly involved in ongoing conflicts.[5]

Although the new international order and the UN itself appear to be egalitarian, the existence of inequalities (power differentials, economic dependencies, etc.), among actors perpetuates pre-existing stratifications, which enable stronger powers to maintain their privileged positions. Thus, the great powers have exclusive veto rights in the Security Council while the General Assembly usually serves as a deliberative body. With some major changes, such as the delegitimation of colonialism as a norm, it can be said that the UN emerged as a modified version of the League of Nations. Ian Clark points out:

We could point to the United Nations Security Council and say with justification that the order inaugurated in 1945 was one overwhelmingly in favour of the major powers. It imposed a system of collective security in which order would be enforced upon smaller states if they resorted to violence, but because of the veto the same could not be imposed upon the Great Powers.[6]

An important result of this stratification has been the establishment of an international patronage system based on the convergence of the "national interests" of superpowers and other great powers with those of the developing nations.[7] Alliances between the superpowers and developing countries reflected ideological affinities as well as economic and geostrategic interests. They also led to direct or indirect interventions of external powers in disputes between and within developing nation-states.[8]

The role of the UN in African conflicts has been limited to exercises in "damage-control," focusing on the impact of crises rather than dealing with the roots of conflicts. Although this criticism of the UN can be substantiated by the history of the role of the organization since its creation, the uneven allocation of power among states and the absence of an authoritative executive body have contributed a great deal to this deficiency.

The international norms established in the post-World War II order have been characterized mainly by an emphasis on ideal goals. For example, the ambiguities inherent in the concept of self-determination became manifest in clashes over the imperatives of territorial integrity sanctioned as the right to self-defense. Africa, more than any other continent, displays the consequences of such contradictions. Former colonies emerged as independent states following periods of nationalist struggles in which the demand for self-determination, legitimated as an international norm, played a primary role in the transition from subordinate status to sovereignty. In addition, the legacies of colonialism, such as the division and amalgamation of peoples created by arbitrary colonial boundaries, presented definitional problems such as determining which peoples belonged to what state and, most importantly, which peoples could exercise their right to determine their own political destinies. The delegitimation of the colonial order in the international arena led to the institutionalization of the principle of self-determination. The promulgation of the UN Charter and subsequent anti-colonial resolutions confirmed the principle legitimating the entrance of Third World polities into the international system of nation-states.

The United Nations and the post-World War II international order

UN Resolution 1514 (XV) was the first attempt to put into effect the right of self-determination in accordance with the provisions of the UN Charter. The key issues in this resolution were the concepts of self-determination and the doctrine of territorial integrity. The following principles were declared on December 14, 1960:

Article 1: The *subjugation of peoples* to alien subjugation, domination, and exploitation *constitutes a denial of fundamental rights*, is contrary to the United Nations and is an impediment to the promotion of world peace and co-operation.

Article 2: All people have a right to self-determination; by virtue of that right they *freely determine their political status* and freely pursue their economic, social and cultural development.

Article 3: Inadequacy of political, economic, social or educational preparedness should never serve as a pretext for delaying independence.

Article 4: All armed action or repressive measures of all kinds directed against *dependent peoples* shall cease in order to enable them to exercise peacefully and freely their *right to complete independence, and the integrity of their national territory* shall be respected.

Article 5: Immediate steps shall be taken, in Trust and Non-Self-Governing territories or all other territories which have not yet attained independence, *to transfer all powers to the people of those territories, without any conditions or reservations*, in accordance with their freely expressed will and desire, *without any distinction to race, creed or color*, in order to enable them to enjoy complete independence and freedom.

Article 6: Any attempt made at the partial or whole disruption of the national unity and the territorial integrity of a country is *incompatible with the purposes and principles of the Charter* of the United Nations.

Article 7: All States shall observe faithfully and strictly the provisions of the Charter of the United Nations, the Universal Declaration of Human Rights and the present declaration on the basis of equality, non-interference in the internal affairs of all States and respect for the sovereign rights of all peoples and to their territorial integrity.[9]

Although this document reflects the principles of the UN it also highlights the contradictions inherent in the various paragraphs, provisions that have been difficult to implement due to the ambiguities surrounding self-determination itself. The lack of a consensus on the definition of "people" and the absence of an order of priority in these principles facilitated the ascendancy of "territorial integrity" as the overriding norm. This doctrine was used by Ethiopia to nullify the guaranteed rights of "all" peoples to the right of self-determination without incurring expulsion, as provided in Chapter II, Article 6 of the Charter.[10] The UN's structure, in which membership is based on state sovereignty and the prohibition of interference in the "internal affairs of all States," makes the organization unable to respond to any violations that a sovereign state may commit against non-state "people" fighting for self-determination. The UN's incapacity to enforce these norms and arbitrate in disputes involving claims to self-determination has led to the resort to armed struggle by aggrieved parties.

Enfranchisement of colonized peoples in the first decades of decolonization through the implementation of the right of self-determination, as specified in the UN Charter, proved to be problematic. It was applied to entire ex-colonial territories, not to separatist or irredentist claimants within them. (Only in Trust Territories was the choice available, as when the British Cameroon Trusteeship was split between Nigeria and the Republic of Cameroon in 1961.) In Africa, the new international order inaugurated an era of conflicts emanating from the contradictions between the concept of self-determination and its application to African conditions. Some of the disputes that can be traced to this contradiction include those waged by the Eritreans and the Ogadeni Somalis in the Horn, the Saharouis in the Maghreb, and the Namibians in Southern Africa. These conflicts are examples of cases that have fallen through the cracks of a *lex imperfecta* that characterizes the post-World War II international and regional order. Nevertheless, despite these weaknesses, the emphasis on a search for legal norms and universal principles has generated a series of resolutions that have attempted to grapple with some of the unresolved problems.

UN Resolution 2625 (XXV) was adopted in 1970, a decade after Resolution 1514 (XV). It stated the following operational principles for implementing the right of self-determination by a people:

The establishment of a sovereign and independent State, the free association or integration with an independent State or the emergence into any other political status *freely determined by a people* constitute modes of implementing the right of self-determination by that people.

Every State has the duty to refrain from any forcible action which deprives people referred to above in the elaboration of the present principles of their right to self-determination and freedom and independence. In their actions against, and resistance to, such forcible action in pursuit of the exercise of their right to self-determination, *such peoples are entitled to seek and receive support* in accordance with the principles of the Charter.

Nothing in the foregoing paragraphs shall be construed as authorizing or encouraging any action which would dismember, or impair ... *the territorial integrity*, or political unity of sovereign and independent States conducting themselves in compliance with the principle of equal rights and self-determination of peoples as described above.[11]

This revision in the view of self-determination attempts to narrow its scope by including associational relationships with existing states. Thus, self-determination is expanded to include political arrangements other than full political independence. According to Resolution 2625 (XXV) then, the exercise of the right to self-determination could result in something other than a "sovereign and independent state." Association or even integration with *another* state would be possible as long as it could be determined freely by the "people" exercising their right of self-determination. Thus federal and confederal arrangements, or union with an established sovereign state, could be legitimated as an exercise of self-determination. (As noted above, this has only happened in the case of the Trust Territories of Togo and Cameroon on whom the UN conferred special juridical status in order to make such amalgamation possible.)

These theoretical modifications are in line with the Charter, but politically the contradiction between the exercise of the universal right of a people to self-determination and the exercise of sovereign rights of a *state* to maintain territorial integrity remains unresolved. Since political legitimacy is already conferred on existing nation-states, entities that do not possess legal status in international law and custom are at a disadvantage in expressing their demands through the channels available in the existing international order. Claimants to the right of self-determination are thus forced to search for allies or sponsors among member states in order to have their grievances heard.

Despite these normative restrictions and the built-in tensions of the post-

World War II international order, the main tenets embodied in the UN Charter have shown a remarkable resilience. However, since 1945, when the UN was established as a collective security system against future aggressors, the international order has seen the emergence of disputes of greater complexity than were envisioned at the time of the signing of the Charter. The rise of superpower rivalry, the politics of bipolar tensions, and patronage politics on the basis of spheres of influence, were factors inhibiting the ability of the UN to function according to its principles.[12] Although the UN and the larger post-World War II international order are based on a concept of a large global system of states, national sovereignty and power are still jealously guarded by individual members. Thus, the imperatives of states to protect their "national" interests have led to various modifications of the original norms established in the post-World War II era. Part of the problem of viewing the UN as an embodiment of a new international order has been reconciling its role, as originally conceived, with its actual functional capacities. As John W. Holmes put it:

It took many years for Western policy-makers to adjust their view of the United Nations as a crusade against sin, and that adjustment has not been made easier by the latter-day assumptions of the Third World that [that] is indeed what it should be, provided that it is they who now define sin ... It is not, as heralded, a replacement for the balance of power but as a place in which power can be balanced or mustered more soberly.[13]

Forty-five years later, at the beginning of the 1990s, the larger system within which the UN was nested began to undergo transformations. The changes enunciated by Gorbachev's *perestroika* and *glasnost* had their reverberations on US–Soviet relations as well as superpower involvement in the Third World. The status quo of a bipolar world, and the power relationships that shaped a global order defined by superpower rivalry, finally collapsed in 1991 with the dissolution of the Soviet Union. The UN began to function as an international arena for the restoration of equilibrium in the post-Cold War era and a forum in which the grievances of the past could now be addressed free from the constraints of the Cold War. Its role became increasingly visible in the early 1990s through its involvement in Kuwait, Somalia, Eritrea, and the former Yugoslavia.

The post-World War II regional order: Africa

The right of African peoples to self-determination, the rallying cry against colonialism, was quickly subordinated to the principle of territorial integrity of the successor to the colonial state. In the OAU Charter the affirmation of the right of all peoples "to control their own destiny" is qualified by the imperative to "safeguard and consolidate the hard-won independence as well as the sovereignty and territorial integrity of our states."[14] Self-determination functioned quite well in the struggle to achieve independence from European colonialism. But in the post-colonial era self-determination, with its attendant demands for political participation, threatened the stability and order of the new, fragile states. The new African heads of state, unable and at times unwilling to confront complex problems of governance of multi-ethnic and segmented societies, opted to limit the applicability of the right of self-determination to cases of Africans struggling against European or white rule. In cases where the right of self-determination was invoked against acts of expansion by neighboring African states, the territorial integrity of sovereign states was upheld. The new status quo was upheld by the OAU which relegated self-determination to nothing more than a rhetorical clause. Rupert Emerson noted in 1969 that:

self-determination has become the bright and shining sword of our day, freeing peoples from the bondage of empire. Yet the sword must be recognized as double-sided – sharp and cutting on one side of its blade but blunt and unserviceable on the other.[15]

The emergence of an African regional order, symbolized by the establishment of the Organization of African Unity in May 1963, was characterized by the institutionalization of the two concepts of self-determination and territorial integrity. Nkrumah's famous dictum, "Seek ye first the political kingdom" was realized in the rapid transformation of former colonies to independent states claiming their right to self-determination.[16] Although the aspiration of a unified continental government did not crystallize, regional norms and beliefs about self-determination were enshrined in the Charter of the OAU.

We, the Heads of African States and Governments . . .

CONVINCED that it is the inalienable right of all people to control their own destiny;

CONSCIOUS of the fact that freedom, equality, justice and dignity are essential objectives for the achievement of the legitimate aspirations of the African people . . .

CONVINCED that, in order to translate this determination into a dynamic force in the cause of human progress, conditions for peace and security must be established and maintained;

DETERMINED to safeguard and consolidate the hard-won independence as well as the sovereignty and territorial integrity of our States, and to fight against neo-colonialism in all its forms . . .

HAVE agreed to the present Charter. (Charter of the OAU, September 13, 1963)[17]

The right to self-determination had been an integral part of the rising wave of African nationalism and the cornerstone of the anti-colonial movements of the late 1940s and 1950s. Its primary utility was in the mobilization of internal and external forces to precipitate the demise of the colonial order. An enduring problem was defining who constituted a "people" and determining by what means a decision on "peoplehood" is reached.

Two intimately interrelated questions habitually appear as soon as the issue of self-determination is posed: Who constitutes the self to be determined, and by what means and by whom is the determination to be undertaken? The range of possibilities under both headings is large, and the choices made may drastically affect the outcome. At the extremes, self-determination may encompass the whole of an assumed macro "national" territory, giving no heed to minorities which may have quite different alignments in mind, or it may operate at the level of small and separable local entities such as villages and urban precincts, always considering that the end result must be a reasonably coherent territory or territories.[18]

These definitional and operational problems were an integral part of the ambiguity inherent in the concept of self-determination as discussed earlier. What is significant in the African case is that the right of peoples to self-determination was limited to those "peoples" formerly under *European* rule. This *de facto* limitation of self-determination to one decade of decolonization (1957–1967) has been the dominant characteristic of the institutionalization of self-determination as a regional norm. Pan-Africanist ideals of the nationalist era and the emergence of juridical states led to what Mayall has described as the "domestication" of the norm.[19] In Africa it served to delegitimate European colonialism and to proscribe the subjection of "peoples," but the OAU Charter's prohibition of interference in the internal affairs of a sovereign state overrode the primacy given to self-determination in the pre-independence period.

The point is that in the emerging regional order of an African state system the importance of self-determination was diminished by the contending principle of the territorial integrity of sovereign states. Thus, the delegitimation of the colonial order and the emergence of indigenous sovereign states led to the emphasis on norms reflecting the immediate concerns of the decolonization period. In situations where the decolonization process has been contested, such as in Eritrea and Somalia, the principle of self-determination of peoples directly confronts that of territorial integrity of established states. The political calculus based on the fragility of new African states generated a consensus on the adoption of the principle of territorial integrity as the cornerstone of the second phase of African nationalism after 1960.[20]

Article 3 of the OAU Charter reflects the primacy accorded to the principle of territorial integrity over that of self-determination.[21]

The Member States, in pursuit of the purposes stated in Article II, solemnly affirm and declare their adherence to the following principles:
1 the sovereign equality of all Member States;
2 non-interference in the internal affairs of States;
3 respect for the sovereignty and territorial integrity of each State and for its inalienable right to independent existence;
4 peaceful settlement of disputes by negotiation, mediation, conciliation or arbitration.[22]

Although the OAU Charter pays tribute to the "inalienable right of all people to control their own destiny," the above Article – in particular principles 2 and 3 – confirms that the emphasis was on the rights and prerogatives of states. The post-colonial regional order that emerged was based on the legitimation of statehood linked inextricably to the consolidation of territorial boundaries. The dominant norm, which served to consolidate the embryonic African states, was that of territorial integrity.

Pan-Africanism, as envisioned by Nkrumah and others, soon encountered the contradiction between the ideal and the real aspects of power facing independent Africa. The symbolic value of Pan-Africanism, with its emphasis on continental unity, had neglected the crucial role of territorial integrity. Pan-Africanism as a supranational ideology rejected the artificial boundaries created by colonial powers. The pre-independence movements rode the crest of the waves of Pan-African continental nationalism, a philosophy that underscored *subjective* values of symbolic unity rather than the objective tasks of attaining statehood and sovereignty.[23]

Although Pan-Africanism was ascendant in the late 1940s, the symbolic value of Ethiopia as the oldest anti-colonial "state" was one of the first and strongest threads woven into the fabric that was to emerge as the African regional order.[24]

The OAU and the consolidation of the regional consensus

The Organization of African Unity (OAU) was established in Addis Ababa, Ethiopia, on May 25, 1963, five months after the annexation of Eritrea into the Ethiopian Empire.[25] The OAU, like the UN, upheld such goals as freedom, justice, peace, and economic and social development. Although the OAU's Charter and structures borrowed a great deal from its international prototype, its dual goals of unity and maintaining territorial boundaries led it to suppress the right to self-determination in favour of the right to territorial integrity (even for those African peoples subjugated by a sovereign African state). Gino Naldi comments on the effects of the fusion of these principles with the aspirations of African unity.

Somewhat paradoxically unity is interrelated with the defense of sovereignty, independence and territorial integrity. This is not only an attempt at bolstering the fragile unity of many African states but constitutes an affirmation of the principle of *Uti Possidetis*, or the permanence of inherited colonial frontiers, and a rejection of the irredentist claims of other African states.[26]

Unlike the UN, the OAU's emphasis on states' rights de-emphasizes the rights of "peoples" and subordinates their rights to those of the state. Jon Woronoff notes this important distinction between the two organizations:

Unlike the Charter of the United Nations and many other historic documents, the Charter of African Unity made no pretension of creating an organization for the people as opposed to the leaders. The Charter boldly began "We the Heads of African States and Governments."[27]

The statist line of the OAU in turn gave birth to a series of norms linked to the sovereignty of African states and their leaders. Robert H. Jackson argues that a "negative sovereignty" grew out of the anti-colonial movements, a doctrine that empowers rulers and subordinates demands of self-determination to a racialist nationalism.

In contemporary Africa as in dynastic Europe sovereignty is a right of rulers rather than peoples ... Self determination in sub-Saharan Africa is the right of black Africans to have a government of their own race within the inherited framework of the ex-colonial state and a corresponding right not to suffer having a neighboring government of white men.[28]

Whereas military victories by liberation movements may secure control over disputed territories over extended periods of time, the absence of sovereignty denies them protection from punitive actions by established states invoking rights of "territorial integrity." An official hearing at the OAU confers a modicum of legitimacy which may then provide further opportunities to obtain fully-fledged recognition. On the other hand, failure to acquire legitimacy from the regional order resulted in exclusion or isolation, as demonstrated in the Eritrean case.

The jealously guarded sovereignty of African states militated against the establishment of a central body with legally binding powers, leaving the task of confronting African conflicts to interested sponsors and transnational patrons. The absence of an African "security council" with binding powers has made diplomatic efforts for the recognition of non-state bodies, such as liberation movements, even more difficult. The OAU's reliance on consensus as a prerequisite to policy-making and the amendment or reform of existing principles has bound existing regimes to an organizational status quo established at a specific historical period and encumbered by time-bound imperatives. As things stand, the OAU must depend on the "good offices" of leaders or find other ways to circumvent its lack of authority to implement steps to resolve conflicts, particularly if they are considered potentially injurious to member states. Claude Welch assessed the OAU's role in its first decade as follows:

A regional organization, whose strengths derive primarily from its ability to speak for all members, cannot effectively utilize exclusion as an operating principle. The costs of unanimity are diffuseness and principles of sweeping neutrality.[29]

In brief, the OAU's operating motto appeared to be that "if you are not with us then you are against us." This tendency to interpret unanimity as "unity" permitted a variety of localized and regional conflicts to proliferate. Behind the facade of institutionalized unity a multitude of conflicting interests were permitted to play out their deadly games. The conflict in the Horn was testimony to both the lack of unity in the new regional order and its political impotence.

From the outset, different visions of what the role of the OAU should be in the African order led to the factionalization of African states. The very creation of the OAU signalled a compromise between the continental philosophy of Pan-Africanism and the more narrowly defined nationalisms of member countries. Inter-African splits became pronounced, for example, over the Algerian war, the question of Mauritanian statehood, the Congo crises, the Western Sahara question, and the Libya–Chad disputes. Even before the signing of the OAU Charter the differences among member countries became obvious in the composition and orientation of the various groupings that emerged between the late 1950s and 1963.

Three groups – Brazzaville, Casablanca, and Monrovia – emerged in the three years preceding the formalization of the regional order. The central issue of contention was the disparate visions of independent Africa. The Brazzaville group espoused gradualist and peaceful means of decolonization.[30] The Casablanca group proposed a unitary united government for Africa.[31] The Monrovia group emerged as a mediator between the Brazzaville and Casablanca camps and succeeded in reaching a moderate stance which served as the basis for the OAU Charter.[32] Recourse to passive mediation in inter-African disputes became a hallmark of African organizational politics and left a trail of unaddressed grievances.

The first test of the OAU came almost before the "ink was dry" on the Charter. A border dispute between Algeria and Morocco broke out, eventually resolved through the mediation of heads of state. Bypassing formal OAU structures (such as the Council for Conciliation, Mediation, and Arbitration) became a precedent that turned into a norm for the resolution of inter-African conflicts by the OAU. This pattern was justified as facilitating the peaceful settlement of disputes among member states and gave the leaders latitude to exercise, at their discretion, their interpretations of various conflicts. The structural gap – the absence of a decision-enforcing body – led to informal caucusing or the formation of *ad hoc* committees as a forum for policy-making, which underscores the OAU's procedures for settling conflicts.

The settlement of inter-state conflicts was limited to mediation by heads of state. Prestige, personality, and power plays thus became the defining characteristics of the African mode of resolution. More importantly, quid pro quo arrangements between leaders striving to protect their "national interests" determined whether issues such as the intermittent Ethio-Somali border disputes became part of the OAU's agenda. In cases where there was no state to raise a specific problem, such as that of Eritrea, the issue never came before the OAU, thus effectively blocking recognition of the continent's longest war.

Pan-Ethiopianism: the development of a regime of truth

In order to understand Ethiopia's impressive diplomatic capability its doctrine of Pan-Ethiopianism must be examined. A doctrine based on coerced unity, Pan-Ethiopianism was presented by various regimes as an expression of African "unity" and utilized as a legitimation of Ethiopia's territorial expansion in the post-colonial era. In the post-World War II era, through a combination of diplomatic statecraft and a modernized army, Ethiopia arose as a dominant power capable of manipulating the various Western, Middle Eastern, and African interests to consolidate its hegemony over the Horn. Whereas the rest of the new African states emerged from colonization as juridical entities with dependent economies and hastily trained, makeshift armies, Ethiopia acquired a larger territory, a modernized army, and a host of Western powers vying for its favors.[33]

That Ethiopia emerged from the colonial era not only unscathed but economically strengthened and geographically expanded was a demonstration of its power and status. Utilizing its new-found identity as a champion of African nationalism in the Pan-Africanist arena, it legitimated its anachronistic system of absolute monarchy and neutralized any challenges to its hegemony from its newly incorporated territories.[34]

Pan-Ethiopianism, the doctrine that claimed neighboring territories by virtue of cultural similarity and conquest, was left unchallenged by the new African states. That modern Ethiopia was a conquest state forged by Shoan emperors, and that it was involved in the brutal oppression of fellow Africans, were facts either conveniently forgotten by Pan-Africanists, or even more typically not "discovered" until much later.[35] In any event, the myth of Ethiopia as a political "Zion," enhanced by anti-colonial and anti-Western sentiments, had already acquired currency in African political activist circles during the 1940s. A combination of wishful thinking and the fusion of the empire's Pan-Ethiopianism led to the validation of Ethiopia's claims by Pan-African activists and theoreticians alike.

Pan-Ethiopianism was a far cry from the demand for independence and self-determination for African colonized peoples. Ethiopian policy since World War II has been remarkable for its Janus-like duality. The face turned toward the rest of black Africa is suffused with the glow of African independence, anti-colonialism, and self-determination; another, less readily visible, face scowls at such demands as challenges to Ethiopia's position in the Horn and the continent. Ethiopia's maintenance of this dual role without losing its legitimacy in the African arena was based largely on its ability to portray challenges to its hegemony as a threat to the African regional order. The demands for self-determination by the Eritreans and the Ogadeni Somalis were overshadowed by the Pan-Ethiopianist mission of reunifying "Ethiopian" peoples torn asunder by European colonialism. Artfully woven into these heroic endeavors was the need for Ethiopia to gain "access to the sea," "redress fascist aggression," and protect the security of the region. Territorial expansion was thus welded, in a bewildering fashion, with decolonization and, in the Eritrean case, a dubious unity based on claims of pre-colonial linkages.

The new African order was based partly on an idealistic vision: the quest for an African symbol untainted by European domination. This search led to the adoption of Ethiopia as the epitome of African independence. The mythical allure of Biblical Ethiopia and Menelik's victory against Italy at the battle of Adowa in 1896 served to underscore this symbolic image of an independent African country; the expansionist nature of the Ethiopian empire was not considered.[36] Ethiopia used its traditional mythology and newly acquired Pan-Africanist legitimacy to establish and maintain norms that enabled it to rise to hegemony. In the international arena, Ethiopia's legitimacy was enhanced by its membership in the League of Nations. But it was not until the consolidation of its alliance with the USA that its international legitimacy was established effectively. The Ethio-American alliance provided a new source of economic and military support, enabling it to pursue its interests in the region.

Ethiopia's aspiration to regional[37] hegemony was facilitated by the skillful manipulation of the former colonizers and their rivals. Its imperial system under Menelik II had coexisted and cooperated with the colonizing powers in the first scramble for Africa. Menelik's later successor, Haile Selassie, exploited the symbolic legitimacy of Menelik's legacy and post-World War II anti-fascist sentiments to extend Ethiopia's boundaries under both regional and international orders, orders that proscribed such territorial expansion. Harold G. Marcus describes the Emperor's charisma and diplomatic skill which led to his portrayal as:

the hero of romantic liberals and even celebrated by the militant left. His was a world image: the tiny monarch standing before the globe's representatives and with tall dignity seeking fulfillment of the promise of collective security.[38]

Ethiopia's acquisition of Eritrea in the 1950s was a manifestation of its transition from a dominant power to a regional hegemon.[39] That it was able to make such a transition without losing its legitimacy as an "anti-colonial" power was a testament to its increasing influence in the politics of the region.

Haile Selassie's political acumen and the success of his "image manage-ment"[40] sustained Ethiopia's image as the representative of the "new Africa." Never mind that Ethiopia's post-war foreign policy was derived from tenets antithetical to nascent African nationalism, the exercise of self-determination, and the introduction of democratic participation within the framework of modern nation-statehood.[41] Its alliance with the USA, too, was in stark contrast to some radical African nations' clear stand against imperialism and neo-colonialism (for example, Nkrumah's Ghana, Sekou Toure's Guinea, and Nyerere's Tanzania). Despite the ideological and objective differences among the various African states, regional consensus on "territorial integrity" legitimated Ethiopia's claims to areas under former European control.[42] In the Horn, the death knell of self-determi-nation was sounded by Ethiopian invocation of territorial integrity based on pre-colonial historical linkages. Ethiopian claims were couched in terms that made its motivation appear Pan-Africanist. The demand of the Eritreans for self-determination was equated with atavistic religious and ethnic secessionism, an image abhorred by the Pan-Africanist order. This ability to establish a "congruence of social purpose"[43] facilitated Ethio-pia's manipulation of the terms of political discourse in the region.

Ethiopia's key participation at the helm of the emergent regional order was to prove fatal to radicals in their attempts to chart a progressive leadership for post-colonial Africa. Nkrumah's Pan-Africanist vision of a continental government was abandoned in favor of a less radical leadership provided by Emperor Haile Selassie. The incessant difficulties of imple-menting a continental government infrastructure for the envisioned United States of Africa in the immediate post-independence years led to friction between the Casablanca and Monrovia factions. Thus, imperial Ethiopia, legitimated by the new regional and international order, stepped in as a moderator between the two contending groups. The institutionalization of the African order and the establishment of the OAU thus became a forum through which Ethiopian interests would be maintained.

This early acquisition of both regional and international legitimacy created favorable conditions for the rapid modernization of Ethiopia's military. The Cold War politics of the 1950s were exploited adeptly to sustain the growing needs of a new army. The geostrategic interests of the USA in acquiring a foothold on the Red Sea littoral coincided with parallel Ethiopian claims over Eritrea's sea ports at Massawa and Assab. This convergence of interests initially characterized the Ethiopian–US alliance and was later to be replayed under different circumstances between the post-imperial Ethiopian regime and the Soviet Union.[44] The acquisition of Eritrea, which served geostrategic interests for superpower patrons of the imperial as well as the Marxist regime(s), remained a locus of conflict and a source of challenge to Ethiopian hegemony.

The military benefits reaped by Ethiopia from these alliances also had an economic analog. The introduction of air transportation and cottage industries provided an impetus for economic modernization. The establishment of schools and a national university funded primarily by the USA and staffed largely by expatriate personnel created a modern bureaucracy.[45] The international visibility derived from such strategic linkages was also instrumental in the generation of widespread sympathy and aid during Ethiopia's recent famines.[46] This particular residual of strategic alliances was crucially important, not only as a prop to Ethiopia's otherwise moribund economy but also as a partial buffer between the regime and its domestic and regional opponents. The impulse by the international community to fulfill a humanitarian goal through donations of aid portrayed Ethiopia as a victim of "natural" rather than political disaster, and deflected any criticism from the Ethiopian state's role in contributing to the conditions of famine.[47]

Diplomatically, one of Ethiopia's significant achievements was its influence in shaping the nature of discourse concerning conflicts in the Horn. It established and maintained a regime of truth,[48] successfully characterizing the Eritrean conflict as secessionist and Arab-inspired. It was able to block effectively any overt discussion of the conflict on the African agenda. The Eritrean response, with its insistence on the right to self-determination and its portrayal of Ethiopia as an African colonizer, developed in isolation from regional norms.

The Eritrean challenge to Ethiopian hegemony through armed struggle was overshadowed by a regime of truth legitimated throughout the international and regional orders. Attempts at conflict resolution by external "mediators" from 1989 to 1990, while breaking Eritrea's three decades of isolation, were effectively countered by Ethiopia's promotion of its regime of truth.[49] Herman J. Cohen, US Assistant Secretary of State, reflected the ascendancy of Ethiopia's claims in his 1990 statement to the US Congress:

Ethiopia will be able to achieve a durable peace only by means of a negotiated, political solution. The outlines of that solution are not hard to see. Ethiopia must remain whole.[50]

Thus Ethiopian hegemony in the Horn was facilitated by its diplomatic effectiveness which, buttressed by military and economic assistance from superpowers, enabled it to maintain a stalemate with the Eritrean liberation struggle for thirty years.

From May 1991 all of this began to come apart. EPLF victories in Eritrea and the ousting of Menghistu's regime by the Ethiopian People's Revolutionary Democratic Front (EPRDF) forced American diplomats quickly to reassess their policies in the Horn. By 1993 the United States was one of the major donor countries contributing to the Eritrean referendum and the first nation to recognize Eritrea's independence, with the international community following suit.[51] The UN Security Council accepted Eritrea's application for membership on June 28, 1993.[52]

Immediately following the EPLF's liberation of Eritrea in May 1991, talks were held between the provisional government and the OAU. An eighteen-member OAU team attended the Eritrean referendum in April 1993 and declared the results as free and fair. After the declaration of Eritrean independence on May 24, 1993, an invitation was extended to the new nation to join the regional organization. On June 4, 1993, Eritrea became the fifty-second member state of the OAU.[53] Eritrean acceptance of OAU membership, however, did not lead to acquiescence to the norms, rules, and modes of operation of the organization. In a continuation of its challenge to the status quo, the Eritrean president addressed the need for a new vision and a re-structuring of the organization.

My pleasure to be amongst you today to reclaim the seat in this august body is boundless ... But this pride and joy does not rest in our mere accession to the OAU. Nor does it derive from a symbolic or spiritual gratification that we feel in rejoining the family from which we have been left out so long ... The sad fact remains that the OAU has become a nominal organization that has failed to deliver on its pronounced objectives and commitments ... [We] cannot hide – at least on the basis of our observation from without – our disappointment of [the OAU's] track record. To mince our words now and applaud the OAU would neither serve the desired purpose of learning lessons from our past or reflect positively on our honesty and integrity ... Although the OAU has often championed the lofty ideals of unity, cooperation, economic development, human rights and other worthy objectives, it has failed to seriously work for their concrete realization ... We must put our act together if this continent is to be delivered from its multiple problems ... The first step in this direction is an honest admission of our past errors and shortcomings. This will require a new vision as well as the political courage to make a sober analysis of why and how we went wrong.[54]

No longer excluded from the international and regional organizations, the government of independent Eritrea called for a reassessment of the norms, rules, and structure that had failed to achieve their goal of resolving regional conflicts. Rather than representing a threat, Eritrea's inclusion in the regional body may provide the catalyst for a fundamental transformation of the post-colonial African order which may result in the prevention of future wars in the continent.

In order to understand the complex and costly path that led to Eritrean independence it is important to understand the genesis of the conflict. An in-depth examination of the Eritrean conflict, with its origins in the 1940s and 1950s, demonstrates that the long and costly delay in addressing Eritrean demands for self-determination involved historical timing and the reconfiguration of the international state system after World War II. The next chapter explores the internal and external factors that led to the territory's association with Ethiopia, and the violations of Eritrean self-determination which resulted in the launching of armed resistance to Ethiopian domination.

3   Eritrea and the African order

Introduction

In 1894, an Eritrean chief, Bahta Hagos revolted against Italian settlement of the highlands and warned his people that "it is very difficult to find a cure once the red snake has bitten."[1] The red snake of Italian colonialism was finally vanquished in 1941. However, in its place came a fraternal black snake advocating African "liberation through unity" as a cure for colonialism.[2] In the 1940s, Eritrean nationalists echoing Pan-African tenets of unity declared that union with Ethiopia would safeguard them from "foreign administration" and "mutilation of [their] territory."[3] In the 1950s, the conditional union was effected, through a UN-sanctioned federation of Eritrea and Ethiopia. By 1962 Ethiopian unity proved as coercive and dominating as the red snake, driving Eritreans to launch an armed struggle to sever ties with Greater Ethiopia. Eritrea's persistent struggle to determine its own destiny and safeguard the basic rights of its inhabitants was denied legitimacy in the name of protecting Ethiopian unity, a "cause" upheld by the notion of Pan-African unity.

This chapter will discuss the rationale for coerced unity facilitated by Pan-Africanism as the doctrine of post-colonial Africa. I argue that the African consensus to deny legitimacy to the Eritrean struggle against Ethiopian hegemony was based on the validation of an enforced unity by states over the rights of people to self-determination in the post-colonial African order. I begin with a discussion of Pan-Africanism and Ethiopian portrayals of the Eritrean struggle as an "Arab" threat that excluded Eritrean nationalists from the African arena. I also argue that, contrary to the portrayals of Eritreans as Pan-Arabists, the anti-colonial struggles waged by Eritrean nationalists in the 1940s and 1950s were manifestly Pan-Africanist.

The support for unity with Ethiopia as a response to Italian colonialism and the British military administration was a reflection of the romantic notion of African unity as a panacea for the problems of nation-building. The failure of the Ethiopian–Eritrean federation and the establishment of the ELF in 1961, followed by Ethiopia's incorporation of Eritrea in 1962, were clear demonstrations of the contradictions inherent in the advocation of a coerced unity by the newly independent African states.

The allure of Pan-Ethiopianism (discussed in chapter 2) as a principle of the emerging Pan-Africanist philosophy found resonance among the newly decolonized African states. Ethiopia's image as an anti-colonial power paved the way for its later emergence as a leader of independent Africa.

The Eritrean nationalists' defiance of Ethiopia was dismissed as a sectarian insurrection deemed unhealthy for the post-war African order. The alliances forged between the early nationalists and Arab states – due in part to a lack of African support – further served to alienate a great number of African states. The Eritrean demand for self-determination, skillfully distorted by Ethiopia, came to be viewed as a danger to Africa rather than the actualization of Pan-Africanist tenets. Understandable as these views may have been in the heyday of Pan-Africanism, the persistence of these views until the 1990s requires an in-depth examination of the philosophical underpinnings of Pan-Ethiopianism and Pan-Africanism.

This chapter analyzes Ethiopia's hegemonic exercise of diplomacy and the Eritrean response, which isolated the conflict and deprived it of legitimation in the African political arena for three decades. Special attention is paid to the ways in which the Ethiopian state manipulated the predominant norms of the post-colonial African order by defining the Eritrean challenge to Ethiopian hegemony as a Pan-African (encompassing all black African states) threat. Consequently, the Eritrean response to this exercise of diplomatic sanctions will be examined in light of the historical and political developments which contributed to the Eritreans' failure to gain access to legitimating institutions.

Ethiopia's success in containing the Eritrean challenge was due (at least in part) to its ability to portray the conflict not only as a threat to its expanded territorial boundaries, but also as harmful to the newly established African state system. The regional consensus that Eritrean secession would lead both to further African balkanization and Arabization of the Red Sea area legitimated Ethiopia's coercive rule over Eritrea. The Eritrean challenge to Ethiopian hegemony was thus successfully barred from the African politico-diplomatic arena for decades by identifying it as a threat to the African regional order.

Pan-Africanism: the rationale for coerced unity

In twentieth-century Africa the underlying philosophy of the post-independence regional order has been that of Pan-Africanism,[4] a doctrine with its roots in the early political movements against European domination.

Pan-Africanism may be regarded as a general label descriptive of a variety of interrelated political, economic, cultural, and racial interests and aspirations, ultimately focused on the African continent but not necessarily operative solely in that habitat.[5]

Modern Africa's political identity sets Pan-Africanism apart from other "Pan" movements in the world.[6] These latter movements can be characterized by their focus on ethnicity, language, history, and tradition. By contrast Pan-Africanism was an attempt to transcend these particularistic affiliations and construct a supranational political identity based on the shared experience of European colonialism of the continent.[7] The philosophy of Pan-Africanism, which encompasses Africans in the continent as well as in the diaspora, has its roots in the negation and subordination of a specific African identity.

Institutionalized slavery and colonialism led to the unravelling of the indigenous systems of rule and to the partial disintegration of the traditional social order: in effect, "things fell apart."[8] Both phenomena had a common element: the imposition of racial humiliation. Patrick Manning explains the linkage of these shared experiences and their impact on post-colonial Africa.

Slavery helped, ironically, to create one Africa out of many. The irony is that the conditions of slavery, by the very arrogance and insensitivity of the oversimplified categorization of "the blacks," ultimately faced all black peoples with the same structures and the same dilemmas. These facts – the experience of slavery and the ideology of racism – brought responses among black people which led to the development of a Pan-African identity to match their common dilemma. Africans came to recognize each other as brothers and sisters, and to construct a common identity out of the repression and denigration they shared. The creation of one Africa, initiated by slavery, was taken to completion by the impact of colonialism ... and by the new forms of racism which developed in the twentieth century.[9]

These commonalties were to have an enduring impact on the development of African-centered philosophies and ideologies of independent Africa.

Pan-Africanism, African Socialism, and various millenarian and syncretic movements need to be understood as an articulation of an identity that can be claimed as Africa's own. Colin Legum captures the essence of Pan-Africanism:

It is not, and has never been, a unified or structured political movement. It is a movement of ideas and emotions ... Operating within it are several greatly differing trends: at one extreme the political conservatives and nationalists; at the other the radicals and revolutionaries.[10]

Unity was emphasized even in the fusion of revolutionary theories with African radicalism in the post-independence era, producing what Neil MacFarlane described as

a pronounced stress on the maintenance of national unity and a subordination of the resolution of contradictions within the people to this unity.[11]

The adoption of "progressive" ideologies inspired by Marxism, too, justified unity based on class analyses as a mechanism for transcending the various socio-cultural and economic divisions of African societies.

The Pan-Africanist emphasis on unity had a resonance deeply rooted in the shared African experience. Slavery created a diaspora which developed its own variant of Pan-Africanism, "Black Zionism," seeking return to Africa.[12] A socio-cultural legacy has been the equation of distant Ethiopia with the African "promised land." This identification of Ethiopia as a focus of all that was noble in Africa laid the foundations for the receptivity with which Ethiopian claims were embraced in the period of anti-colonial activities. This view was especially prevalent among the diaspora and African students in Europe, the West Indies, and the United States. The 1935 Italian invasion of Ethiopia by Mussolini and Emperor Haile Selassie's speech at the League of Nations further stimulated the anti-colonialist fervor among Pan-Africanists.[13] The restoration of the emperor to his throne in 1941 (though requiring Allied help) was hailed as a victory for Africa.

Ethiopia's post-war claims over the Horn were advocated by the Pan-Africanist, T. R. Makonnen, who lobbied for the return of Italian Somaliland and Eritrea to their "motherland Ethiopia."[14] These views carried into the post-independence African arena, embraced by various political activists-turned-leaders. A good example is Nnamdi Azikwe's tribute to Ethiopia as

the last vestige of black autocracy. It represents the type of government which the forefathers of Africans established in this continent ... [T]hat country will go down as one of the few survivors of the great powers of history ... [T]he continued existence of Ethiopia after its contemporaries and their descendants had vanished from political history, is, and should be, an object of admiration.[15]

This "Ethiopianism"[16] of early Pan-Africanism provided the building blocks of the international and regional support for Ethiopian unity, later symbolically institutionalized as territorial integrity.

Colonialism, too, left a legacy of boundaries cementing the separation of African polities. These arbitrary boundaries became the symbols of the physical fragmentation of the continent by outside powers. Anti-colonial African nationalists upheld the "unity" of the continent and once again looked to Ethiopia as a source of inspiration.

Thus, the notion of unity – both in the romantic and realistic sense – has remained a strong bonding principle for the disparate entities that comprise modern Africa. Both slavery and colonialism, integral parts of the African experience, were condemned for their disintegrating effects; slavery severed familial and social units while colonialism erected artificial barriers between African peoples. The African response was to view unity as a common basis for the construction of a free and independent future. This partly explains the overriding consensus on the threat of "balkanization."

The Eritrean nationalist perspective regarded the attempt by the post-colonial system to right historical wrongs as overzealous in its attempt to rectify the past through the wholesale acceptance of unity as a guiding norm.[17] The discrepancy between Pan-Africanist perceptions and the Ethiopian reality was noted by Margery Perham. Perham's language, undeniably condescending, nevertheless accurately described the lack of fit between the African image of Ethiopia and the reality of the empire:

> Long before Italy's aggression [Ethiopia] had been a kind of Zion to all those Africans ... found mainly in the United States, in the West Indies, and in southern Africa. They projected their emotions upon the distant, unknown kingdom, where, had they known it, Negroes were still enslaved ... [Italy's invasion of Ethiopia in 1935 triggered] a nationalism with a difference, an emotion aroused by the sense of a common race with distant, and unknown Ethiopia.[18]

That African unity was used to justify the violation of the basic rights of Africans by Africans has not eroded its appeal as a common political desideratum. In fact, with the institutionalization of the African state system and the establishment of the OAU, unity was enshrined as the primary purpose in the organization's Charter. For example, Article II speaks of the promotion of "unity and solidarity of African states."[19] The OAU further underscores the means through which this unity should be upheld, advocating adherence to the principles enumerated in Article III:

1. The Sovereign equality of all Member States;
2. Non-interference in the internal affairs of the States;
3. Respect for the sovereignty and territorial integrity of each State and for its inalienable right to independent existence; and
4. Peaceful settlement of disputes by negotiation, mediation, conciliation or arbitration.[20]

The process of Eritrea's decolonization – its passage from colonial status to association with the Ethiopian empire – led to its exclusion from the jurisdiction of sovereign entities considered legitimate by the African interpretation of the principle of self-determination. Despite Eritrean appeals to the United Nations and later attempts to involve the OAU in addressing grievances, the Eritrean liberation movements continued to be faced with the question of legitimacy. The new regional norms and rules institutionalized by the OAU left no room for either mediation or arbitration of the Eritrean–Ethiopian conflict.

The threat of balkanization – the African analog to the American fear of communism – became an accepted norm used to block any reforms or changes in the regulation of inter-African conflicts.[21] The term "secessionist," used to designate the Eritrean conflict, carried negative connotations which placed Eritrean aspirations for independence in an unfavorable light. Secession from an established African entity, regardless of the reasons for it, was viewed as akin to treason by the newly established African states.[22] The association of the Eritrean liberation movements with Arab states, especially the ELF's Pan-Arab alliances, also touched a raw nerve in the collective African memory of the past evils of the Arab-brokered slave trade.[23]

The ELF and the EPLF issued several declarations which unequivocally affirmed their self-identification as an African people. But their continued assertions were not given credence.[24] The Ethiopian portrayal of the Eritrean conflict as an impending "Arabization of the Red Sea" was generally accepted both at the OAU and the UN. The Eritrean challenge to Ethiopian hegemony took on larger-than-life proportions when it was extrapolated to the stability and order of African regimes. In sum, the rejection of Eritrean demands by the African order was based on a number of factors (some pragmatic and others of a perceptual nature) aptly utilized by Ethiopia. These included: (1) the view of Arab aid to the Eritrean liberation fronts as a form of cultural or racial treason; (2) acceptance of Ethiopia's self-image as a champion of African independence despite its authoritarian and undemocratic rule; and (3) unwillingness to credit the historical and geographic determinants that led to the association of Eritrean nationalists with Arab states.

At best, it would be naive, or at worst, condescending, to assume that African leaders were ignorant about the Eritrean–Ethiopian conflict, although they were certainly misinformed. In any case, it appears that their silence on the issue was a function both of Ethiopian military prowess and effective diplomatic leverage strong enough to block any official recognition. Where diplomatic efforts did not suffice as deterrents, the Ethiopian state resorted to helping those groups who opposed regimes critical of Ethiopia's hegemony. This assistance included Ethiopia's "unofficial" aid to the southern Sudanese groups opposing Khartoum's centralist rule, which permitted Eritrean offices in the Sudan.[25] A second example is Ethiopian sponsorship of the Somali Salvation Front (SSF) and the Somali National Movement (SNM), which opposed Said Barre's rule.[26]

Ethiopia's role as a champion of African liberation was also carefully nurtured by its "official" aid to OAU-recognized liberation movements such as the Zimbabwe African National Union (ZANU), SWAPO, and the African National Congress (ANC).[27] Inter-Eritrean rivalry and the ability of Ethiopia (albeit with superpower support) to reverse the guerrillas' impressive military victories also led to cautious assessments of the possible consequences of overtly interceding in the conflict. The dominance of the Ethiopian line in official diplomatic circles and the portrayal of the Eritrean conflict as an Arab-sponsored conspiracy rallied the black African majority to the Ethiopian side.

Finally, the inability of the Eritrean nationalists to provide an alternative to the hegemon's "regime of truth" contributed to the general misreading of Eritrean resistance. The Eritrean nationalists' focus on internationally based claims of self-determination and expressions of their challenge to Ethiopian hegemony as "colonization" undermined any chances of a hearing in an arena where "colonialism," for all intents and purposes, had ceased to exist with the end of direct European administration. The Eritreans' choice of an outdated political paradigm of Ethiopian "colonialism," coupled with the support of erstwhile allies such as Libya, Syria, and Iraq, did not endear their cause to the African states as a struggle deserving of fraternal support.

Ethiopia's hegemonic dominance also enabled it to control the flow of information about the conflict. Its access to both the OAU and the UN provided it with "a new instrument for the pursuance of its traditional objectives," where "new organizational forms and procedures ... have been put at the service of power politics."[28] Scholars of various disciplines and ideological proclivities, as well as policy-makers, were influenced by the information disseminated by the Ethiopian empire-state and its "Afro-Marxist" successor. The net result was akin to what Edward Said summed up as:

an institutional tendency to produce out-of-scale transnational images that are now in the process of reorienting international social discourses and processes.[29]

In their own portrayals of the Eritrean–Ethiopian conflict Eritrean nationalists claimed the right to exercise national self-determination on the basis of their identity as a former Italian colony whose decolonization was thwarted by Ethiopian intervention. The unilateral Ethiopian action to terminate Eritrea's special status as an autonomous unit within the Ethiopian empire formally altered Eritrea's status from a distinct political and geographic entity to a province of Ethiopia. The subsequent passivity of the UN and the unwillingness of the OAU to address the Eritreans' demands together facilitated the transformation of the Eritrean grievance from a "colonial" one into an "internal" matter falling under exclusive Ethiopian jurisdiction.

Ethiopia's control over Eritrea thus had two supporting constituencies: an international community that acquiesced in the willful abrogation of a UN resolution, and a regional one (the OAU) which followed suit. The confusion of these two aspects in the Eritreans' demand for independence has led to an emphasis on the colonial origins of the Eritrean problem without due attention being paid to the evolution of Ethiopia's hegemonic dominance, a transformation accomplished through manipulation of the norms and regulations formulated to abolish colonialism. It is hardly surprising, therefore, that Eritrean demands for redress were directed both to the UN and the Ethiopian state. The absence of any powerful member state of the OAU willing to mediate on behalf of the Eritrean liberation fronts on the basis of their right to self-determination effectively closed the doors for an African-sponsored resolution of the Eritrean conflict.

With the neutralization of the appeal to the right of self-determination by Ethiopia's invocation of the principle of "non-intervention," Eritrean nationalists fell back on claims of colonialism to explain Ethiopia's oppressive rule and the occupation that followed.[30] The Eritrean nationalists' view of Ethiopia as a colonizing state was a constant theme underpinning the Eritreans' identification as a colonized people with the legal right to self-determination on the basis of the post-colonial world order. However, Ethiopia's disavowal of any "colonial" capabilities and its self-proclaimed status as an anti-colonial regional power successfully circumscribed the Eritrean argument for decades. In the diplomatic arena in particular, the Eritrean demand for self-determination, which should have had universal resonance, was undermined through the Eritrean nationalists' insistence on calling Eritrea a "colony" of Ethiopia. Thus, their demand for redress was shelved because of the incompatibility of their discourse with that of the predominant political language of the post-war regional and international order.

Eritrea: outside looking in

From the outset, the Eritrean case went against the grain of Africa's post-colonial order and its attendant philosophical, ideological, and political premises. Its historical timing, arising as it did twenty-two years before the establishment of the OAU, turned it into an orphan of the new state system. Eritrea challenged Ethiopia's claim to be the champion of African anti-colonialism, and exposed, from the first, the flaws in the norms and rules of the new regional order.

From 1961 to 1981 the failure of the ELF, ELF–PLF (the Eritrean Liberation Front–People's Liberation Front), and the EPLF to gain African recognition left armed struggle as the only means of attaining independence. Not surprisingly, successful military campaigns further exacerbated African fears of balkanization. The fact that Eritrea was challenging Ethiopia also made it difficult for them to obtain the sponsorship needed to gain a hearing in the OAU, with its headquarters in the Ethiopian capital of Addis Ababa.[31] Lacking access to the OAU the Eritrean nationalists sought assistance from the Arab states, a move that placed them in yet another unfavorable position – that of being identified as instruments of Arab expansionism.

Despite their protestations to the contrary, the Eritrean nationalists were unable to shake off this label. This identification was exploited by Ethiopia to justify its mission of preventing not only the balkanization of the continent, but also the Arabization of the Red Sea. Under these circumstances the Eritrean nationalists could do little but continue to assert their determination to achieve independence through armed struggle. Their diplomatic efforts became reactive, that is, they responded to the parameters set by the Ethiopian hegemon. The established norms of postcolonial Africa (norms based on the sanctity of colonial boundaries and respect for the territorial integrity of sovereign states) coincided with Ethiopia's hegemonic interests. Despite their ability to hold a military stalemate, the Eritrean nationalists were unable to break through the African diplomatic impasse for three decades.

Post-colonial Africa adopted a number of international norms governing state behavior and established a sturdy regional state system.[32] Some scholars, like James Mayall, have argued that "the legitimate exercise of the self-determination principle [is confined] to the withdrawal of European imperial power."[33] Mayall contends that this selective interpretation has resulted in a "domestication" of self-determination on the basis of an African nationalism which equated the principle with freedom from European colonialism.[34] The early Pan-Africanist philosophy emphasized the rights of peoples to self-determination and upheld the need for unity of African peoples in the face of European colonialism. Pan-Ethiopianism, with its emphasis on the unity of the peoples of the Horn, adopted the concept of unity to validate a coercive unity of the Eritrean and Ogaden Somalis.

Independent Africa's acquiescence to Ethiopian claims also reflected a continuity with the romanticized pre-independence view of Ethiopia as a black Zion. Very few of the African intellectuals who rose to positions of leadership questioned the appropriateness of looking to monarchical Ethiopia for leadership. The few objections that did arise came from the Pan-African Freedom Movement of East and Central Africa (PAFMECA) established in 1958. Richard Cox notes that even PAFMECA, aware of Ethiopia's position, refrained from a direct attack and chose to paraphrase its criticism as the need for "democratisation of all Independent African States ... [intended] ... as a dig at Ethiopia, which was then regarded as an anachronistic State."[35] No concrete steps were taken to pressure Ethiopia to follow the tide of democracy envisioned by PAFMECA leaders. In fact, any further criticisms were stopped by Ethiopia's application to join the East African federation and its hosting of the second PAFMECA meeting of February 1962. The cooptation of this regional grouping enabled Ethiopia to regain "the mainstream of Pan-Africanism, partly through the medium of PAFMECA itself."[36] In addition to providing the location for Pan-African conferences, Ethiopia silenced any criticisms over its non-democratic nature by successfully lobbying for the resolution on the sanctity of colonial borders.

This resolution was passed at the Cairo OAU Summit in 1964, and despite its inapplicability to both the Ogadeni and Eritrean cases,[37] it was nevertheless used to legitimate the hegemonic *fait accompli*. Further political challenges to Ethiopia were pre-empted by quid pro quo arrangements with East African countries such as Kenya and Tanzania. A cooperation treaty was signed with the Kenyan government, which was threatened by Somali claims on the Northern Frontier District. Tanzania, whose leader, Julius Nyerere, was widely acclaimed as an African democrat, was pulled into the hegemonic net by Ethiopia's timely assistance to his regime during the military uprisings of 1964.

In the end, Ethiopia's value as the symbolic inspiration of African activists overshadowed the shared colonial experience of the Eritreans. It mattered little that the Eritrean experience under Italian colonialism (1869–1941) and the racial humiliation suffered under Mussolini's fascism had strengthened the Eritreans' African identity. Nor did it matter that the three major Eritrean political parties of the late 1940s – the Unionist Party (UP), the Liberal Progressive Party (LPP), and the Moslem League (ML) – were unequivocal on the subject of their African identity (unlike Ethiopia). Italian colonialism and the fascist "racial laws" had demarcated the racial lines between natives and Europeans. The UP was the only party which channeled these anti-colonial sentiments towards Pan-Ethiopian unity, reflecting thereby the general Pan-African tendency. The LPP and ML, by contrast, focused on forging an "internal" unity of Eritrea's diverse populations by demanding independence for all Eritrean citizens.

In fact, the UP's line was remarkably similar to that of black Zionism and the romantic perspective on Ethiopia held by Pan-Africanists in the diaspora. Although Pan-Africanism as an ideal was never articulated explicitly by the UP, its demand for unification with Ethiopia was regarded by Pan-Africanist ideologues as an integral part of the continental drive for unity. In fact, the UP's drive for union with Ethiopia was propeled by bitter anti-Italian and anti-British sentiments. Eritrean Moslems were viewed with equal hostility; the UP emphasized Christianity as the primary bond between the Eritrean highlanders and the Ethiopian empire. The UP's "Zionism" was thus based on a religious premiss rather than an organic unity of the Ethiopian and Eritrean peoples.

The LPP, also known as "Eritrea for Eritreans," advocated immediate independence and attempted to propagate a common Eritrean identity without distinction of creed. Unlike the clergy-supported UP, its platform underscored the shared experience of colonialism of Christian and Moslem Eritreans and rejected the Pan-Ethiopianist unity through political evangelism. Ethiopia – like many in the regional and international communities – considered the LPP's demand for an independent Eritrean nation as secessionist rather than an articulation of the rights of an African people emerging out of colonialism.

The third major party, the ML, like the LPP, advocated independence after a ten-year British trusteeship as a guarantee against Eritrean Christian domination and Ethiopian intervention. In view of these dual threats, the ML's choice of trusteeship made it a target for the UP's accusations of collaboration with colonial powers. The ML's insistence on guarantees of equality for Eritrean Moslems provided a propitious target due to its opposition to Christian domination and its disavowal of any organic links with the Ethiopian empire. The alienation and disaffection of the Moslem intelligentsia with both the Pan-Ethiopianism of the UP and the LPP's effervescent Pan-Eritreanism led to the introduction of Pan-Islamic tendencies. The ML's demands for independence and equal rights for all Eritrean citizens were underplayed while the religious factor was emphasized. The resulting image was a distortion of the Eritrean conflict as a Moslem–Christian rivalry, publicized by Ethiopia as the modern enactment of Islamic attempts to encircle the Christian kingdom.

By launching an armed struggle in 1961 Eritrean nationalists had hoped to attract UN intervention.[38] Any chances of successfully overcoming hegemonic domination through legal processes based on documented violations of the UN federal framework was pre-empted in 1962 by Ethiopia's annexation of Eritrea as the fourteenth province of the empire. In the mid-1960s, the ELF turned to the Ba'athist states of Syria and Iraq, and to radical Pan-Arabist states like Libya, who provided arms, money, and ostensible solidarity. It is hardly surprising that the ELF's goals were stated in terms that reflected the legacy of Arab Socialism. Arab aid, however, was neither substantial nor consistent.[39] Furthermore, the tenuous link between the Eritreans and the Arab world was enhanced by the Ethiopian–Israeli alliance to eliminate the armed struggle. The early ELF leaders, such as Idris M. Adem and Osman S. Sabbe, used attestations of Pan-Islamic solidarity to gain access to the Arab states. In the end, as was noted earlier, the Arab link could not save the ELF from its own weaknesses: confessional rivalry and a patronage-based form of leadership led to fragmentation among the ranks and resulted in the establishment in 1970 of a new secular organization, the EPLF.

The EPLF's political platform reiterated unequivocally the "Africanness"[40] of the Eritrean peoples and denied that it had any intentions of creating an Arab state. From 1970 until the late 1980s its ideological tenor and goals could be described as Afro-Marxist. That orientation, however, actually worked against the EPLF: the adaptation of Marxist and Maoist terms of reference to describe the feudal nature of Haile Selassie's empire helped to strengthen Ethiopia's international position as the regional bastion against communism in Africa. Then, with the Ethiopian revolution of 1974 and the demise of the emperor, the ELF and EPLF found themselves echoing the *Dergue*'s diatribes against feudalism, anti-imperialism, and Zionism.

In any event, the emergence of the Soviet Union as Ethiopia's primary ally[41] left the Eritrean nationalists in the political and ideological lurch. Soviet military aid to the *Dergue* in 1977–1978 enabled the embattled Ethiopian army to re-establish control over areas liberated by the two Eritrean fronts. While Ethiopia's revolutionary transition from an anachronistic feudal empire to a Marxist–Leninist republic altered the terms of ideological reference, the same goals remained regarding the Eritrean problem. To the existing repertoire of balkanization and arabization Marxist Ethiopia added "narrow nationalism": Eritrean resistance now became an obstacle to the "progressive" alliance of all classes and peoples.

Ethiopia's new rulers joined the Afro-Marxist camp, which hailed the emergence of its progressive leadership. However progressive, the Ethiopian revolution failed to break with its imperial past in one critical area: control over Eritrea remained a primary goal of the state, though now it was couched in appropriate Marxist terms, and echoed by Afro-Marxist states. Again, Eritrea's demand to exercise the right of self-determination and its claims for redress after Ethiopian violations were glossed over. As was the case in the 1960s, the 1970s and 1980s witnessed further adept utilization of ideological, military, and diplomatic means to consolidate Ethiopia's hegemony. The orchestra changed, but the music remained the same: Ethiopia's territorial integrity was upheld while Eritrea's right to self-determination remained unaddressed in the African arena.

Part II

4   The origins of the Eritrean conflict

Introduction

The origins of the Eritrean conflict can be traced to 1941–1951 when the first generation of anti-colonial nationalists failed to construct a coalition capable of establishing a unified Eritrean nation-state to counter Ethiopia's claims. From the outset, the decolonization of Eritrea was complicated by six factors: (1) the overriding interests of the liberating Allied forces which delayed the process of decolonization; (2) an international consensus which favored Ethiopian territorial claims; (3) Ethiopia's intervention in the internal Eritrean political arena; (4) the absence of any cohesive political institutions capable of reconciling the divergent interests of multi-ethnic Eritrean society; (5) the politicization of long-standing religious and regional rivalries among the inhabitants; and (6) the absence of a neutral and effective international decolonizing agency.

The defeat of Italy by British-led Allied forces in 1941 did not result in either the immediate transformation of the territory into a trusteeship or full independence. On April 8, 1941, Eritrea was placed under the British Military Administration (BMA) pending an international decision on the fate of the former Italian colony.[1] The BMA was a caretaker government for Eritrea as an occupied enemy territory following the terms of the Hague Convention of 1907. Its tasks were to:

govern humanely ... maintain law and order, and harness the resources of the country to the Allied war effort ... The BMA ... was required to function at the minimum cost and had no mandate to introduce large-scale reforms or innovations, which might incur additional financial expenditure.[2]

These constraints on the caretaker government were incompatible with the demands for reforms expressed by the anti-colonial Eritrean nationalists of the 1940s. Italian colonial rule had imposed a harsh and effective central administration, which in later years had glorified fascism and established a quasi-apartheid society replete with laws governing racial separation.[3] Italian settlers had mixed freely with the population and there was already a small population of Italo-Eritreans. But in 1935, Italy sought to eliminate such colonial "permissiveness," inspired by the Nazi ideology of racial superiority adopted by Mussolini.

The defeat of Fascist Italy had been viewed as liberation by the population. From the outset, Eritrean expectations were much higher than the caretaker government was willing or able to meet. A Report submitted by Brigadier Stephen H. Longrigg for the BMA's first year gives a clear indication that the caretaker government was aware of the basis for the inhabitants' expectations. He stated:

> We had unfortunately made promises or half-promises before the occupation which we have been unable (or not always willing) to implement, thereby giving the natives some grounds for complaints.[4]

The "liberation" of Eritrea was primarily an effort to bring about the defeat of the Axis powers rather than a premeditated noble endeavor to free Eritreans from fascist colonial rule. As they pushed out Italian forces in the Horn of Africa, the British did make promises to the populations of both Eritrea and Ethiopia that both would be free from alien rule.[5] Once the Axis powers were defeated their priorities immediately shifted to the establishment of spheres of influence in the post-war international order.

The international debates about the fate of Eritrea and the other Italian colonies of Libya and Somalia were initiated formally in 1945. A Council consisting of the foreign ministers of Britain, France, the USA, and the USSR (CFM) held its first meeting in London in September 1945. At this time Ethiopian claims over Eritrea and Somalia were rejected by the CFM. The USA proposed a UN collective trusteeship for ten years followed by independence; this was opposed by Britain. The USSR preferred individual trusteeship and expressed its desire to administer Tripolitania. Meanwhile, France proposed that Italy return to its former colonies as an administrative power. A second meeting was convened in Paris in April 1946 to reach agreement between the "big four." Here, Britain proposed the partition of Eritrea between Ethiopia and the Sudan, reunification of Ogaden with Somalia, and immediate independence for Libya. The USA and USSR supported the earlier French proposal for Italy's administration of its former colonies.

It was only when agreement was found to be impossible, that the CFM decided to send the Four Powers Commission of investigation (FPC) to the colonies to hear the wishes of the inhabitants themselves. The FPC visited Eritrea from November 8, 1947 until January 3, 1948 and encountered a population divided between supporters of union with Ethiopia, supporters of a "Greater Eritrea" incorporating the Tigrigna speakers of the northern province of Tigrai, and proponents of total independence for Eritrea within the boundaries prior to 1935 (i.e. before the Italian invasion of Ethiopia and expansion of its colonial boundaries to include the province of Tigrai). The FPC reported that the population was divided with a slight majority opting for independence and the rest for union with Ethiopia. The British and American delegates reported that 55 percent favored independence or an international trusteeship leading to independence, while 44.8 percent opted for union with Ethiopia. The French and Russian delegates reported that 52.17 percent favored independence or preliminary international trusteeship and 47.83 percent opted for union with Ethiopia.[6]

The "national" interests of the "big four" – Britain, France, the USA, and the USSR – were aimed at either maintaining or expanding their colonial possessions or, in the case of the emergent superpowers, establishing new bases and alliances. Britain's interests were to ensure the economic well-being of its two colonies, British Somaliland and the Sudan. Its proposal was to partition Eritrea between Ethiopia and the Sudan and to restore the Ogaden to Somalia.[7] France sought to maintain the colonial status quo and to prevent precedents of early independence for its colonies in the Horn and the Maghreb. American and Soviet efforts focused more on competition to establish footholds vacated by Italy as well as replacing Britain as the paramount international power in the Horn.[8] The one common denominator that made the fulfillment of these externally motivated goals possible – partially or wholly – was imperial Ethiopia's desire to incorporate the territory.[9] These various international interests were accompanied by the equally disparate goals of Eritrean nationalist factions whose visions of a future Eritrea were shaped by different socio-historical experiences.

In the emerging new international order which delegitimated colonialism the claims of the restored Ethiopian empire to the territory and its astute manipulation of big power rivalries to attain its goal distorted the decolonization process and the implementation of the right of self-determination of the Eritreans as a colonized people. Internally, the population emerging out of Fascist Italian rule, which had restricted the emergence of indigenous political groups, found itself facing continued European rule by the British, the possible return of Italian rule as a trustee, or the prospect of partition between neighboring Ethiopia and Anglo-Egyptian Sudan.

During this period, when international powers were haggling over solutions that were beneficial to their own national interests, the political climate in Eritrea changed from jubilation at liberation from Italian rule to fragmentation of the anti-colonial nationalist platform. British support for partition and the continued Italian presence in the territory caused anxiety and suspicion regarding European collusion at the expense of the inhabitants. The tense political climate was compounded by neighboring states which claimed Eritrea on the basis of pre-colonial linkages. Both Ethiopia and Egypt claimed the territory based on the fact that at certain periods of history they had controlled parts of what now constituted Eritrea. Ethiopia stressed racial, linguistic, cultural, and religious similarities with the highland areas while Egypt emphasized its links with the coastal areas inhabited by Moslems. Italy, despite its status as a defeated power, lobbied actively for its return as a trustee for its former colonies. Of the three claims the possibility of restoring Italian rule was met with outright hostility in Eritrea, with the exception of the settler community.

The debate among the four powers regarding the disposal of the former Italian colonies lasted from 1945 to 1948 without yielding a unanimous solution. The treaty of peace with Italy had stipulated that if the four powers could not reach an agreement on the fate of Italy's colonies within one year "the matter should be referred to the General Assembly of the United Nations for a recommendation."[10] Accordingly the CFM submitted the case to the UN on September 15, 1948.[11]

The UN began its deliberations on Eritrea on September 21, 1948. On May 13, 1949, the First Committee recommended to the General Assembly that "Eritrea, except the Western Province be incorporated into Ethiopia."[12] This recommendation was rejected by the General Assembly, whose members demanded more information about the wishes of the population before moving forward. On November 21, 1948 the General Assembly passed resolution 289 A(IV) to send a UN Commission to Eritrea to "ascertain more fully the wishes and the best means of promoting the welfare of the inhabitants."[13] This resolution entrusted the Commission to take into particular account "the interests of peace and security in East Africa ... and ... Ethiopia's legitimate need for adequate access to the sea."[14] The Commission, made up of five member countries (Burma, Guatemala, Norway, Pakistan, and the Union of South Africa) opened its offices in Asmara on February 15, 1950. It held a total of seventy public and private meetings with Eritrean individuals and party members between February 24 and April 5, 1950.[15] In addition to conducting hearings and field trips to various parts of Eritrea the Commission also distributed questionnaires and consulted with the caretaker government.[16]

On December 2, 1950, the UN finally passed a resolution to federate Eritrea with imperial Ethiopia as a compromise solution to the long and messy decolonization process. The Eritrean–Ethiopian federation (1952–1962) was short-lived due to the incompatibility of Ethiopia's absolutist monarchy and the nascent pluralist system in Eritrea. This incompatibility ultimately intensified, first as resistance, then rebellion, and finally an armed struggle for Eritrean national liberation that persisted until 1991.

Competing visions of Eritrean nationalism

On May 5, 1941, a diverse group of Eritreans (Christians, Moslems, young intellectuals, and traditional elders) established the first political organization to communicate Eritrean wishes to the BMA. Above all, they desired an end to Italian domination over Eritrea. The leadership of this anti-colonial patriotic association consisted of twelve members divided equally between six Christians and six Moslems.[17] It became known as the *Mahber Fikri Hager Ertra* (MFHE).[18] The MFHE was forced to operate clandestinely because of the BMA ban on official political parties.[19] Its membership included old and new elites, those with ties to the pre-colonial ruling classes, and self-made individuals and intellectuals. Among its founders were young Eritrean intellectuals such as Gebremeskel Woldu, Woldeab Woldemariam, and Ibrahim Sultan. All three were born under Italian colonial rule and were employed in clerical positions. Although they were from different regions and practiced different religions they shared an anti-Italian platform.[20] During the first two years of the BMA the MFHE functioned as a voluntary association which formed the basis for the political parties that later emerged.[21] The MFHE served as

a communicator . . . through which new ideas, even forbidden ideas, could circulate . . . a proving ground for political leaders, where they could demonstrate the support they could garner among a significant segment in the population.[22]

From 1941 to 1944 the MFHE remained a clandestine anti-colonial organization which embraced both Christian and Moslem nationalists and served as a common arena where traditional resistance groups, syncretic movements, and economic interest groups interacted.[23] It provided what James Coleman referred to as "an indispensable precondition for the rise of nationalism."[24]

The continued presence of Italian colonial administrators, the post-war economic crises that weakened Eritrea's new export industries, and rising urban unemployment were all concerns shared by the various sectors and regions. These issues served as a basis for unity among urban and rural elites who viewed the presence of foreigners as the source of economic, social, and political problems. Beyond the shared anti-Italian sentiments and a desire for freedom from colonial rule the MFHE had little in the way of a clear political agenda. The members of the MFHE, especially the traditional elite, regarded the defeat of the Italians as an opportunity to restore their pre-colonial power and status. The new elites, products of the Italian colonial system and beneficiaries of Western education, wanted to retain their new status and prospects for social mobility. Coleman, in a study of African anti-colonial elites which is certainly applicable to Eritrea, argues that such an elite-led movement is characterized by

an urge to recapture those aspects of the old which are compatible with the new, which it recognizes as inevitable and in some aspects desirable ... In brief, nationalism is the terminal form of colonial protest.[25]

The MFHE drew on the existing informal associations of the urban intelligentsia, traditional rulers, and rural elements whose grievances coalesced in anti-colonial sentiments. The founders were born during colonial rule and were therefore exposed to Western ways through education or apprenticeship, both under the Italians and during British occupation. Gebre-Medhin describes these anti-colonial leaders as "socially dislocated elements of the first-generation Eritrean intelligentsia, most of whom had rural backgrounds but had Western liberal aspirations."[26] Trevaskis emphasizes their urban-centered nature, suggesting that "no Eritrean class was better fed with British liberal ideas than the Asmara intelligentsia, [and] none was so starved of British reforms".[27] Coleman corroborates this view in his general assessment of African elites who headed similar anti-colonial nationalist movements:

[T]hose who in terms of improved status and material standards of living have benefitted most from colonialism; in short ... those who have come closest to the western world but have been denied entry in full terms of equality ... They are the Africans whom [colonial] policy has done most to create but least to satiate.[28]

Pre-existing local, socio-economic, and class divisions did not sharpen until the introduction of an external regional actor: the Ethiopian imperial state. With the help of the Eritrean Coptic Church, religious and kinship ties between Ethiopia and the Christian highlands became the rallying point for MFHE elements proposing union with the empire. The Eritrean Church's alliance with the Ethiopian empire changed the equilibrium in favor of the pro-union elements, using the pulpit to "convert" people to support union with Ethiopia. Ethiopian sponsorship (imperial and ecclesiastical) precipitated the resurgence of ethnic, religious, and provincial cleavages that had been subordinated to the more universal anti-colonial and nationalist sentiments.

While Eritrea's fate was being debated by the four powers and Ethiopia's support for the pro-union elements within the MFHE was increasing, another faction emerged advocating independence. This pro-independence faction was organized by Woldeab Woldemariam, who left the MFHE in 1944 and established another clandestine group in 1945, later known as *Ertra n'Ertrawian* (Eritrea for Eritreans). Woldeab's group opposed the dominance of the Coptic Church and sought to preserve the liberal pluralism introduced by the BMA. The group proposed a fifteen-year trusteeship before independence, both to prevent partition and to allow ample time for the development of Eritrean social, economic, and political institutions. Woldeab sought the support of those traditional elites who were opposed to Ethiopian rule.[29] A self-made, educated man born to Tigrayan immigrants, he lacked the support of a ready-made constituency that was available to the MFHE through traditional elite membership. Woldeab was an editor of the BMA-sponsored Tigrigna-language Eritrean weekly *Nai Ertra Semunawi Gazeta*. Thus prohibited from overt political activity as an employee of the BMA, he still managed to find support among the notables of the Akele Guzai region, where elite opposition to Ethiopian rule was particularly acute. Soon a small select group among this pro-independence traditional elite began to lobby for the inclusion of Tigrigna-speakers of the highlands and neighboring Tigrai province of Ethiopia.[30] The 1935 Italian invasion of Ethiopia had expanded Eritrea's boundaries to include Tigrai and provided some Eritrean and Tigrayan nobility opposed to Ethiopian control the impetus for the creation of an independent "Greater Eritrea." This irredentist movement, referred to as *Tigrai-Tigrigni* was said to be led by a "principal chief of the [Akele Guzai] region ... and was known to be anti-Ethiopian and Pro-British."[31] This movement was limited to a select circle of Eritrean highland notables and Tigrayan nobility, and very little is known about its emergence and very quick demise. Although the concept of a "Greater Eritrea" disappeared due to lack of grassroots support, cultural and linguistic affinities with neighboring Tigrai continued to be invoked by officials of *Ertra n'Ertraw-ian* into the late 1940s.[32] The religious and ethnic factionalism within the MFHE aroused justifiable anxiety among the association's Moslem members. They were faced with the threat of partition and incorporation with the Sudan or a future as a minority in Christian-dominated Eritrea.

During the second half of the 1940s the political atmosphere in Eritrea was charged with a bitterness against Italian rule and mistrust of British intentions.[33] This was further aggravated by the BMA's insensitive hand-ling of the Eritreans' demand that Italians be evicted from their former positions of power.[34] In addition, the British government's proposal to partition Eritrea between Ethiopia and the Sudan made the inhabitants feel like political hostages to be exchanged in deals made between external powers. In the absence of concrete support for their wishes for indepen-dence some nationalists began to view union with Ethiopia as the only way to liberate themselves from European domination.[35] Those nationalists for whom union with Ethiopia represented a worse fate than European domination began to reconsider the possible return of Italian rule as an alternative. There were also the staunch advocates of independence who regarded the gradual encroachment of Ethiopian power as a threat to their future.

For the majority of the Tigre people who inhabited the lowlands, engaged in a struggle for emancipation from the *Nabtab* (the ruling class of the Beni Amer), union with Ethiopia signified a return to the capricious rule of aristocracy.[36] For some of the lowland traditional rulers and chiefs union with an imperial power signified an opportunity to preserve their power and status. Nevertheless, the close links of the MFHE with the Ethiopian Coptic Church threatened to leave Moslem lowlanders a minority in an absolutist empire. Kinship, religion, and provincial interests which had been submerged in the anti-colonial coalition re-emerged, setting the stage for the fragmentation of Eritrean political parties.

In October 1946 the BMA lifted the ban on political parties and encouraged the institutionalization of political activities.[37] By this time, the MFHE had fragmented and only its name existed as a testimony to the earlier attempt by the anti-colonial nationalists of 1941 to forge unity in the face of continued European occupation. The "love of country" that had united the disparate members was not sufficiently strong to withstand the continuous disagreements over the future of the country. After the BMA's announcement allowing political parties to register and organize, the MFHE underwent a second internal struggle over the nature of an impending union between Eritrea and Ethiopia. A proposal to reconcile the former members of the MFHE who had opted for separation from Ethiopia and the unionists within the MFHE was proposed by Woldeab Woldemariam and Moslem and Christian notables. The proposal was for a "conditional union" which allowed Eritrean autonomy in social, cultural, and economic affairs. Woldeab argued that in the face of imminent partition of the territory between Ethiopia and the Sudan, "conditional" union would serve as a compromise between the pro-independence and pro-union factions of the MFHE. Gebremeskel Woldu, president of the MFHE since 1941, agreed to call a meeting of both sides to discuss the proposal. Woldeab, in consultation with some elders, drafted a twelve-point proposal.[38] The draft outlined the need for freedom of expression and religion, autonomy over internal affairs, the preservation of Eritrean languages and cultures, and equal rights under the law for Christians and Moslems. This draft was essentially a framework for federal union, although the term "federation" did not come into use until later. At that time the "conditional" union was referred to as *"hibret b' wou'l."* A date was set for Sunday November 23, 1946 to convene an assembly or *Waa'la* at Bet Giorghis, Asmara, to discuss the reconciliation of the two factions. Members of the MFHE and notables from both sides were invited to attend the *Waa'la*.

This attempted *rapprochement* between the two factions was seen as a threat by the radical pro-unionists and Abune Markos who were supported by the Ethiopian empire. Conditional union which allowed Eritrea considerable autonomy from the empire was not compatible with the goals of the Eritrean Coptic Church nor those of the empire. As the time for the *Waa'la* at Bet Ghiorghis approached, the radical unionists under Tedla Bairu and Abune Markos, and their imperial backers, began to lobby actively for unconditional union. They recruited young people, smuggled guns and bombs across the border, and started preparing to sabotage the reconciliation meeting.

On the eve of the *Waa'la*, Abune Markos held an all-night meeting of the MFHE, during which Gebremeskel Woldu was demoted from his post as president[39] and replaced by Ato Tedla Bairu.[40] When the *Waa'la* was convened the next day, the pro-independence factions were greeted by a new, unsympathetic leadership and found themselves surrounded by the armed members of *Mahber Andinet*, the youth section of the radical unionists. Before the discussions could begin, Tedla Bairu pre-empted further discussion of the agenda by questioning Woldeab Woldemariam's eligibility to speak on behalf of Eritreans. Claiming to speak on behalf of indigenous (*Dekheabat*) Eritreans, Tedla Bairu raised the issue of Woldeab Woldemariam's Tigrayan parentage and therefore his "Ethiopian" ancestry and concluded that his earlier stand on trusteeship and his current advocacy of "conditions" were not in the best interests of Eritreans. Woldeab Woldemariam responded that as a person born and raised in Eritrea, he had a right to express an opinion on the future of his beloved country. Tedla Bairu insisted that Woldeab Woldemariam wished to "deprive Eritreans of their privileges as 'Ethiopians'."[41] Needless to say, the meeting was deflected from its original intent to discuss the twelve-point draft about the proposed "conditional" union and the members dispersed without discussing the original agenda. The *Waa'la* at Bet Ghiorghis became a symbol of the irreconcilable differences and personal rivalries that characterized Eritrean national politics until the end of the decade.

The personal affront that Woldeab Woldemariam suffered at the *Waa'la* led to numerous debates in the newspapers that further exacerbated the political and social divisions between the two factions. The bitter media feud continued through April to May 1947, with Tedla Bairu portraying Woldeab Woldemariam as a political opportunist and Woldeab Woldemariam responding by characterizing Tedla Bairu's tactics as "Hitlerian" ethnic cleansing.[42] The BMA soon put a stop to these vitriolic exchanges and announced that the weekly newspaper was intended not for personal opinions but to serve as a forum for the exchange of political ideas of the general Eritrean public.[43]

Party politics in transitional Eritrea, 1946–1950

The failure of the Bet Ghiorghis *Waa'la* signalled an end to the MFHE as an anti-colonial nationalist coalition. For all intents and purposes, the MFHE ceased to function as a cohesive organization on November 23, 1946. The victory of the radical unionists and the Coptic Church supported by the Ethiopian empire heralded an ominous future for the non-Christian and non-elite members of the MFHE. Soon after the *Waa'la*, Ibrahim Sultan, a member of the MFHE since 1941, invited all the Moslem communities to send representatives to Keren to attend a meeting. On December 4, 1946, the first Eritrean political party, *El Rabita El Islamiya* (Moslem League), was established.[44] Said Bubaker bin Osman al Mirgani, the Mufti of the Eritrean branch of the *Tariqa Khatimiyya*, was chosen as President. Ibrahim Sultan was elected Secretary General. The Moslem League (ML) rejected any partition of Eritrea, opposed any form of union with Ethiopia, and demanded Eritrean independence. It was willing to accept a ten-year trusteeship under the British or another international power.[45]

During the same period, the unionists reconstituted the remnants of the old MFHE and the new radicals supported by Ethiopia to form a new political party. As a reflection of its declared aim of union with Ethiopia it changed its name to *Mahber Fikri Hager Ertra: Ertra m's Ethiopia* (Love of Country Association of Eritrea: Eritrea with Ethiopia). On December 3, 1946, Abune Markos appointed a new leadership consisting of Ras Kidanemariam Ghebremeskel (Honorary President), Dejazmatch Beyene Beraki (President), and Saleh Ahmed Kekiya (Vice-president). A second meeting was held on December 27, 1946, where the new leaders appointed an executive committee with Ato Tedla Bairu as Secretary General, Fitawrari Taha Adem (Treasurer) and Fitawrari Haregot Abay (Deputy Assistant Secretary).[46]

On February 18, 1947, the third party, *Mahber Netzanet Ebyet Ertra: Ertra n'Ertrawian* (Independence and Progress Party: Eritrea for Eritreans) – also known as the Liberal Progressive Party (LPP) – was established in Adi Kheih. Ras Tesemma Asberom was elected President, Dejazmatch Maascio Zewelde as Vice-president, and Grazmatch Seyoum Maascio as Secretary-General. Ras Tessema Asberom announced in his opening speech that the goal of the LPP was the creation of an independent Eritrean government free of any European control.

This country has belonged to Christians and Moslems for thousands of years. We have lived in harmony with our respective religions and helped each other. Today, we express our desire and that of our people for independence ... We notified the [British] administration in writing last year. Then, as now, our wish is to be independent and our country to be administered by its own people.[47]

The LPP objected to the role of the Coptic Church in political affairs. This was clearly expressed in Dejac Abraha Tesemma's public address:

The *Waa'la* intended as a forum where we could resolve our differences was disrupted. This disruption was legitimized by religious leaders who intervened in

public affairs ... Eritrea or Mereb Mellash belongs to Christians and Moslems alike
and does not belong to either one of us. We are children of one mother.[48]

The LPP differed from the ML in that it did not indicate a willingness to
accept European trusteeship. That the LPP and ML shared a common
political agenda of independence was reflected in the presence of Ibrahim
Sultan and Abdel Kadir Kebire and other members of the ML at the
founding of the third political party.

One month later, a branch of the LPP was established in Mendefera,
Seraie on Saturday, March 8, 1947. This branch called itself *Mahber
Netzanet'n Limaa'tn Ertra: Ertra n'Ertrawian* (Independence and Develop-
ment Party of Eritrea: Eritrea for Eritreans.) The leaders of the LPP–Seraie
branch were Dejac Sebhatu Yohannes (President), Azmatch Berhe
Gebrekidan (Vice-president), and Grazmatch Asberom Woldeghiorghis
(Secretary).

The leaders of the LPP–Seraie branch were outspoken in their demand
for independence and alliance with the ML on the basis of that common
political aim. They opposed the Church's role in fomenting religious rivalry
and objected to the UP's propaganda that the LPP–ML alliance was
tantamount to a betrayal of one's religion. Azmatch Berhe Gebrekidan, a
highly respected leader of the Seraie province, reiterated the LPP's demand
for independence and opposition to union with Ethiopia.

Because we have chosen independence – because we have accepted the stand taken
by our brethren in Akele Guzai – they call us *Rabita* and say that we have converted
to Islam. This does not offend us because those who refer to us by that name disagree
with the goal of our party. Party members should not insult or criticize those who
have established parties based on democratic laws ... A unified people have chosen
independence and hope for independence ... In these times that we live in, not to
wish for independence ... is to build a house in the middle of a river or on sand.
When the wind blows such a house will be swept away without a trace ... [T]hose
who look for chains ... put it on their own necks and ask to be strangled will in the
end suffer dire consequences.[49]

These different parties went on to establish their respective newspapers and
headquarters, inaugurating a decade of intense political dialogue regarding
the future of Eritrea.

The ban on political parties from 1941 to 1946 had shrouded in secrecy
the political activities of the different factions and had engendered a mutual
suspicion and distrust that was a reflection of Eritrean domestic affairs and
the debates about its future in the international arena. Ibrahim Sultan
captured the overall feelings of mutual distrust and hostility both in the
domestic and international debates about transitional Eritrea in his
statement:

If we look at the meetings held in London, Paris or Washington, we see acute
rivalry, accusations and counter-accusations ... In this world there is no under-

standing and no peace. We, Eritreans, are part of this world and the chaos and lack of trust that is evident in the international arena is also reflected in our relationship with each other.[50]

As the MFHE now receded into the background so did the ideals of "patriotism" and "love of the country of Eritrea." Political activities took on a more ominous meaning as the UP found itself competing for power and membership with the two pro-independence parties. The UP took the verbal offensive in its propaganda. The Coptic Church served a crucial role by using its pulpit and numerous clergy to preach union with Ethiopia. Funded by the empire, the UP recruited *shifta* (bandits) to threaten or eliminate rivals. Gebremeskel Woldu, the former president of the MFHE lamented the failure of the Eritrean leaders to cooperate and warned that factionalism would lead to tragedy.

We have reached a crucial juncture ... That *Mahber Fikri Hager*, given its capabilities has accomplished many things in the past cannot be denied ... By the same token, observers will note that its name is nobler than its needs. Numerous wounds have been inflicted that have not yet been healed. These should be discussed and resolved ... [but] it will have to [be] left to history ... It behooves us not to be arrogant in our work. Our tasks should be conducted with love, harmony and consultations not by giving orders and accepting orders ... Three parties have merged as a result of arrogance and factionalism. So that gaps can be bridged it is important to seek common ground ... To work "politically" at this juncture is wrong. In my opinion, at this time it is necessary to work in a "diplomatic" way. In order to do this one must try to understand the "psychology" of the people i.e. their history and way of life, what they hate and what they love. Independence cannot be attained by gossip, slander, lies, distortion and manipulation. If we all work with love and humility ... then our association's name can reflect its deeds ... If we are to honestly serve our country and people we should look at the misery of our people not our selfish interests! *ehh!* ... *ehh!* ... *ehh.*[51]

Geberemeskel Woldu's poignant words could serve as an epitaph to the MHFE.

Disputes between the three parties led, in the end, to brute force, corruption, and terrorism. Political violence by "unknown assailants" against prominent pro-independence persons began to occur frequently. Among the first victims was Ato Woldeab Woldemariam, who suffered severe wounds from a bomb on July 7, 1947, but survived the attack.[52] The UP's new Secretary General, Tedla Bairu, proved to be authoritarian and intolerant but also a shrewd and skilled negotiator for the empire. He was ruthless in eliminating opposition to union with Ethiopia and attacked aggressively the ML and LPP's platforms.[53] The leadership of UP–Massawa branch, who were wary of his quick ascent to power, declared themselves "independent" and demanded "conditional union."[54] The UP continued to rally its supporters against the pro-independence supporters and targeted especially the ML's willingness to accept European trusteeship as a conspiracy to restore Italian rule over Eritrea. Images of the Fascist racial laws were vividly invoked to cast doubt on the ML's stated goal of independence.[55]

While the political battle raged on, three new associations and two new parties emerged in 1947. *Mahber Jeganu Wetahader* (Eritrean War Veterans Association (EWVA)) was established in August 1947 and was dedicated to ensuring that the Italian government fulfilled its obligations to its former colonial soldiers. The second organization was the *Mahber M'huran Eritrawian* (Intellectual Association of Eritreans (IAE)), another brainchild of Woldeab Woldemariam. Very little is known about this association except that it demanded independence and its president was Gheregziher Woldemariam, one of the few Eritreans who was a university graduate in those days. The *Mahber Italo-Eritrei* (Italo-Eritrean Association (IEA)) was established by Guido De Rossi. On September 29, 1947 some members of the EWVA and the IEA established a new political party and registered as the New Eritrea Pro-Italia Party (NEPIP). Its leadership included Omar Mohammed Baduri (President) and Blatta Mohamed Abdella Ali (Vice-president). The NEPIP demanded Italian trusteeship to be followed by independence.[56] The third party, *Hezbi-al-Watani* (National Party of Massawa (NPM)) was established by members who seceded from the ML.

When the FPC visited Eritrea from November 7, 1947 until January 3, 1948, it encountered four parties (ML, LPP, NPW, and NEPIP) demanding independence, and the UP which demanded union with Ethiopia. The FPC completed its report on August 31, 1948 but was unable to reach a unanimous decision. When Eritrea's fate was not resolved according to the schedule mandated by the FPC the matter was submitted to the UN. Representatives of the Eritrean political organizations were invited to submit their views at the UN meeting in New York scheduled for April 1949. This decision was greeted by an increase in political harassment of pro-independence politicians. On March 30, 1949, Abdel Kadir Kebire, President of the ML–Asmara branch, was assassinated on the eve of his departure to attend the meeting in Lake Success, New York.[57]

Fragmented nationalism

The matter of Eritrea's disposition was submitted to the United Nations for deliberations in May 1949 at the end of which the Bevin–Sforza proposal to partition Eritrea was raised. This plan was essentially a "gentlemen's agreement," ultimately rejected by the General Assembly.

From April 5 to May 13, 1949 the UN General Assembly deliberated the Eritrean question. Representatives of the major parties and organizations were heard. Ibrahim Sultan of the ML opposed any annexation of Eritrean territory to either Ethiopia or the Sudan. He expressed his party's preference for a direct UN trusteeship should Eritrea be granted immediate independence. Mohammed Abdulla of the NEPIP also opposed annexation of Eritrea by Ethiopia and argued for an Italian trusteeship to be followed by independence. Tedla Bairu of the UP expressed his party's desire for union with Ethiopia and opposed any form of partition of the territory. The LPP representatives were not present at the UN hearings in New York, although delegates from the Italo-Eritrean Association (IEA) were present. The IEA opposed both union with Ethiopia and the partition of Eritrea.

By the end of November 1949, nineteen Italians and two Eritreans, all supporting Eritrean independence, had been murdered.[58] Outraged Eritreans and Italians bitterly accused the BA of "inertia" and negligence in its duties as an administering authority in their newspapers. These attacks were considered to be inflammatory, and on December 19, 1949, the BA closed down the three Eritrean political newspapers and four Italian newspapers.[59]

The BA's 1949 Annual Report to the Foreign Office in London aptly summed up the deteriorating political conditions in the territory. It delineated the negative political and economic impacts of the Bevin–Sforza partition plan, the threat of which had led to an increase in *shifta* activities and the rise of anti-Italian sentiments. The BA's investigations into *shifta* activities "under a 'partisan' cloak"[60] resulted in a search of the *Mahber Andinet*, where unauthorized arms and incriminating documents were seized. The leaders of the *Mahber Andinet*, described by F. G. Drew, Chief Administrator of the BA, as "storm troopers," were imprisoned and put to trial and the organization was banned on April 6, 1949.[61] In his report of the situation of Eritrean party politics at the end of 1949, Drew declared:

It is regrettable to have to record that methods of political propaganda in Eritrea have in some quarters not yet progressed beyond those of murder, intimidation and bribery.[62]

Gebremeskel Woldu's prediction that the political violence and aggressive and authoritarian methods used by the UP would lead to the disgrace of Eritrean patriotism had come true.[63]

On November 21, 1949, the General Assembly passed Resolution 289 A(IV) to send a five-member commission to properly reassess the political wishes of the Eritreans, to ensure the maintenance of "peace and security" in East Africa, and to devise ways to guarantee the "rights and claims of Ethiopia ... in particular [its] legitimate need for adequate access to the sea."[64] The UN rejection of the Bevin–Sforza plan and partition as a final solution was a source of relief to all Eritrean political parties. Nevertheless, the postponement of a solution gave rise to anxiety and heightened tensions while party officials prepared to resubmit their views to the United Nations. The failure of the Bevin-Sforza plan showed that despite the deep-seated differences among the various Eritrean political organizations, partition was rejected as an option. The inability of the pro-independence parties to speak with one voice also highlighted the strength and cohesiveness of the UP.

In May 1949, the NEPIP changed its name, rejected its earlier proposal for Italian trusteeship, and became the New Eritrea Party (NEP). The NEP sought an alliance with the ML and began to lobby actively for independence. A number of influential ML members felt "the vigorous Italian support for independence most embarrassing."[65] This was to prove a liability for the ML and especially for Ibrahim Sultan, who found it increasingly difficult to maintain the diverse coalition of the League intact in the face of UP attacks and international indifference.

In June 1949, a coalition of the major pro-independence parties was established.[66] *Selfi Natznet* or Independence Bloc was led by Ibrahim Sultan of the ML and united all the pro-independence parties and organizations around a common demand for independence. The Bloc included the ML, LPP, NEP, IEA, the NMPM (National Moslem Party of Massawa), and two other affiliated organizations, the EWVA and IEA. The IAE, although not a signatory to the Bloc's Charter, was also included at this first meeting.[67] The Bloc demanded immediate independence of Eritrea within its 1936 boundaries.

On July 25, 1949, a ceremony inaugurating the Bloc was held in Asmara, attended by officials of the BA, the Italian representative (Count di Gropello), the Ethiopian representative (Colonel Nega Haile Selassie), and a number of journalists. The Bloc's program, circulated to the public, declared the following:

Independence Bloc

THE FOLLOWING POLITICAL ORGANIZATIONS:

Rabita el-Islamiya (Moslem League)
Mahber Natznet'n Limaat'n Ertra (Liberal Progressive Party)
Mahber Hadas Ertra (New Eritrean Party)
Mahber Jeganu Wetahader (Eritrean War Veterans Association)
Mahber Italo-Eritrei (Italo-Eritrean Association)
Mahber Hezbi el-Watan (National Moslem Party of Massawa)

(a) Understanding that the political aspirations of the Eritrean people is for immediate independence;

(b) Observing the United Nations' principle of the right to self-determination of a people;

(c) Knowing that the people of Eritrea, without distinction of race, religion, and political affiliation, unanimously reject the partition of Eritrea;

(d) Taking into consideration the decisions of the executive bodies of the above mentioned organizations which met on June 22–26, 1949 in Dekhimehare and on July 24, 1949 in Asmara;

HAVE ESTABLISHED "SELFI NATZNET" INDEPENDENCE BLOC

The goals of *Selfi Natznet* (Independence Bloc) are:

(1) Immediate independence for Eritrea;
(2) Establishment of a democratic government;
(3) Maintenance of Eritrea's territorial integrity;
(4) Prevention of partition outlined by the Bevin–Sforza plan intended to incorporate Eritrea with either Ethiopia, the Sudan, or any other country.

Signed by the Secretaries of the following political parties

Mahber Rabita el-Islamiya	Ibrahim Sultan
Mahber Ertra n'Ertrawian	Seyoum Maascio
Mahber Hadas Ertra	Mohamed Abdella
Mahber Jeganu Wetahader	Ali Ibrahim
Mahber Italo-Eritrei	Filippo Casciani
Mahber Hezbi el-Watan	Ahmed Abdelkadir Beshir[68]

The Bloc's program reflected a growing sophistication of the pro-independence parties and an understanding of the terms of reference of the UN Charter as it applied to the decolonization process. Point by point it countered claims put forward by Ethiopia, Britain, and Italy. The Bloc presented itself as a coalition to safeguard Eritrea's territorial integrity, preserve its colonial boundaries, and pursue the establishment of an independent, democratic Eritrean government. A new party, the Independent Eritrea Party (IEP) joined the Bloc in 1950 increasing the official membership to six. Not much is known of the origins of the IEP except that its members had been former unionists in the Keren area who defected to the Bloc and that its President was the indefatigable Woldeab Woldemariam, who was also the editor of the party organ, *Hanti Ertra* (One Eritrea).[69]

The emergence of the Bloc ten months prior to the arrival of the UN Commission for Eritrea was the first organized challenge capable of countering the unionist forces. From July until November 1949, the UP's prospects for obtaining a majority for its platform for unconditional union appeared very slight. The inclusion of the former pro-Italian groups was a necessary step to close the ranks, but it gave rise to anti-Italian sentiments that were quickly seized by the UP. The UP accused the Bloc's leadership of receiving funds from Italy through the Italo-Eritrean Association and of serving Italian interests. In November, the UP leadership reversed its earlier rejection of the Bevin–Sforza plan and opted to accept partition. They informed the UN Commission that:

while not departing from its basic desire for reunion of Eritrea with Ethiopia, it might be that one solution for the whole country would not be considered workable ... the Unionist Party ... indicated that if the majority of the inhabitants of the Western Province were found to oppose reunion, it would not oppose a separate solution for that Division, provided that the remainder of Eritrea were then unconditionally joined with Ethiopia.[70]

This change of policy by the UP led many members of the ML from the western province to abandon the Bloc and join the unionists. Sheikh Ali Radai emerged as a leader for dissident elements who opposed Ibrahim Sultan's leadership of the ML and established a separate party, the Independent Moslem League (IML). The IML joined the unionist camp after "receiving guarantees from the Ethiopian Government that it would respect Muslim institutions."[71] The IML's crossing over to the UP was followed by three more groups which seceded from the Bloc and formed three separate parties which joined the unionists. The Liberal Unionist Party (LUP), led by Dejazmatch Abraha Tessema (one of the founders of the LPP) and Grazmatch Seyoum Maascio, opposed the inclusion of Italo-Eritreans in the Bloc and proposed conditional union with Ethiopia. The Independent Eritrea United with Ethiopia Party (IEUP) also opposed the Bloc's Italian affiliations. The IEUP's platform was a strange mix: a willingness to agree to independence to be followed by union with Ethiopia. The Moslem League of Western Province (MLWP) was established by former ML members who opposed the Bloc's demand for immediate independence and the inclusion of the Italo-Eritreans. The MLWP demanded a separate solution for the western province: British trusteeship for ten years to be followed by independence. When the UN Commission arrived in Eritrea in February 1950, it encountered a polarized population, split roughly between the Independence Bloc and the UP and its allies. Political assassinations, bombing, and terrorism had reached a peak.

The fragile coalition of the Bloc fell apart due to the same factors that brought down the coalition of the MFHE in 1946. Internal factionalism, external interference, and the absence of an effective and neutral decolonizing agency. The UN Commission Report for Eritrea indicated an awareness of these factors in its statement.

These political shifts are indicative of the state of feeling and uncertainty which has been engendered in Eritrea by the long delay in applying a final political solution. The continued uncertainty also is a root cause of the insecurity and violence which have marked the past months.[72]

The UN Commission for Eritrea, consisting of delegations from Burma, Guatemala, Norway, Pakistan, and the Union of South Africa arrived in Asmara on February 15, 1950, amid violent demonstrations following the assassination of Nasser El-Din Said, a member of the ML–Asmara branch.[73] The unrest was not limited to Asmara and was evident in all the territory. *Shifta* activities increased in the western province, Akele Guzai, Red Sea coastal areas, and Seraie. The Bloc and the LPP suffered a great loss when the Vice-president of the LPP-Seraie branch, Azmatch Berhe Gebrekidan, was murdered in 1950. Italians, British officers, and American soldiers also became victims of *shifta* activities. Italian-owned concessions, businesses, gold mines, shops, and property were burned and destroyed.[74]

From February 24 until April 5, 1950 the Commission held a total of seventy public and private meetings with party representatives and community leaders.[75] It is interesting to note that while all party leaders, officials, and political figures were listed in the Commission's list of visits and hearings, Woldeab Woldemariam, who had been a prominent figure in Eritrean politics since the early 1940s, was conspicuously absent.[76] One reason for this glaring omission was that he was an employee of the BA, which prohibited its employees from holding public office while working for the administering authority. Despite these constraints he continued to write newspaper articles and participated actively in Eritrea's political parties. During the UN Commission's hearings he suffered a fourth unsuccessful attempt on his life on March 30, 1950.[77] Following this attempt the BA announced new security policies to contain the growing political tension. These included collective punishments on whole villages that did not report *shifta* activity and rewards for those who cooperated with the BA.[78]

The UN Commission proceeded with its triple tasks of ascertaining the wishes of the inhabitants, protecting Ethiopia's interests, and ensuring peace and stability in East Africa amidst the escalating political violence in Eritrea. After holding consultations with the parties, inhabitants, and interested governments, the Commission concluded that "a majority of the Eritreans favour political association with Ethiopia" while noting the existence of "large groups who oppose the movement of union with Ethiopia."[79] The members of the UN Commission were not unanimous in their conclusions. The delegations from Burma and the Union of South Africa argued that the welfare of the population could be ensured by federation of Eritrea and Ethiopia. The delegation from Norway proposed "complete and immediate reunion."[80] Burma and South Africa proposed a federation under which

Eritrea [would] be constituted a self-governing unit of a federation of which the other member shall be Ethiopia under the sovereignty of the Ethiopian Crown.[81]

The delegation of Burma proposed that the constitutional head should be the emperor of Ethiopia but that the "governmental structure ... shall consist of a federal government and governments of Ethiopia and Eritrea."[82] These three members of the Commission, constituting a majority, noted that

a solution based on the principle of economic and political association with Ethiopia, may not at the moment command general support in Eritrea, where passions have been inflamed by political propaganda and *the resort to violence by irresponsible elements.*[83]

The remaining two members of the Commission, Guatemala and Pakistan, disagreed with the majority's assessment of the wishes of the inhabitants, the future of the Eritrean economy, and the primacy of the Ethiopian demand for access to the sea, highlighting instead the exercise of the Eritrean people's self-determination as a means of ensuring peace and security in East Africa. The Burmese and Pakistani delegations submitted a separate memorandum which reported the negative and undue pressures placed on the pro-independence parties and elements of the Eritrean population. In light of the fact that federation and/or union authorized the subordination of Eritrea to Ethiopia – a solution that appeased the desire of "irresponsible elements" perpetrating acts of violence in the name of furthering unity with Ethiopia – the minority opinion questioned the validity and integrity of federation as the best solution for Eritrea. They linked the acts of political violence to the UP and the Ethiopian-sponsored clergy, and went so far as to accuse the BA of complicity.

It was evident at the hearings held in the highlands, where the bulk of the adherents of the Unionist Party are found, that the organization of those present was semi-military. Quite a number of them wore uniforms and distinctive marks, notwithstanding an order from the British Administration prohibiting the use of uniforms on such occasions. It was apparent that the Unionist cause enjoyed the favour of the Administering Authority in the region.[84]

The minority memorandum noted that the assassination of pro-independence party leaders and officials, the asylum granted to *shifta* gangs by Ethiopia, the Eritrean Coptic Church's threats to excommunicate pro-independence Eritreans, and Ethiopia's financial support for the UP constituted deliberate political intervention in the free expression of popular sentiments. It also pointed out that the BA's preference for partition, which would increase its colonial possession, had led to a neglect of Eritrea's economy. The inviability of an independent Eritrea was a factor cited by the majority opinion, Western governments, and the Ethiopian empire to argue that Eritrea, economically, would benefit greatly from its association with Ethiopia.

It should also be considered that since the present Administering Power in Eritrea is interested in a certain political solution of the problem and hopes that at least a part of that territory may be added to its possessions, it should not be surprising that far from improving the existing conditions, that Power is not even concerned about their deterioration, for the more that the Eritrean economy suffers the more probabilities there would be [for] that Power to carry out its political plans.[85]

The Guatemalan and Pakistani representatives held that the denial of independence to Eritrea constituted a violation of the principles and spirit of the UN Charter.

All peoples have the right to be free. The Eritreans have the right to independence, since a majority of the population claims it and there are no juridical reasons justifying any other procedure.[86]

They noted that the countries of that region were under either colonial control or trusteeship and therefore did "not present any danger to the peace of Ethiopia, nor, in general, to the peace and security of that area of the world."[87] After refuting the majority's assessment of the political, economic, social, cultural, and geostrategic reasons for union they warned prophetically that the denial of Eritrean independence would lead to future conflict and instability in the region.

The *annexation of Eritrea*, in part or in whole, to Ethiopia, or the annexation of a part of Eritrea to the Sudan *against the will of a large portion of the Eritrean population would create constant internal friction*, giving rise, *inter alia*, to political measures of repression and to political persecutions *which would jeopardize the internal tranquillity of Ethiopia and peace and security in that part of the world.*[88]

The Guatemalan and Pakistani members of the UN Commission concluded that Eritrea should be placed under direct UN trusteeship for ten years, followed by independence, and recommended:

(1) That Eritrea, within its present boundaries, shall be an independent sovereign state.

(2) That this independence shall become effective at the end of a period of ten years from the date on which the General Assembly approves this recommendation.

(3) That during this period mentioned in paragraph 2, Eritrea shall be placed under the International Trusteeship System with the United Nations itself as the Administering Authority.[89]

They also recommended that the administering authority should be appointed by the General Assembly and be assisted by representatives from the United States, Ethiopia, Italy, a Moslem country, a Latin American country, and Eritrean representatives from the Coptic Christians, Moslems, and other minorities.[90] They underscored the need for trade and economic agreements between Eritrea and Ethiopia and called for the establishment of Massawa and Assab as free zones. Finally, they recommended that the UN's organization, Unesco, establish a university with Asmara as its headquarters to serve not only Eritrea but the surrounding countries. The memorandum concluded with a call for the UN to design a budget for financing these proposals.

5   The federation years: 1952–1962

It must be remembered that Ethiopia has always contended that
Eritrean autonomy was impracticable, and that full and complete union
alone, would meet the needs of the two countries ... As senior partner
in the Federation, Ethiopia has a right to expect Eritrea to follow her
leadership loyally; in return for financial and other aid she has a right to
expect Eritrea to listen to her advice and be considerate of her interests.
What she cannot legitimately demand or expect is Eritrean subservience
... It is for Ethiopia to make her choice. The temptation to subject
Eritrea firmly under her own control will always be great. Should she
try to do so, she will risk Eritrean discontent and eventual revolt,
which, with foreign sympathy and support, might well disrupt both
Eritrea and Ethiopia herself ... It is to her own interest as well as
Eritrea's that she should ensure that the Federation survives in the form
its authors intended.[1]

Trevaskis, Eritrea: A Colony in Transition.

The disposal of Eritrea

Trevaskis, a former British official in Eritrea captured the peculiarities and
possible outcomes of the Eritrean–Ethiopian federation. By agreeing to the
federation, the empire operated on two different levels. The first was a
continuation of imperial patronage of Eritrean leaders upon which Ethiopia depended to produce policies beneficial to the empire. The second was a
manipulation of the legal provisions which guaranteed the autonomy of the
Eritrean government over its internal economic, social, and political
affairs.[2] Trevaskis' analysis predicted that it would be difficult for imperial
Ethiopia not to fall back on its traditional mode of rule but hoped that it
would show foresight and act in accordance with the internationally
sponsored resolution.

On December 2, 1950, the UN General Assembly passed Resolution 390
A(V) to federate Eritrea with Ethiopia as "an autonomous unit ... under
the sovereignty of the Ethiopian Crown."[3] On December 14, 1950 the
General Assembly elected Mr. Anze Matienzo to serve as the UN Commissioner in Eritrea.[4] His tasks were (1) to consult with the BA, the Ethiopian

government, and Eritrean inhabitants; (2) to prepare a draft for the Eritrean Constitution; and (3) to advise and assist the Eritrean Assembly in its consideration of the Constitution. Resolution 390 A(V) was a "middle-of-the-road formula" which attempted to reconcile the wishes and welfare of the inhabitants while at the same time ensuring "the interests of peace and security in East Africa and the rights and claims of Ethiopia."[5]

The UN Commissioner was entrusted with the task of drafting a Constitution for Eritrea to be ratified by the Ethiopian emperor. A key issue of contention between the Commissioner and the Ethiopian Foreign Minister, Ato Aklilu Habtewold, was the role and scope of the Ethiopian representative to Eritrea.[6] The task of reconciling the wishes of the population for autonomy and the empire's propensity for control presented Matienzo with legal, ethical, and personal dilemmas during the two years of transition.

Matienzo arrived in Asmara on February 9, 1951. Consultations with the BA, the Ethiopian government, and the inhabitants of Eritrea were held during May–July 1951. The political violence that had characterized Eritrea since 1949 had increased in 1950 and by 1951 created an atmosphere of fear and insecurity. In his final report the Commissioner expressed his fears that:

renewed *shifta* activity had coincided with the moment when recommendations of the General Assembly should be implemented in an atmosphere of confidence. Although such activities might for the time being be due to common banditry ... during the consultations, or when the Eritrean Assembly was convoked, it could again be politically exploited as it had been in the past.[7]

Matienzo held meetings at the UN headquarters in Asmara as well as paying visits to the various districts. The polarization of Eritrean parties into unionist and pro-independence camps and the rifts between their constituencies had not been altered by the UN Resolution 390 A(V). The Independence Bloc had become the Eritrean Democratic Front (EDF). The coalition of parties within the EDF consisted of the ML, LPP, NEP, IEP, IEA, and EWVA. The pro-unionist parties were led by the UP and consisted of the IML, LUP, MLWP, and IEUP. The UN Commissioner sent written invitations to all political parties, religious leaders, and representatives of foreign communities. Professional organizations and economic and cultural associations were invited to apply for a hearing. Press announcements were also published to facilitate communications.[8] The officially registered parties and organizations were invited to express their views on the following questions:

1 THE ASSEMBLY

Should there be one or two Assemblies?
For what periods should the Assembly or Assemblies be elected?

2 THE EXECUTIVE

Of what should the Executive consist?
How should it be nominated?
Should it be nominated for a set term of office?
Should the Assembly be able to dismiss it at any time?
Should the emperor of Ethiopia be represented in the Executive and should he take part in consulting the government?

3 ELECTORATE

Should universal suffrage be established?
If so, what form should it take, if the traditions of the territory are to be respected?
Since it seems advisable, in principle, to adopt the system of indirect voting, what should be the best method of putting it into effect, taking into account the movements of nomadic tribes who form part of the electorate?

4 GENERAL POINTS

What should be the official languages of Eritrea?
Should Eritrea have a special flag?[9]

All the parties submitted their views and questions in writing to the Commissioner and attended the hearings, except the "acting head of the Coptic Church."[10] Predictably, the EDF and the UP and their allies took opposing stands on almost all the questions presented by the Commissioner. On the question of how many assemblies the future Eritrean government should have the EDF, the Grand Mufti, and the representatives of the Arab and Greek communities asked for two assemblies with a senate and house of representatives. The MLWP, IML, and NP also asked for two assemblies and two separate administrations for the Moslem and Christian communities. The UP, LUP, IEUP, the Coptic Church, and the representatives of the Jewish and Indian communities asked for a single assembly.

The EDF attempted to ensure the widest exercise of the autonomy granted to federal Eritrea while the UP supported any means which narrowed the gap with monarchist Ethiopia. The EDF proposed that the executive be nominated jointly by the two assemblies for a period of two years. The UP and the Coptic Church proposed that the executive be nominated by a single assembly conditional upon the emperor's approval. The unionists opposed the empowerment of the assembly to dismiss the executive. The Grand Mufti proposed an executive office of twelve ministers, to be elected by both assemblies for five years.

All the parties generally agreed to use indirect elections based on the customs and traditions of the country. The EDF asked for proportional representation of Moslem minorities in the highlands and the Christian minorities in the lowlands. It also proposed direct elections be held in urban centers such as Asmara, Massawa, and Keren. The two most divisive issues during the consultations were the selection of the Eritrean flag and official languages. The EDF proposed Arabic and Tigrigna as the official languages, an Eritrean flag, and separate federal flag other than the imperial green, yellow, and red flag of Ethiopia. The use of Arabic and a separate Eritrean flag were opposed by the UP which preferred to adopt the Ethiopian flag. Bitter arguments underlined the existing religious and cultural divide between Moslems and Christians and after debates the Moslem population, too, rejected the use of Tigrigna and opted to use only Arabic as the official language.[11]

After these consultations were completed the Commissioner left for Geneva to draft an Eritrean Constitution to complete the last steps of Eritrea's decolonization. The First Panel of Legal Consultants (FPLC) met with the Commissioner in Geneva from November 23 to December 20, 1951. The fears and anxieties expressed by the EDF were taken into consideration by the panelists who stated that:

It is true that once the Federal Act and the Eritrean Constitution have come into force the mission entrusted to the General Assembly under the Peace Treaty with Italy will have been fulfilled and the future of Eritrea must be regarded as settled; but it does not follow that the United Nations will no longer have any right to deal with the question of Eritrea. The Federal Act and the Eritrean Constitution will still be based on the resolution of the United Nations and that international instrument will retain its full force. That being so, *if it were necessary either to amend or to interpret the Federal Act, only the General Assembly, as the author of that instrument would be competent to take a decision. Similarly, if the Federal Act were violated, the General Assembly could be seized of the matter.*[12]

The opinion of the panelists was transmitted to the Ethiopian Foreign Minister in January 1952, who interpreted these safeguards as a violation of Ethiopia's sovereignty and interference in its internal affairs. The Ethiopian response to the Commissioner expressed this sentiment in a memorandum:

[T]he mere adoption of a recommendation by the United Nations concerning a Member thereof, or *its territory* could not constitute a perpetual servitude over such a Member.[13]

Thus, even before the Eritrean Constitution had been drafted the Ethiopian empire regarded Eritrea as "its territory" and regarded the exercise of autonomy by the Eritreans according to the Constitution designed by the UN as a violation of Ethiopian sovereignty. The FPLC's opinion, on the other hand, served to calm the fears of the EDF and give rise to the general Eritrean public's feeling that the UN resolution granting them autonomy would be guaranteed according to international law. The Second Panel of Legal Consultants (SPLC) met from January to February

1952, to prepare the provisional draft of the Eritrean Constitution to be enacted after ratification by the Ethiopian emperor. Copies of the draft were immediately submitted to the BA and the Ethiopian government. The Ethiopian Foreign Minister went to Asmara in late March and stayed until April during which time he continued to reiterate his government's objection to the limitation of the powers of the Ethiopian representative to Eritrea, the inclusion of human rights, and the emphasis on democratic pluralism included in the draft.

While the UN Commissioner, the Ethiopian government, the BA, and the panelists were discussing amendments and changes to the draft of the Constitution, the population was preparing for elections. On January 29, 1952, the BA issued Proclamation 121 establishing sixty-eight electoral districts and criteria for voter eligibility and office holders for the Eritrean Assembly.[14] The general procedure was for indirect elections except for the urban centers of Asmara and Massawa where direct elections were to be held. People were qualified to vote in both the indirect and direct elections if they were male inhabitants "descended from a parent or grandparent wholly of blood indigenous to Eritrea," twenty-one years of age and over, residents of a constituency for at least one year, of sound mind, and without prison records.

Eligible officials for election to the Eritrean Assembly were required to be over thirty years of age, to verify a two-year residency in their constituency, not be declared bankrupts, and could not be under a contract of employment with the BA.[15] Eritrean women were not eligible to vote or hold office regardless of their age or level of education; nor were Italo-Eritreans or any others of mixed parentage. The exclusion of such persons served to diminish the support of EDF members, such as the Italo-Eritrean Association and long-standing members of foreign communities permanently settled in Eritrea.

In the indirect elections, the districts first elected delegates to an electoral college which then elected members of the Assembly by secret ballot. Direct elections were held in Asmara and Massawa on March 25/26, 1952, and the second stage of indirect elections (where the electoral colleges elected members of the Assembly) was held on March 26, 1952. In the indirect elections in the rural areas the results were recorded by the UN Commissioner as follows:

Unionists and Liberal Unionists	32
Democratic and Independent Front	18
(Moslem League and other parts of the EDF)	
Moslem League of the Western Province	14
National Party	1
Independent Moslem League	1
	Total 66

These figures changed slightly when on May 12, 1952, an EDF delegate and a MLWP delegate were elected, thus increasing the EDF's total seats to 19 and that of the MLWP to 15, bringing the total to 68.[16]

The Eritrean Assembly was inaugurated on April 28, 1952. The chief administrator of the BA gave the opening speech followed by the representative of the emperor. The next day the Assembly, dominated by a strong Unionist plurality, voted by secret ballot to elect Ato Tedla Bairu as president and Sheikh Ali Radai as Vice-president of the Assembly, ensuring the UP's leadership of the first Eritrean government.[17] The Assembly also approved the use of English, Arabic and Tigrigna as the languages to be used in the Assembly. On May 3, 1952, the Assembly deliberated on the draft of the Constitution submitted by the Commissioner. Matienzo stated that "Eritrea's autonomy will be guaranteed by the Constitution [which] is based on democratic values."[18] This draft described the Eritrean government as a "semi-presidential" system whereby the Chief Executive would be elected by the Assembly and empowered to appoint the secretaries of the executive departments. The Assembly met to deliberate the various articles of the draft Constitution from May 12 to July 10, 1952, and proposed and passed amendments. Some of the key amendments were:

1 a single chamber for the Assembly;
2 four-year Assembly terms;
3 regular sessions to be specified by law;
4 closing of regular sessions requiring the Chief Executive's consultation with the President of the Assembly;
5 special sessions convened by the Chief Executive requiring a written request from one-third of Assembly members;
6 quorum raised from one-half to two-thirds of members;
7 granting of Eritrean citizenship to federal nationals in accordance with the laws of Eritrea;
8 denying the representative of the Ethiopian emperor the power to comment on draft legislation submitted to the Assembly;
9 adopting a distinct flag, seal, and arms for Eritrea.[19]

On July 10, 1952, the Assembly unanimously adopted the Eritrean Constitution, with the various amendments. The UN Commissioner signed the Instrument of Approval on August 6, 1952. On September 11, 1952, the Federal Act was ratified by Emperor Haile Selassie I. Eleven years after the termination of its status as an Italian colony Eritrea's transition from colonial status to federal unit under the sovereignty of the Ethiopian empire was completed.[20]

After the ratification of the Federal Act by the emperor, the British flag was lowered with great pomp and ceremony on September 15, 1952, and the federal (Ethiopian) flag was raised. It was not until the next morning that the Eritrean flag (olive branches on a sky blue background) was raised in front of the Eritrean government building in a low-key ceremony attended by a small gathering of officials. Eritrea was pronounced an "autonomous unit"[21] under imperial sovereignty and the short-lived decade of Eritrean party politics came to an end. Two days later, on September 18, 1952, a 3,000-man Ethiopian brigade moved into Eritrea, ostensibly to replace the much smaller British army.[22] The UN-sponsored federation legitimated Ethiopia's imperial presence in Eritrea.

Federation: a prelude to annexation?

Federation inaugurated a decade of constitutional and legal infringements by the Ethiopian empire that nullified the Eritrean Constitution. The federal government stripped away the safeguards on the autonomy of Eritrea's political, social, and economic institutions. Although large-scale Ethiopian settlement was prevented by Eritrean objection, Ethiopian armed units were sent into Eritrea to pre-empt any Eritrean resistance to federation.[23] The first half of the federation period, 1952–1955, retained the facade of democratic trappings. But even the appearance of democracy was gradually eroded by the new administration's collaboration with pro-Ethiopian members of the first Assembly.

On September 30, 1952, Proclamation number 130 was issued by Emperor Haile Selassie, declaring the federal Ethiopian court to be the territory's final court of appeal. This was in violation of Articles 85 and 90 of the Eritrean Constitution.

ARTICLE 85

Judicial power

Judicial power shall be exercised by a Supreme Court and by other courts which will apply the various systems of law in force in Eritrea. The organization of these courts shall be established by law.

ARTICLE 90

Jurisdiction of the Supreme Court

The Supreme Court shall have jurisdiction in the following matters:

1 *As a court of last resort* with respect to appeals from final judgments in points of law, and also to the extent provided by law with respect to appeals both on questions of law and fact.[24]

This imperial act infringed upon the judicial authority of the Eritrean government and bypassed the Eritrean Constitution as the supreme law of the land. The subsequent increases in Ethiopian import tariffs drove up the cost of living in Eritrea by 20 percent. In October 1952 protests and demonstrations were held denouncing the economic hardship imposed on the population. Opposition newspapers such as *Dimtzi Ertra* (Voice of Eritrea) were closed down. This, too, constituted a violation of Section II, Article 30 of the Constitution:

ARTICLE 30

Freedom to express opinion

Everyone resident in Eritrea shall have the right to express his opinion through any medium whatever (press, speech, etc.) and to learn the opinions expressed by others.[25]

In July 1953, the empire tightened its control and curbed mobility by passing a law that required all Eritrean males in urban areas to carry identity cards at all times.

Omar Kadi, jurist, former President of the IML, and editor of the pro-unionist newspaper *Andinet'n Me'belnaan / Unione e Progresso* (Union and Progress)[26] was one of the few members of the Eritrean Assembly to lodge a letter of protest to the President of the Assembly, on May 25, 1953. In this letter he pointed out that the legal maneuvers of the federal government were unconstitutional and eroded Eritrea's autonomy. Omar Kadi demanded to know why the Eritrean government "was negligent in its obligations and in its competence?"[27] Public disquiet increased but any overt opposition was stifled or subverted by the distribution of funds and titles to certain Assembly members.[28]

The systematic erosion of Eritrean constitutional rights was even more flagrant after 1955. Intimidation, coercion, and military might now came into play. Outspoken members of the Eritrean Assembly were either threatened or arrested for violations of federal (i.e. Ethiopian) laws. In May 1955, Ibrahim Sultan was put on trial, accused of defaming a foreign (Sudanese) official. This trial was important not only because it targeted the most visible proponent of autonomy but also because it was a clear show of power in the unionist-controlled Assembly, to muzzle any dissent from the former leader of the Independence Bloc. Two months later Tedla Bairu resigned as Chief Executive and was replaced temporarily by Sheikh Idris Mohamed Adem until the scheduled elections. What little autonomy the Eritrean government exercised was eliminated in 1956 with the Ethiopian-engineered election of Asfha Woldemichael, who had served as the representative of the UP branch in Addis and worked for the Ethiopian emperor.

During Asfha Woldemichael's tenure as Chief Executive the pace of dismantling the federation accelerated. Among the major bills he passed were the change of the name of the Eritrean government to that of Eritrean "administration," the adoption of the Ethiopian flag, and the introduction of a large number of Ethiopian administrators and teachers into Eritrea. The renaming of the Eritrean government as merely an "administration" was more than a cosmetic change. It stripped away the official existence of any government other than the imperial government of Ethiopia. The other symbols of a distinct Eritrean political entity – the flag, seal, and arms – were replaced by those of the empire. The arrival of Ethiopian administrators and teachers also signified a direct violation of Eritrea's right to administer its internal affairs. Article 5 of the Constitution clearly demarcates the jurisdictions of the federal and Eritrean government:

ARTICLE 5

Matters coming within the jurisdiction of Eritrea

1 The jurisdiction of the government of Eritrea shall extend to all matters invested in the federal government by the Federal Act.

2 *This jurisdiction shall include:*

(a) the various branches of law (criminal law, civil law, commercial law, etc.);
(b) the organization of public services;
(c) internal police;
(d) health;
(e) education;
(f) public assistance and social security;
(g) protection of labor;
(h) exploitation of natural resources and regulation of industry, internal commerce, trades and professions;
(i) agriculture;
(j) internal communications;
(k) the public utility services which are peculiar to Eritrea;
(l) the Eritrean budget and the establishment and collection of taxes designed to meet the expenses of Eritrean public functions and expenses.[29]

The intervention of the federal government and the authorization of Ethiopian citizens to hold key positions in the administration and educational institutions of the country were the beginnings of a policy of *Amharization* or Ethiopianization.

Eritrean leaders, and especially the Moslem minority in the Assembly sent petitions to the UN protesting against these violations of the Constitution but to no avail.[30] By 1958, the Assembly was little more than a rubber stamp for imperial demands. The Assembly began to lose any credibility with the people as the Ethiopian empire's "federal" representatives continued to combine coercion and legal manipulation to create a pliable Assembly.

During March and April 1958, eighteen prominent Moslems, including Omar Kadi, were arrested for sending a telegram to the UN Secretary-

General protesting Ethiopian violations of UN Resolution 390 A(V). The Ethiopian Crown invoked its rights as a federal government to administer foreign relations and regarded this action as a crime against the empire-state. The Eritreans, on the other hand, continued to adhere to the belief that the UN, as the international instrument of the decolonization of Eritrea, would safeguard their autonomy. The eighteen accused Moslems who had signed the petition to the UN appealing for a review of Eritrea's status were charged with interfering in federal jurisdiction regarding internal disputes.[31] Omar Kadi was sentenced to ten years while the others were detained for short terms or released on bail.[32] The Moslem communities were outraged and felt persecuted, especially since there was no official protest from other members of the Assembly.

Resistance to Ethiopian hegemony

Formal opposition to these encroachments of the federal government were not forthcoming due to fear of retaliation and the corruption of some Eritrean officials. But grass-roots resentment against the Ethiopian empire and the federation found expression in the lyrics of popular songs. The reaction of the inhabitants seems to have been one of incredulity at the increasing harshness of life during the federation:

Ata Ane'ye Gerimuni	(I am amazed at what's happening.
Marcia Indietro' do	I never thought we would go
N'kheid Mesiluni	backwards in history
Kabzi Khulu's Mussolini'	Would Mussolini have been
do Me'Hasheni?	better for me?!?!)[33]

Popular protest increased along with economic hardship and censorship.[34] Increased political repression led to the flight of established political leaders from Eritrea to Egypt and the Sudan.[35]

The third Eritrean Assembly elections were held on September 5–7, 1960. While leaders like Ibrahim Sultan were forced to flee Eritrea, the three trusted "kingsmen" – Asfha Woldemichael, Sheikh Hamid Ferej Hamid, and Keshi Dimetros (Melaake Selaam) – were re-elected as Chief Executive, President, and Vice-president respectively of the Assembly. A week later, 300–400 students went on strike in Asmara demanding the restoration of the Eritrean flag, seal, and arms. They were immediately imprisoned despite protests from outraged parents. Some were even sent to Ethiopia to serve out their prison terms.

By this time, resistance to further Ethiopian erosion of Eritrean autonomy had achieved an inexorable momentum, and a chain of events in 1961 and 1962 signalled an impending flashpoint in the confrontations between Eritrea and Ethiopia. In late 1961 the American consul in Asmara noted "some firming up of the Eritrean opposition against further Ethiopian encroachments," including the growing reluctance of the "normally ... subservient" Eritrean police to submit to the empire and a new resolve by the "usually spineless" Eritrean Assembly, under "increasing criticism from constituents," to act as more than a "rubber stamp" of imperial wishes.[36] By October 1961 reports of *shifta* activity had increased, especially under Hamid Idris Awate in the Agordat region of the western lowlands. Awate is credited with firing the first shot at an isolated Ethiopian garrison in the western lowlands. Awate had "taken to the field again" not merely as a bandit but for more significantly political reasons, to "nullify concessions granted by the Eritrean government" to both Eritrean and Ethiopian officials.[37]

In November 1961, *Melaake Selaam* Dimetros, the Rasputin-like Vice-president of the Eritrean Assembly and "one of the leading instruments for Ethiopian policy" in Eritrea suffered an attempt on his life, and one of his assailant, Ghebremedhin Hailu, was killed in the attempt. According to the American consul in Asmara, "the general feeling [in Asmara] was one of regret that the Vice-president of the Assembly had escaped unscathed."[38] Ghebremedhin's funeral reportedly was also well attended. Notwithstanding Dimetros' own unsavory reputation in Eritrea the American consul concluded:

the assassination attempt ... constitutes a warning to the Ethiopian government and its instruments in Eritrea to be more prudent in pushing their annexation policies here and in trying to rig local elections to suit their purposes ... But whether or not the warning will be heeded is another matter.[39]

Expressions of grass-roots resentment became bolder. The earlier reaction of the 1950s when public sentiment was reflected as incredulity at the gradual erosion of constitutional rights was replaced by anger directed at the elected officials of the Assembly. By early 1962 folk singers in Asamra's numerous beerhouses were drinking to the accompaniment of such warnings:

Assembleia B'Haki F'redu	(MP's do the right thing
Kabti Reshan	So that you may leave
B'dehan K'twerdu	your offices safely.)[40]

In May 1962, propelled by rumors that the Eritrean Assembly was considering a resolution to unify the territory with Ethiopia, hundreds of high-school students held a demonstration demanding Eritrean freedom. The demonstration was well organized and peaceful. The American consul noted in his report that:

it was a surprising and courageous move in this police state. Symptomatic of general discontent ... this incident was apparently triggered off by a widespread rumor that the Eritrean Assembly was about to vote for full union with Ethiopia.[41]

The demonstration reflected the existence of organized resistance aiming "presumably to encourage – if not to frighten – the Assembly members in order that Ethiopian pressures would be resisted."[42] These demonstrations were held during the meeting of the UN Committee of Seventeen on Colonization in Addis Ababa. The night before the Committee was to depart, Robert Blake, the American delegate to the UN Committee received a leaflet written in English dated June 3, 1962 signed by an organization calling itself the "Association of Eritrean Intellectualists." Despite the awkward use of the English language the leaflet's message was clearly an appeal to the UN and the outside world to heed the violation of Eritrean rights and aspirations to freedom. It stated:

In these years, we lost our men, who became Refugees, our factories which were working till 1955, and our flag which were waving till 1956. Now, if you go and see what the Ethiopians are doing . . . in Eritrea, you may call it the Second Algeria or the Second South Africa . . . even the students . . . from 300–400 . . . are in jail . . . in search of Indipendent, as every countries did for Freedom. We are not the herd of sheep needing a foreign shepherd to rule us. . . . we have indeed many learned Eritrean brothers whose new task will not be too heavy for their strong shoulder.[43]

Such warnings and political activity asserting Eritrean rights had repercussions on the Eritrean administration. The Assembly adjourned until June 18 without passing any acts of reunification.[44] The political climate in Eritrea reflected an emboldened Eritrean population and administration.

Emperor Haile Selassie's visit to Eritrea from June 16 to 28, 1962 seems to indicate growing imperial concern over the turn of events. During his visit the emperor clearly demonstrated that he considered himself the only sovereign over the country. In a direct and arrogant violation of the Eritrean administration's jurisdiction over its own police forces, he promoted twenty-three officers. In addition, he bestowed numerous titles on members of the Assembly and assorted chiefs. Nor did he try to coopt only the elite. In a shrewd attempt to restore his popularity among the peasantry, he "took upon himself for two years the payment of tribute, a revenue item in the Eritrean budget which is exacted from country villages in lieu of income tax."[45] These displays of royal largess, though, were accompanied by declarations to restore "internal order."[46]

The Eritrean Assembly, which convened on June 19, 1962, three days after the emperor's arrival in Asmara, rejected the Chief Executive's proposal to allocate large sums for the police.[47] Such a show of autonomy while the royal entourage was still in the city was a clear signal that times had changed. The American consul noted:

First, the acquiescence of the Eritrean Assembly cannot be taken for granted even though its members may have been suborned with money, titles or decorations, and second, should unilateral action be attempted, it is possible that it may cause a violent "reaction."[48]

In a speech given on the eve of his departure from Asmara, the emperor made no reference to the Eritrean Administration or the Eritrean people. Rather, he talked about "this part of Our Empire" and, alluding to the activities of Eritrean exiles in the Middle East, he "castigated dissident elements . . . as 'tools of foreigners'."[49]

During the ten years of federation Ethiopia had inadvertently created the conditions that united the bellicose and disparate Eritrean nationalists. By July 1962 it appeared unlikely that indirect Ethiopian rule could contain successfully the burgeoning resistance. The challenges to Ethiopian hegemonic control – legal, social, economic, and political – by the Eritrean Administration and armed confrontations with the Awate-led armed group signalled the inviability of imperial rule through Eritrean emissaries.

The termination of the Eritrean–Ethiopian federation

On November 14 1962, with a sizeable Ethiopian army surrounding the Eritrean administration building where the Assembly convened, Eritrea was declared a part of the Ethiopian empire.[50] The acquisition of a new territory for the expansion of Greater Ethiopia had been accomplished through diplomatic, military, and extra-legal means. Annexation, which ended the territory's brief "democratic" interlude, was the anti-climactic end to a gradual usurpation of the right to self-determination for Eritrea. The Eritrean–Ethiopian federation was primarily an appeasement of Ethiopia's expansionist claims which attempted to reconcile two antithetical political systems: parliamentary democracy and absolutist monarchy.

The Eritrean–Ethiopian federation was UN-sponsored, Ethiopian-backed, and adopted as a compromise solution by a significant elite stratum. It was a quintessential illustration of the lack of consensus and failure of will among the three sets of competing participants: the international powers (the UK, Italy, USA, USSR, and the UN), the regional power (Ethiopia), and the domestic (Eritrean) contenders for power. The federation also served to sharpen the divisions among the Eritrean groups, helped draw the battle lines between the proponents and opponents of closer ties to Ethiopia, and moved Eritrean nationalists closer to violent confrontation with the Ethiopian regime.

The UN resolution served to articulate and legitimate Ethiopia's claims over Eritrea based on pre-colonial historical linkages. The terms of reference – underwritten by the UN – that highlighted and legitimated the primacy of Ethiopian interests (access to the sea) had already prejudged the issue. It is in this light that one can argue that Ethiopia's assiduous attempts to subordinate Eritrean interests to those of the empire, and its ability to use the external and internal rivalries for its own ends, all add up to the development of hegemonic dominance. Where military might had achieved the aims of a Greater Ethiopia during the reign of Menelik II and his predecessors, the new international order prohibiting outright colonization prevented the use of these traditional means of acquiring territory.

Diplomatic effectiveness, alliance management, selective coercion, and other legal and extra-legal means all combined to legitimate Haile Selassie's acquisition of Eritrea. The Eritrean–Ethiopian federation, envisioned as a mechanism of decolonization, succeeded in constructing a new legal entity which only affirmed the existence of Eritrea by virtue of its association with the empire. Through effective diplomatic lobbying, manipulation of great power interests, and intervention, Ethiopia acquired the legal means to achieve its hold over Eritrea. In the words of Bereket Habteselassie, the UN's guarantee of Eritrean autonomy which was "grafted onto a feudal system was like an antibody imposed on a body politic that was not able or willing to receive it."[51] Outright illegal means, such as blackmailing the UN Commissioner, were also used to ensure that requisite institutional safeguards for Eritrea were not implemented.[52] The inherent legal as well as structural contradictions that exist between a federal arrangement based on decentralization with a degree of autonomous participation, and an absolute monarchy were either optimistically or opportunistically ignored.

The absence of a common vision among the Eritrean political parties and organizations reinforced the international consensus reached on the "right" of Ethiopia to be an actor in the resolution of Eritrean affairs. Resolution 390 A(V) paved the way for the Ethiopian presence in Eritrea and the empire's acquisition of new territory by means other than an outright military takeover which had characterized former colonial conquests. The Eritreans of the 1940s and 1950s were faced with the opportunity to create a "nation" from the artificial amalgamation of its disparate regional inhabitants. Italian rule had effectively forged a territorial entity by demarcating the boundaries of its "first-born" colony. With the demise of Italian colonialism even the boundaries that had encompassed colonial Eritrea were challenged by external powers. An example of this was the British government's push for the partition of Eritrea between the Sudan and Ethiopia.

Internally, the Eritreans of this era had not developed a clear sense of what separated them from their neighbors to the northwest, south or east. They had barely begun to interact as equal members of the new postcolonial society. The process of separating primary affiliations of kinship, regionalism, and religion from that of a common national identity that embraces all its inhabitants was to take another thirty years. An encompassing nationalism requires extended interaction among the constituencies. In Eritrea, as in the continent as a whole, the creation of a consensus defining a common experience, the compilation of a shared political lexicon, the development of sets of symbols and ideology were all in their embryonic stages in the two decades following Italian rule.[53] The incubation period of nationalism is also subject to influences emanating from the international and regional political orders within which this process takes place.[54] As such, the evolution of a common identity in the face of an external threat, which began with the loss of autonomy in the 1950s, should not be mistaken for a fully-fledged national identity.

In the Eritrean case, in the light of the territory's historical and socio-cultural fragmentation, the process of creating an Eritrean nation was derailed by competing external rivalries and the competing loyalties they engendered. Domestically, the Eritrean–Ethiopian federation (1952–1962) culminated in the collapse of the fragile alliances of Eritrea's disparate socio-political groupings. Regionally, it attested to the ability of the Ethiopian hegemon's capacity to manipulate both the new international order and the existing political vacuum in neighboring Eritrea to acquire a historically contested area. Internationally, it reflected the simultaneous hypocrisy and idealism of the new international order as demonstrated by the UN's capitulation to the imperatives of powerful national interests at the expense of the rhetoric of self-determination and humanitarianism.

Eritrean nationalism, permeable to competing external threats, underwent a qualitative transformation during the federation period, culminating in the establishment of an anti-Ethiopian liberation struggle. Thus, Ethiopia inadvertently strengthened the fragmented nationalism that had begun to disintegrate under the onslaught of imperial diplomatic and military power. Coercion and isolation were the means by which Ethiopia attempted to negate the existence of the Eritrean "problem." Although successful in containing internal dissidence imperial Ethiopia's repressive policies provided the impetus for the organization by the Eritrean people to attain their independence through armed struggle, when legal recourse to the international order (which had sanctioned Ethiopia's hegemony) had proved futile. There is little question, then, that modern Eritrean nationalism was a by-product of Ethiopian hegemonic domination. Of equal importance to the shaping of modern Eritrean nationalism was the dual failure of the post-war international order to fulfill its noble goals of freeing all peoples from alien rule as promulgated in the UN Charter and of first-generation Eritrean nationalists to unite around a common goal.

By 1962 the charade of "federal autonomy" was over and Eritrea was annexed as the fourteenth province of Ethiopia, so ending the unequal and uneasy political association between Eritrea and Ethiopia. Ethiopian success at reviving a reconstructed past based on pre-colonial historical linkages fragmented the common bond of the Eritrean opposition which had fostered a distinct Eritrean identity. However, the coercive unity imposed by the hegemon through appeals to a glorious Christian imperial past alienated Eritrea's significant Moslem population – a population that would spearhead the armed resistance against Ethiopia's hegemonic domination.

6   Secular nationalism: the creative radicalism of the ELM

The politics of protest

Organized Eritrean response to Ethiopian hegemony began in the late 1950s. Eritrean nationalists had three tasks: (1) to reconcile the fragmented nationalism that characterized the Eritrean political parties of the 1940s and late 1950s; (2) to construct a viable Eritrean national identity; and (3) to mobilize the nationalist forces against Ethiopian hegemony. In contrast to the party politics of the 1940s, the late 1950s were marked by organized, clandestine resistance to the increasing Ethiopian domination of Eritrean affairs.

The new leadership, who replaced the party politicians and traditional power brokers, were the leaders of the first liberation movement, the Eritrean Liberation Movement (ELM), established in 1958. The urban-based ELM used secularization as a strategy to reconcile the Moslem–Christian schism. However, the ELM's attempt at secularization was stymied by the formation in 1961 of a rival organization, the Eritrean Liberation Front (ELF). The ELM continued along the path of civil disobedience and liberation by coup until 1965.[1] That year, in a bloody confrontation that thereafter would characterize the relations between Eritrean liberation movements, the ELM's decision to launch its own armed struggle was violently crushed by the ELF.

This chapter examines the development of organized Eritrean resistance to Ethiopian hegemony at the end of the federation years. The period, which extends from 1958 through annexation to 1965, was characterized by (1) the politics of protest and civil disobedience; (2) a secular nationalism which temporarily transcended religious, ethnic, and urban–rural divisions; (3) a clandestine organization which established a wide network of resistance; and (4) the politicization of Eritrean culture. I argue that, despite the ELM's brief existence and its abrupt demise in 1965, the radicalization of Eritrean society (particularly the youth) had far-reaching effects on the Eritrean nationalist resistance. The creative mobilization strategies which bypassed traditional patronage networks succeeded in temporarily unifying the fragmented nationalism of the earlier decade.

98

The third quarter of the 1950s bore testimony to the efficiency of the Ethiopian Crown in undermining the federal and constitutional guarantees of Eritrean autonomy. By 1958 the Eritreans had come to realize that the facade of federation could not accommodate the autonomy granted to Eritrean institutions under UN Resolution 390 A(V). In an environment characterized by swift and brutal repression, opposition to increasing Ethiopian domination was driven underground.

New leaders, strategies, and means of resistance emerged in the struggle to salvage Eritrea's future as a distinct political entity. The party leaders and traditional elites of the 1940s were replaced by young exiles who focused on the task of reconciling the fragmented nationalism which had contributed to the failure of Eritrea's bid for nationhood. Their first venture was to organize widespread acts of civil disobedience, ushering in an era of organized political protest.

The clandestine politics of protest permeated a wide constituency and popularized the nationalist struggle through a creative mobilization of social and economic grievances against Ethiopian violations of federal guarantees. The use of the cultural arena as a vehicle for national reconciliation and mobilization was one of the most significant developments of this period. Social gatherings, sport, and tea-houses were transformed into mobilization centers for youth, workers, and small traders. The new leadership gave birth to a creative use of cultural symbols in order to overcome the schism between the Moslem and Christian populations, a schism that had been so skillfully exploited by the Ethiopian empire-state. In contrast to the earlier decade of fragmented nationalism the leaders of the late 1950s organized clandestine cells around a social and political platform on which all Eritreans could unite.

The Eritrean Liberation Movement (ELM)

The *Harekat Tahrir Eritrea*[2] (Eritrean Liberation Movement) was established in November 1958 by five young Moslem Eritrean exiles residing in Port Sudan. The group included Mohamed Said Nawud, Saleh Ahmed Iyay, Yasin el-Gade, Mohammed el-Hassan, and Said Sabr.[3] They were all in their twenties and without prior affiliation to the political parties of the earlier decade. Port Sudan was ideally suited for their purpose because it served as an entrepôt for news, arms, and the sizeable human traffic (commercial and nomadic) that crossed the Eritrean–Sudanese border. M. S. Nawud, the principal leader, had contacts with the Sudanese Communist Party (SCP), which at that time was one of the best organized of such groups in black Africa.

The SCP's influence on the ELM was reflected in the adoption of SCP structures of recruitment and mobilization. The ELM's clandestine cell structure and the emphasis on literary study circles were also distinguishing features of the Sudanese nationalist movements.[4]

The founders of the ELM, all Moslems, were conscious of the harmful effects of the religious divisions which had pitted Christian against Moslem in the 1940s. From the outset, the ELM's leaders attempted to overcome the religious hostility fanned by the Ethiopian and Eritrean Coptic Churches in the competition for power during the British administration. The preamble to the ELM Charter emphasized that Moslems and Christians were brothers, and that their unity was what made Eritrea a nation.[5] They also appeared to have been conscious of the class divisions that had resulted in the cooptation of traditional ruling elites by the imperial Crown. Thus their recruitment efforts were directed at the working class, petty traders, teachers, and students, social groups from which the leadership itself was derived.[6] The ELM's political platform also challenged the traditional model of conducting politics through patronage and inter-elite alliances.

The new politics of protest developed simultaneously on various levels: a redefinition of a politically distinct, pluralist, and secular Eritrean state; a reassertion of the Eritrean demand for independence on the basis of Ethiopia's violation of Eritrean constitutional rights; a rejection of Pan-Ethiopianism; and a denunciation of elite nationalism based on patronage politics and confessionalism. The failure of the anti-colonialist elite politicians to construct a common platform served as a lesson that new methods, networks, and institutions were crucial to the survival of a secular, independent Eritrea.

The first clear indication of these new methods was the organization of clandestine cells at the grass-root level. The cells consisted of a basic group of seven, each of whom was entrusted with the task of recruiting six other members. Induction into the organization included an oath to support the aims outlined in the organization's preamble, an undertaking to donate 3 percent of earnings to the nationalist cause, and attendance at bi-weekly meetings.[7] This structure was in stark contrast to the previous decade's mode of political organization, which had depended on the goodwill of elites (party politicians and traditional rulers) and circumscribed mass political activity. The ELM's mobilization appealed to Eritreans of different ages, faiths, and economic classes. It spread throughout the towns and cities, creating what Markakis has called an "amoeba-like" movement in Eritrea's urban centers.[8]

Although the initial impetus for this new opposition had sprung from Eritrean Moslems living in Port Sudan and initially took hold in the lowlands, it quickly began to attract recruits from the highland Christian sector, particularly in the capital city of Asmara. The first cells were organized by such leaders as Saleh Ahmed Iyay (a worker from Keren) and

Yasin el-Gade (a tailor from Asmara), who returned to their towns to establish clandestine cells. Among the Tigrigna speakers in the highlands the movement was called *Mahber Shew'ate* (Association of Seven) and it quickly became a Pan-Eritrean organization emphasizing a common Eritrean identity and discouraging confessional rivalry.[9]

Means and ends: the emergence of creative radicalism

The increasing strong-arm tactics of the Ethiopian Crown forced politics out of the formal arena of Assembly meetings and reinstated it into the hidden, informal areas of social activities. Tea-houses (*enda shahi*) located around the bazaars, soccer stadiums, and schools became the centers for clandestine mobilization and recruitment.[10] The evening radio broadcasts of Woldeab Woldemariam from Cairo, although banned by the Ethiopian imperial government after the Suez Crisis in 1956, had already garnered an audience which continued to frequent the tea-houses to discuss the latest issues. Secondary schools under pressure from Ethiopian "Amharization" policies provided a ready-made network of alienated elements, including students, teachers, and civil servants of the Eritrean Ministry of Education. The banning of all political parties and labor unions led to the politicization of social organizations such as soccer teams. The Eritrean team, *Adulis*, traveled to the Sudan for national matches, and there ELM members mobilized and recruited members for the new organization. Team members, like Tekie Yihdego, played key roles in spreading the network among the youth in Asmara.[11]

The ELM shunned overt dialogues with the Unionist-controlled Assembly or the traditional elites, through whose internal divisions the bulk of Eritrea's inhabitants had been delivered into the hands of the Ethiopian empire. By 1960 a general sense of betrayal at the hands of traditional rulers had become increasingly evident; the nationalist activities of the ELM gave it voice. Popular folk songs in the beer houses frequented by workers of that period reflected the discontent with the older generation.

Abotat'na Uwano	(Our misguided elders
Ab idom' Kelo	Although they had the power
Limano	They went begging)[12]

Such songs reflected the disillusionment of this younger generation of nationalists. The ELM response to the apparent betrayal of past generations was to advocate liberation by *coup d'état*.[13] The goal of the ELM was to stage a coup to overthrow the federal government and declare Eritrea's independence. Former party leaders, such as Ibrahim Sultan and Woldeab Woldemariam, were asked to support the proposed coup. However, the veteran politicians refused, declining any association with what appeared to them to be a radical, Communist-inspired organization.

Due to fears of infiltration, ELM cells had no autonomous decision-making capacity, and as the movement grew in size the members' ability to act became increasingly constrained by the delays in communicating with the leadership-in-exile. Organizational problems notwithstanding, the ELM achieved considerable success in infiltrating the Eritrean administration's institutions, including recruiting Eritrean policemen and highly placed members of the Eritrean Parliament. The acephalous nature of the ELM cells militated against the quick action needed for any urban-based clandestine opposition organization to be effective. Nevertheless, secrecy enabled the ELM to survive the growing repression by the Unionist-controlled police which was directed against anything deemed harmful to the Ethiopian Crown's systematic erosion of the federal relationship.

Although the ELM's membership continued to grow, the political situation in Eritrea was fraught with ominous signs both for those supporting independence and for former Unionists. In November 1959 the Eritrean flag was replaced by the Ethiopian tricolor; in May 1960, the Eritrean seal of government was abolished; and in the same period the name of the Eritrean government was changed to that of "Eritrean administration."

Another change, which also violated the Eritrean Constitution, was the placement of the Eritrean Ministry of Education under the direct supervision of the Ethiopian Ministry of Education. Ethiopian teachers were transferred to Eritrea to teach Amharic, which had been imperially decreed as a requirement in the curriculum. Teachers wearing army uniforms (apparently to intimidate students) were met with open hostility, which led to student strikes and demonstrations.[14] The imposition of Amharic was further evidence of Ethiopia's violation of the autonomy granted to Eritreans to conduct their own "internal" affairs. Student demonstrators were imprisoned for four months by the Eritrean Chief of Police, Tedla Ukbit. Police repression, incarceration, and the torture of dissidents nurtured the informal resistance already evident in the main urban centers.

In addition to the participation of students and workers, artists and musicians joined the underground conglomerate of radical nationalism. The *Mahber Teatre Asmara* (MTA), a cultural association, was established in 1961 by singers, composers, poets, and university students returning from the Haile Selassie I University in Addis Ababa.[15] MTA served as a recruitment center and fund-raiser. It also provided an outlet for the frustrated population. Dismayed at the poor performance of its "formally elected" representatives, Eritreans flocked to the MTA's bi-monthly cultural shows. Plays, singers, and stand-up comics satirized the federal scheme and warned against the evils of "alien" cultures.[16] Although the shows were censored by authorities the artists camouflaged the political messages in the intricacies of traditional ballads. In the cultural arena both the new and traditional nationalists were united in their desire to combat Ethiopian hegemony. *Shigey Habuni*, a popular song of the mid-1960s, is an example of the creative nationalism resonating within the population.

Shigey Habuni	(Give me my torch
Ay'te'tal'luni	How long can you deceive me
Intay Gher'e Iye?	What have I done?
Shigey Zei'tbuni?	That you deny me my torch?)[17]

MTA performances also included traditional folk songs which appealed to the older generation. An excellent example was a new ballad entitled *Aslamai' Kistanai*, which called upon Moslem and Christian Eritreans to unite. It echoed the ELM's program of unity between the two religious groups and reiterated the dangers of outside intervention.

Aslamai Kistanai	(Moslem and Christian
Wedi Kola Dega	Lowlander and highlander
N'Mikhri Tsela'ee	To the enemy's counsel
Ayt'habo Waga	Do not listen
Ayt'habo Waga	Do not give it value
Keyt'khon Edaga	or you may find yourself
	[Being sold] in the market.)[18]

The ELM redoubled its efforts to publicize its existence and obtain outside recognition and support after it failed to obtain the backing of the exiled Eritrean politicians in the Sudan, Egypt, Somalia, and Saudi Arabia. But before the ELM's coup could be mounted the establishment of a new organization in 1960 – the Eritrean Liberation Front (ELF) – by former political leaders in exile further complicated the simple strategy of liberation by coup espoused by the ELM (see chapter 7). Thus while the first ELM Congress was held in Asmara in September 1960 to discuss the "necessity of armed struggle" in the event of a failed coup,[19] the erosion of the fragile unity nurtured by the ELM was already well underway, spearheaded by the ELF under Idris M. Adem.[20] All this occurred during the 1959–1961 period; in the meantime, the ELM had the political field *within* Eritrea much to itself.

The ELM's ideal of a secular Pan-Eritrean nationalism, activated through its politics of protest and reconciliation, set the foundation for a rich nationalist culture. All this had a profound effect on the defiant youth of the 1950s, the same generation that was later to construct the basis for modern Eritrean nationalism. Although the Moslem–Christian schism and ethnic rivalries resurfaced in the course of the armed struggle in the late

1960s and 1970s, this brief period of reconciliation was never forgotten, becoming part of the reinvigorated social foundation of a pluralist Eritrea. The nationalist symbols engendered during this brief period were later integrated into the EPLF's internal and external nationalist mobilization for a cultural renaissance.[21]

As the feasibility of liberation by coup faded, and as it began to face both the hostility of the rival ELF and the threat to its existence from the empire, in 1961 the ELM declared its aim to launch an armed struggle to liberate Eritrea. The Moslem ELF's decision to alienate the secular ELM from its constituency met with some success but the heavily Islamic bent of the ELF leadership – exemplified by Idris M. Adem and the charismatic Osman Saleh Sabbe – created anxiety among the exiled non-Moslem community, who in turn sought Woldeab Woldemariam's support. The veteran politician joined the ELM in 1962 after a unity meeting was arranged by the Sudanese government which had replaced General Abboud's government. Neither Idris M. Adem nor Osman S. Sabbe attended the meeting, though Woldeab Woldemariam was present, as was ELM leader Mohamed Nawud.

One of the first steps taken by the ELM in its final stage was to widen its constituency among Eritreans living in Ethiopia. Unfortunately the ELM's organizational structure of highly secret cells and its lack of clear and quick communication links with the leadership allowed the ELF (which had already established contacts with Eritreans in exile) to supersede it. In the light of the increasingly repressive measures taken by the Ethiopian regime against the Eritrean population, the ELF's declaration of armed struggle as the sole means of achieving Eritrean independence found an attentive audience. A number of ELM cell members joined the ELF, taking recruits with them.[22] Although the ELF had the disadvantage of being directed from outside Eritrea, it benefited from its association with well-known leaders of the past.

The ELM's decision to launch an armed struggle came too late for two reasons. The first was that the open discord between the ELM and the ELF had alerted the Ethiopian government to the threat of organized opposition. Secondly, in consequence, official surveillance became more acute, making the underground resistance movement's operations more difficult to carry out.

The war of words with the ELF had exposed the ELM to the attention of security offices ... Several of its leading members were arrested in 1961, and its cell structure was gradually dismantled, as the authorities concentrated on gaining information from the one member in each cell who was authorized to contact others.[23]

In September 1961, the first shots were fired which were later hailed as the beginning of the armed struggle. They came from the guns of Hamid Idris

Awate's group of thirteen ELF fighters[24] at an isolated police post in the Barka region. Earlier, both the ELM and the ELF had approached the veteran Awate to join their camps. It was in October of the same year that ELM squads made an unsuccessful attempt to assassinate Keshi Dimetros (Vice-president of the Eritrean Assembly), regarded by many as the Eritrean "Rasputin" because of his fanatical pro-Unionist stand and links with the Ethiopian security forces. Dimetros' escape led to a series of arrests which resulted in the incarceration of many cell members. Penetration of the cells by agents of the Ethiopian empire also made it difficult for the ELM leadership to convene after its first Congress and map out its strategies. ELM members living in Cairo made yet another effort to mobilize support from the veteran Eritrean politicians who once again had become divided along familiar religious lines.[25]

Undeterred by Ethiopian displays of military prowess in the wake of their illegal annexation of Eritrea in 1962, the ELM in 1963 began procuring arms for its intended armed struggle. The most accessible market was within Ethiopia itself, where an arms bazaar flourished as a result of the conflict in the Sudan, in which Ethiopia backed the *Anya Nya* against the Khartoum government.[26] ELM cells were reactivated and proceeded to procure arms to recruit fighters, but the organization soon discovered that many cells had already been infiltrated by the ELF. The rivalry with the ELF made the ELM's preparations more difficult.

Nevertheless, the ELM persisted in the mobilization efforts throughout 1963 and 1964, remaining resolute in its decision to commit units to an armed struggle inside Eritrea. Woldeab Woldemariam, who considered such an exercise foolhardy and dangerous, warned Mohamed Nawud against such a step.[27] When Nawud proceeded with preparations to send a contingent of fifty men into Eritrea, Woldeab Woldemariam resigned at the end of 1964. The ELM leadership notified the ELF of its plans and received an ultimatum from ELF spokesman, Osman S. Sabbe, who pointed out that a liberation front already existed and told Nawud that his organization should unite with it or face elimination. In May 1965, despite these warnings, the ELM went ahead with its plans and dispatched a group of fifty men to enter the Sahel region in Eritrea. The ELM fighters were ambushed and forcibly disarmed by an ELF unit at Ela Tsada. According to different sources the ELM suffered up to forty casualties while others place the number at ten.[28]

In March 1965 secondary-school students in Asmara went on a three-day strike. Their demands included: (1) a UN-supervised referendum on the future of Eritrea and condemnation of Ethiopia's illegal annexation; (2) the expulsion of foreign military advisors and closure of foreign bases (including the American radio monitoring Kagnew station in Asmara) as well as the removal of Israeli military advisors present since 1964 at the invitation of the Ethiopian Governor-General Asrate Kassa;[29] (3) the release of political prisoners; and (4) re-establishment of Eritrean jurisdiction over social and economic institutions.[30] The demonstration confirmed Ethiopian fears of infiltration by the organized resistance. Hundreds of students were arrested and the ineffectiveness of civil disobedience as a strategy for liberation from Ethiopian rule was finally driven home. Many students joined the ELF, thus weakening further the ELM's base of support.

Ironically, in the end, the first Eritrean resistance movement, which had shown so much promise in its early days in 1958 due to its rejection of confessional and ideological rivalry, was mortally wounded by a rival group professing to share its goal of liberating Eritrea by armed struggle. The destruction of the ELM had even more ominous consequences: it ushered in an era of internecine violence based on confessionalism and regionalism, all ostensibly justified by the conviction – shared by subsequent liberation groups – that the "Eritrean arena was only large enough to contain a single movement."

The demise of the ELM

For all its accomplishments, including the reconciliationist ideology that proved to be its most durable legacy, the ELM failed to deter Ethiopia's forcible integration of Eritrea into the empire. It was overtaken and destroyed by a more militant organization which promised to accomplish by guerrilla war what the ELM had been unable to bring about by other means. The ELF, capitalizing on a growing Eritrean nationalist consciousness, took over as the prime opposition movement in 1965.

The politicization of religious rivalry spearheaded by the imperial Crown and the Eritrean Coptic Church had long exacerbated the traditional enmity between the two communities. Religion, in the particular historical period of the region, must be understood as a principle of social order that defined individual and group access to economic and political resources. A detailed account of the origins of inter-religious conflict in the region is beyond the scope of this book. For our purposes, however, it suffices to recall that:

Religious enmity between the two communities of almost equal size was nothing new, nor was religion the real bone of contention now. Muslim pastoralists on the lowlands and Christian peasants on the plateau had never been good neighbors, but the reason was a perennial competition for land, not the difference in faith. *Indeed, their adherence to rival religions probably was the ideological expression of this material antagonism.*[31]

Whatever the base of the old religious rivalry, however, the termination of the Eritrean–Ethiopian federation fueled Moslem fears and in the process, gave the ELF powerful leverage over the disillusioned population already mobilized by the ELM. And by using the very same traditional loyalties the ELM had sought to vitiate, the ELF gained a formidable power base over its rival. The results were predictable: patronage politics based on kinship affiliations (reflected in the ELF's leadership style), combined with the exigencies of getting Arab support to combat the region's unchallenged hegemony. All served to accelerate factionalism and exacerbate the already endemic ethno-religious frictions.

7 Defiant nationalism: the ELF and the EPLF, 1961–1981

Introduction

From its inception in 1961 until its demise in 1981, the ELF's armed struggle against Ethiopia was waged on two fronts: against the Ethiopian army and its backers, and against the internal challenges stemming from its practice of a politics of exclusion. This politics of exclusion mitigated against the creation of a single Eritrean national movement. The patronage system of the leadership fostered factionalism and weakened the ELF's claims to legitimacy both domestically and externally. The challenge to its authority waged by the EPLF in the early 1970s and by the EDM in the late 1970s led to the ELF's fragmentation and demise in 1981.

From its establishment in 1960–1961, the ELF was hampered by the legacy of the 1940s in which the Islamic parties had been alienated by the domination of Ethiopian-sponsored Christian parties. Internally, the ELF's affiliation with the Arab world exacerbated religious and ethnic hostilities. The ascendancy of Moslem militants in the ELF leadership and the discrimination against Christian fighters led to an organizational crisis which ultimately spawned another liberation movement, the Eritrean People's Liberation Front (EPLF) in 1969–1970.

Arab support for the ELF enabled Ethiopia to portray the resistance as an "Arab-inspired conspiracy."[1] The fact that Libya, *Ba'athist* Syria, and Iraq also assisted the ELF led to the portrayal of the Eritrean struggle as a "Communist-inspired" destabilization of Ethiopia.[2] Thus, by defining the Eritreans as both an Arab threat to the African regional order and a Communist threat to the international order, the Ethiopian regime was able to legitimize its military offensives against the Eritrean rebels and gain support from the United States and Israel.

From 1971 to 1981 the defiant nationalism of the Eritreans underwent two major transformations. In the first half of the 1970s the ELF and EPLF were engaged in a contest for power which exploded into civil war from 1972 to 1974. The inability of the ELF and EPLF to take advantage of Ethiopia's instability during the revolutionary upheaval of 1974 revealed the absence of a united front in Eritrea. The *Dergue*'s continuation of war to resolve the Eritrean problem was successful because it exploited the internal fragmentation of the nationalists and the regional and international support for Ethiopia's claims to the territory.

From 1975 to 1977 there was a period of uneasy coexistence and sporadic cooperation between the rival nationalist groups. The next two years, 1978–1980, reflected a change in the balance, with the EPLF developing as the stronger front while the ELF remained entangled in internal factionalism. By 1981 the ELF was replaced by the EPLF as the primary liberation organization in Eritrea, which transformed defiant Eritrean nationalism into a formidable challenge capable of countering Ethiopia's hegemony.

This chapter begins with an examination of the origins and evolution of the ELF from 1961 to 1969. During this period the distinguishing features of the ELF were the power struggles within the leadership and the deficiencies of its political and military institutions. This chapter also examines the external factors (regional and international) that led to the isolation of the Eritrean nationalists during this decade. Special attention is paid to the constraints imposed on the ELF as a result of its links with the Arab world.

The rise of reformists between 1969 and 1971 and the emergence of a major rival organization, the EPLF, are discussed with a focus on the internal, regional, and international factors that characterized Eritrean politics of the 1970s and the 1980s. The failure of Eritrean nationalist resistance in the 1960s and throughout the 1970s to realize its goals can be attributed to its inability to resolve internal divisions. The fragmentation of the ELF in this period is also discussed within the context of the changes taking place in neighboring Ethiopia after 1974 and the changes of superpower patrons of the new regime in 1977–1978. Finally, this chapter examines the demise of the ELF in 1981 and its replacement by the EPLF as the primary military and political force in the Eritrean arena.

Origins and evolution of the ELF

The establishment of the ELF was announced in July 1960 by Idris M. Adem, who had already gathered a large following from among the expatriate Eritrean student community in Cairo. Idris M. Adem also recruited a young law graduate of the University of Cairo, Idris O. Glawdewos, and an enterprising schoolmaster, Osman S. Sabbe to form the provisional Executive Committee, the first leadership structure of the ELF.

In contrast to the ELM, whose organizational structure and leadership were similar to South American urban guerrillas of the late 1960s and 1970s, the ELF's targets for recruitment lay in the rural areas of the western lowlands.[3] This area bordering the Sudan was well suited for arms transfers and provided a constituency based on patronage of the leaders-in-exile. Moreover, the ELF was able to use the trained men from these areas who had been part of the Eritrean field force or the Sudanese army, which the British had used to combat *shifta* activities in the 1940s.[4]

The ELF's leadership, located in Cairo, toured the various Arab nations and their expatriate Eritrean communities of workers and students to raise support for the armed struggle. The ELF adapted the Pan-Arabism popularized by Gamal Abdel Nasser of Egypt and the *Ba'ath* parties of Iraq and Syria. Egypt had been the first state to grant asylum to Eritreans fleeing the repressive Ethiopian regime.[5] Egypt had traditionally been a learning center for Eritrean Moslems, but Nasser's rise to power had turned the Egyptian capital into a Mecca for radical dissidents from Africa as well as from neighboring Arab countries.[6]

The ELF leaders' choice of Arab supporters was more a matter of necessity than a reflection of enduring Arab identity. This is not to minimize the existence of a shared Islamic heritage but to point out that the ELF chose to cultivate the new Arab alliances despite the fact that historical Eritrean–Arab relations have long, hostile roots, leaving bitter memories of raids and slavery.[7] The ELF had no option other than the Arab world in its struggle against the Ethiopian hegemony, which itself enjoyed wide support for its claims of African unity.

The early ELF did not have a clear ideological line. A clandestine Labour Party did emerge, espousing Marxism–Leninism. However, its membership reflected a broad ideological spectrum which included fervent Marxists and Islamic fundamentalists.[8] Generally, emphasis was placed on the right of Eritreans to determine their political fate and the violation of the UN-guaranteed constitutional rights. The collaboration of Eritrean Christians with the emperor during the 1940s and 1950s was highlighted as a key factor leading to the disenfranchisement and discrimination of Eritrean Moslems. It was not until the mid-1970s, when young recruits returned from their various trainings in radical Arab states, China, and Cuba, that a more radical Marxist-oriented philosophy began to emerge in the ELF. By 1977, ELF documents and manifestos were declaring the need to "build a progressive Eritrean workers' movement."[9] Nevertheless, the ELF's patronage system and style of leadership continued to play a more significant role than the influence of younger leaders and officers who attained key roles. Ideology remained a secondary factor to the defiant nationalism that united the disparate elements of the ELF.

From its inception in 1960 until 1962 the ELF did not have an institutionalized leadership structure. The provisional Executive Committee was more an expression of the demarcation of power bases among the three founders than a coherent structure. There was also no clear definition of the respective tasks of the members. In 1962 the Provisional

Executive Committee was replaced by the Revolutionary Command (RC) consisting of the Cairo triumvirate and a twelve-member Executive Committee, comprising Eritrean exiles in the Sudan, Egypt, and Saudi Arabia. In 1965 a Congress was convened in Khartoum which hammered out a revised organizational structure. The existing RC was replaced by a Supreme Council (SC), also known by its Arabic name *Majlis al'thawra*. The SC elected Idris M. Adem as President, Osman S. Sabbe as Secretary-General, and Idris O. Glawdewos as Secretary entrusted with military affairs. The headquarters of the SC was moved from Cairo to Khartoum, and a new Revolutionary Command (headed by Idris O. Glawdewos and also known by its Arabic name *Ki'yada al'Ama*), was established at Kassala to oversee military affairs. The distribution of power at the pinnacle of the SC remained ossified, while the ideological orientation of the ELF continued to reflect its Pan-Arabist influences, emphasizing the disenfranchisement of Eritrea's Moslems.

The ELF's organizational structure was based on a territorial/zonal division similar to that of the AFLN.[10] The territory was divided into four main zones each with its own commander, deputy commander, political commissioner, and officers assigned to deal with security, logistics, and health care. In most of the zones the leadership was held by persons from the local area.

The four zones reflected a division of power among the three ethnic groups. The Beni-Amer dominated Zone 1 and were assured of Idris M. Adem's patronage. Zone 1's leadership was also considerably older and entrenched in patrimonial relations based on kinship and clan loyalties. Zone 2 also had a veteran leader whose ethnic kinship to Idris O. Glawdewos provided a crucial link to the external leadership in Cairo. Zone 3's leadership differed from the first two in that the commander, Ahmed Abdelkerim, was not a veteran soldier but a former student in Cairo recruited by the leadership. He had no visible ethnic affiliation with any of the ELF leadership, so the relationship between the zone and headquarters seems to have been based on reciprocity of demand and supply. Poscia asserts that this zone, due to its lack of a "protecting patron," acted as a "pendulum" that reflected shifts in the constituency commanded by the triumvirate in Cairo.[11] Zone 4 also showed some similarities to Zone 3 in that there were no ethnic links to any of the leaders, but its commander, Mohamed Ali Umaro (another former student), was purported to have a close relationship with Osman S. Sabbe.[12] Another, fifth, zone was established by the leadership to accommodate the increasing number of volunteers from the highland areas. Because Zone 5's leader, Woldai Kahsai, was Christian, it became known as the "Christian division," although the majority of its rank-and-file consisted of adherents to Islam.

The patronage network of the triumvirate in Cairo, based on religious and ethnic affiliation, constituted an important component of the vertical ties that linked the headquarters to the field. However, the absence of any horizontal links between the zones encouraged factionalism. Such a zone system based on patronage affiliations with the leadership was bound not only to create conflicting loyalties as the leaders began to fall out among themselves, but also to accentuate the ethno-religious divisions that demarcated the zones from one another. One consequence of the ELF's patronage-based leadership style and the warlordism of the zone commanders was fragmentation within the leadership and friction between zone commanders and the rank-and-file. Zone commanders continued to have full authority over their respective territories and armies. At the zone level the only change was the appointment of political commissioners who were entrusted with increasing the level of general and political education.

The urban ELF cells remained active in promoting the nationalist cause and were successful in recruiting new members from the secondary schools, universities, and civil servants. The ELF's emphasis on armed struggle as the only alternative to Ethiopian domination continued to find resonance among the radical students and disillusioned civil servants and workers. Former ELM members were contacted and persuaded to join the ELF's call for armed struggle. The ELF portrayed itself as the logical extension of the ELM's urban-based resistance and justified its brutal elimination of the ELM in 1965 as a necessary step. In sum, the ELM's achievements were appropriated by the ELF, which presented itself as the sole liberation front dedicated to bringing independence through armed struggle.[13]

Young recruits from the highlands and lowlands were rudely awakened to the ugly realities of the factional politics of the ELF leadership. The relationships between zone commanders and rank-and-file as well as within the leadership (which still remained outside Eritrea) were constrained by the zonal divisions which encouraged patrimonial relations and factional rivalry. ELF recruits were particularly dismayed by the persistence of the corrosive Moslem–Christian schism within the organization.

The ELF leadership's inability or unwillingness to centralize allowed zone commanders a wide latitude in their dealings with the population. A constant problem for the ELF's military wing (ELA, the Eritrean Liberation Army) was a secure supply of food. Where demands for provisions were not met voluntarily by the villages or encampments threats and raids accomplished the desired objective. This led to the alienation of the population which also faced the same demands from Ethiopian army units.[14] Christian villagers were often subjected to pillage and cattle raids. Such methods tended to engender significant animosity toward the ELF in the countryside.

Ethiopian authorities utilized this discontent to create a specialized agency recruited from these disaffected areas to fight the rebels. Asrate Kassa, Governor-general of Eritrea, established a new anti-guerrilla division, *Commandos 101*, recruited primarily from Christian villages and trained by Israeli military advisors, inflaming the already volatile situation.[15] This cooptation of a segment of Eritrean society into taking up arms against the ELF resulted in discrimination against Christian ELF recruits who were viewed more and more as traitors. The ethnic and religious divisions in the zones thus expanded into the population as a whole, highlighting the traditional animosities which had generated the fragmentation of Eritrean nationalism in the 1940s.

Asrate Kassa used the inhabitants of the territories to achieve a four-fold purpose: (1) to split the society into two camps thus blocking the emergence of a unified constituency to sustain the guerrillas; (2) to enable the Ethiopian government to justify its air-raids and bombardments of the lowland areas and obtain more arms and assistance from two powerful sources: the United States and Israel; (3) to prevent any African states from bringing up the Eritrean issue as an item to be discussed, due to its obviously ethnic and religious conflagrations within the population; and (4) to limit the ELF leadership's scope of operations and resources, inflaming rivalry and conflicts between the zonal divisions. The increased offensives also caused a large displacement of refugees, some of whom joined the ELF. In addition, young students and a large number of these refugees (including a significant number of Christians) joined the ranks of the fifth zone. Ethiopia launched more offensives and widened its attacks from the lowland to the highland areas in the years 1964–1967, causing much destruction of property.[16]

Increasing Ethiopian pressure to destroy the ELF, dissent in the ranks, distrust among combatants, and division within the leadership all limited the effectiveness of the armed struggle. During 1967–1968 large numbers of ELF fighters were captured or gave themselves up to the Ethiopian government.[17] Ethiopia publicized these defections to portray the Eritrean nationalist struggle as a religious and tribal insurgency led by Islamic fanatics.[18]

The ELF leadership in Cairo attempted to bolster its tarnished image and distance itself from the "jihadist" actions of some of the zone commanders. Its first step was to nominate a Christian as the Vice-president to the Supreme Council. Tedla Bairu became part of the independence movement which he had fought against so ardently, first as the President of the pro-Ethiopian Unionist Party (UP) in 1946 and then later as the first Chief Executive of the Eritrean Assembly until his resignation in 1955.[19] Personnel changes in the zone system were also implemented as a response to increasing demands from the rank-and-file.

In 1968 fighters who completed training in Syria and China returned to the field and began to mobilize for reforms. Among these were two young men, Issaias Afeworki and Ramadan Mohamed Nur, who were to have a lasting impact on the future of Eritrean politics. Issaias Afeworki returned from China to become the political commissioner for Zone 5.[20] Ramadan Mohamed Nur, who was also part of the same group sent to China, was reinstated as the political commissioner of Zone 4, a post which he had held since 1966. A meeting of zone commanders and political commissioners was held on June 19, 1968 to enact reforms.

A series of meetings held throughout 1968 and 1969 led to the launching of a rectification campaign aimed at overhauling the entire organizational structure of the ELF.[21] The reforms were directed against the "dictatorship" of the zone commanders, the abuse of civilians, and the corruption of the leadership-in-exile. Proposed reforms included:

1 Elimination of zone divisions and the unification of the military under a centralized administration.
2 Establishment of a leadership in the field rather than in exile.
3 Protection of basic human rights through people's assemblies.
4 Ceasing of intimidation and beatings of civilian population, theft, and rape of women by ELF forces.[22]

At the Adobha conference of August 1969 a 38-member body known as the *Kiyada al-Ama* or General Command (GC), based inside Eritrea, was elected to replace the Cairo-based SC and its RC liaison in Kassala. In the meantime, Sabbe announced the formation of a new body, the General Secretariat (GS) to replace the discredited SC. The GC, however, refused to acknowledge the GS and responded by arresting fighters suspected of being adherents of Sabbe and launching a repressive campaign over the eastern lowlands which were viewed as a Sabbe stronghold.

The GC responded to the reforms with terror and violence in 1970. Some reformists fled to neighboring Sudan. Others chose to hide out in the southeastern regions and formulate a new program under a new leadership. This group consisted of Zone 5 members led by Abrha Tewolde and Issaias Afeworki. The power struggle between the new ELF leadership and the reformists led to the formation of three new splinter groups: the People's Liberation Front (PLF), the Eritrean Liberation Front – People's Liberation Front (ELF–PLF), and the ELF–Ubel.

Fragmentation of the ELF: the PLF, ELF–PLF, and ELF–Ubel

The first task of the opposition was to establish a base of operations in Dankalia and mobilize opposition to the ELF GC. Once contact was established disagreements abounded over organizational unity and distribution of arms and supplies. The groups' leaders agreed to cooperate in a united front but decided to retain their respective leadership bodies until an agreed programme was formulated. The group in Dankalia[23] became known as PLF 1, while that led by Issaias Afeworki became known as PLF 2, and a third group of dissidents, mainly from Zone 1 and led by Adem Saleh, became known as the Ubel group (ELF–Ubel), named for the region from which it developed.

Support for the three opposition groups came from the most unlikely quarter: the newly created ELF General Secretariat led by Osman S. Sabbe.[24] Sabbe provided the funds and transportation for dissenters who accepted his offer but declined to allow the former member of the Supreme Council to participate in the organizational meeting of the Tripartite Unity (PLF 1, ELF–Ubel, and PLF 2) held at *Suduh'Ela*, Dankalia on June 24, 1970.[25] The PLF elected a nine-member political and military leadership and excluded Sabbe from the executive body of the new organization.[26] The *rapprochement* with their old foe, Sabbe, was mutually beneficial. The fighters were able to survive due to the General Secretary's patronage and he, in turn, was able to retain his crucial role as the "unofficial" foreign minister of the Eritrean resistance.

Alarmed by the growing degree of dissent, the GC called a meeting and invited the three groups to send representatives to participate in the preparation for the ELF's first Congress. The unanimous response of the three factions was to demand the overhaul of the GC as a precondition to their participation. The GC held its Congress at Ar, on the Sudanese border from October 14 to November 13, 1971. None of the Tripartite members attended. At the Congress the ELF condemned the reformists as reactionary forces. However, by this time opposition to the heavy-handed methods of the GC was widespread. To pre-empt the development of support from within its own ranks for the reforms of the Tripartite Unity, the ELF adopted a number of earlier demands for reform from the 1969 Adobha conference.[27] The GC was replaced by a new, more representative Revolutionary Council (RC). The ELF reinstated Idris M. Adem as President of the RC and Heruy Tedla, the son of Tedla Bairu, as Vice-president. Abdalla Idris was entrusted with military affairs.[28]

In November 1971, PLF 2 established its own programme, *Neh'nan Elamaa'nan* (We and our Objectives), which clarified the reasons for its secession from the ELF. The programme denounced the ELF's sectarianism, its corrupt leadership, and its misrepresentation of the Eritrean struggle as "Arab" in nature. It reiterated the African identity of the Eritrean people and criticized the ELF's parochialism as an obstacle to the struggle for independence.[29] It redefined the objectives of the armed struggle not only as the attainment of political independence but also a struggle to eradicate social, economic, and gender-based inequalities.[30]

In February 1972 delegates of PLF 1, PLF 2 and ELF–Ubel met in Beirut to request assistance from Sabbe's Foreign Mission. The dissidents revised their earlier stand in 1970 to exclude Osman S. Sabbe and Woldeab Woldemariam from holding office in the PLF's leadership. These two veterans severed ties with the old ELF leadership and formed a liaison office entrusted with publicizing the Eritrean struggle and raising revenue for the dissident groups. Sabbe's role was limited to spokesperson and fund-raiser. A joint committee made up of the three groups was formed to oversee the distribution of military supplies. The establishment of an official alliance between the secessionists and Sabbe was viewed as a threat by the Revolutionary Council, which declared a war against the Tripartite Unity on February 24, 1972 to eliminate this threat.

Conflicts within conflict: challenges to the ELF and to the EPLF

The process of unification of the three factions proceeded in spite of the civil war. In October 1972 a meeting of the three factions was held at Geteb, on the Sudanese border. They elected another joint committee to coordinate military and political activities and draft the conditions for a complete merger after a six-month period.[31] The PLF 1 and PLF 2 agreed to a complete merger on September 1973 and became the Eritrean People's Liberation Front (EPLF). Although the English initials for EPLF remained the same, the Tigrigna version – *Hizbawi Hailtat Harnet Ertra* (HH HaE) – was changed to *Hizbawi Genbar Harnet Ertra* (HGHE) at the EPLF's First Organizational Congress in 1977. The change of name denoted a transition from *Hailtat* (forces) to *GenbarI* (front). The Ubel group was divided on this issue, with some of its members joining the EPLF and others fleeing to the Sudan.

In 1973, amidst the ongoing civil war, the newly reconstituted EPLF faced its first major challenge from within its ranks. A conflict surrounding the ideological correctness of its organizational structure and its alliances with Sabbe's Foreign Mission led to the emergence of organized opposition to the EPLF leadership. This opposition, by former university students espousing a militant Marxist ideology, soon became known as the *Menkaa'e*.[32] These radical intelligentsia accused the EPLF leadership of being "petit bourgeois" nationalists and condemned the organization's alliance with the Foreign Mission led by Sabbe, whom they viewed as a reactionary. They called for the creation of a proletarian party.[33] The strident ideological tone of the *Menkaa'e* group reflected an extreme Marxist–Leninist line. While the EPLF leadership attempted to cope with what they called an "ultra-leftist" threat another clandestine group surfaced led by Solomon Woldemariam, claiming ethnic discrimination.[34] This group, claiming to speak on behalf of fighters from the *Akele Guzai* province contended that their region was not adequately represented in the EPLF leadership. The emergence of this latest splinter group reflecting the parochial grievances nesting within a radical ideological movement was a critical challenge to the EPLF's leadership, which owed its separate existence to its opposition to such ethnic and religious particularism.

The conflict encompassed two antithetical currents joined in their opposition to the EPLF's leadership. The *Menkaa'e* conflict was labelled as a combination of "ultra-leftists" and "ultra-rightists" by the leadership. The demands of the opposition were debated extensively for a year and some of the dissidents recanted. The more uncompromising members were placed under arrest and later executed.[35] The executions were carried out while the EPLF was in a very precarious position, caught between the crossfire of the ELF and Ethiopian armies. The decision to quell internal dissent by force has been characterized by Poscia as "a dark chapter" in the EPLF's history.[36] Nevertheless, one should also note that former *Menkaa'e* members came to hold key positions in the subsequent leadership of the EPLF.

The impact of Ethiopia's revolution

During 1973 and 1974, a chain of events in Ethiopia led to the deposing of Africa's last absolute emperor and to a revolutionary transformation.[37] A number of factors facilitated Ethiopia's "creeping" revolution of 1974: the military's inability to quash the Eritrean guerrillas; corrupt officers profiteering from war; low salaries; the lack of adequate food and water supplies exacerbated by the drought of 1972–1973; and the ineptness of the aging emperor. By September 1974 the revolutionary ferment in Ethiopia had coalesced into an organized opposition against the imperial regime. The Coordinating Committee (*Dergue*), made up of officers from the airforce, navy, and infantry units, rose to power. *Ityopia Tikdem* (Ethiopia First) became the revolutionary slogan. Describing the *Dergue*'s rise to power and its slogan of putting "Ethiopia First," Christopher Clapham provides an historical commentary on the early years of the revolution.

The early performance of the *Derg*, moreover, suggested little more than a fairly straightforward radical nationalism, stopping well short of revolution. Its slogan – it was far from policy – of *Ityopia Tikdem* (Ethiopia First) was nationalism of the vaguest kind, and the initial programme issued in early July 1974 was equally anodyne, combining commitment to the monarchy and to national unity with an attack on corruption and a call for "lasting changes."[38]

Ethiopia sought to legitimate the *Dergue*'s authority through its own version of African Socialism: *Hibret Sebawinet*. Edmond J. Keller defines this new ideology as communalism:

Similar to other brands of African socialism, namely commitment to equality, justice, self-reliance, the dignity of labor, cooperativeness, cultural pride, *and above all national unity*.[39]

These radical changes taking place in Ethiopia, though, did not signal a willingness to accommodate the demands of the Eritrean liberation forces. Aman Andom, "a senior and respected general,"[40] visited Eritrea on August 26, 1974 with a nineteen-point plan to resolve the Eritrean conflict, intended to "bridge the gulf between Ethiopia and Eritrea by granting Eritrea administrative, economic and especially social aid, and a full amnesty."[41] The proposal had a three-fold task: (1) to gain legitimacy for the *Dergue* in Eritrea; (2) to discredit the fronts engaged in a fratricidal war; and (3) to create a compliant Eritrean leadership willing to accept what was portrayed as a more tolerant and progressive Ethiopian regime. In its attempts to attain these goals, the *Dergue* allowed an unprecedented freedom of speech and assembly in Eritrea during a four-month period from August until November of 1974. It bypassed the liberation fronts and directly approached traditional Eritrean notables with its peaceful solution to the long conflict. For the first time Eritreans were able to move freely in areas held by the liberation movements. On October 13, 1974, 30,000 people from Asmara left their homes to intervene in the civil war.[42] This policy of allowing the population to communicate openly with the guerrillas, which was intended to persuade the liberation fronts to renounce the armed struggle, did not succeed. Popular pressure and indignation at the ongoing fratricide resulted in ceasefires between the ELF and EPLF. The grass-roots intervention temporarily halted the two-year civil war.

The *Dergue*, through Aman Andom reiterated its intentions to rectify the imperial regime's destructive policy in Eritrea and bring peace. Yet, despite these overtures to the population, the *Dergue*, like its imperial predecessor, was unequivocal on the issue of Ethiopian unity.[43] The liberation fronts responded to Andom's plan by mobilizing their respective armed units for an assault on the Eritrean capital of Asmara. Intermittent clashes between the ELF and EPLF continued to flare while they moved closer to the city.[44] Although a permanent ceasefire between the Eritrean fronts was not negotiated the liberation fronts agreed to coordinate their activities against the Ethiopian army.

The nationalists' insistence that independence was the only option did not deter Aman Andom, who continued to push for a political rather than a military solution. Lacking credibility among the Eritrean population and unable to convince radical members of the *Dergue*, Andom failed in his goal to resolve the conflict through dialogue. His autonomous decision to pursue a political compromise was a clear indication that he did not consider himself merely a "titular" head of state and thus presented a new threat to the "real" strongman behind the *Dergue*: Menghistu Hailemariam.

> [Aman Andom] was speaking out of turn ... He was winning a national and international audience which was strengthening his personal position. Finally his solution for Eritrea disturbed the most intransigent nationalists ... because it gave too much away to the liberation movements.[45]

On November 17, 1974 Aman was accused of treason and killed in the exchange of fire marking the end of what had been hailed as the "bloodless revolution."[46] On November 23, fifty-seven dignitaries, members of the nobility, and office holders awaiting public trial by the revolutionary tribunal were summarily executed. The executions in Ethiopia were followed by a systematic period of terror in response to increasing guerrilla activities in Asmara. The *Dergue*, like its imperial predecessor, established a special corps – *Nebelbal* (Flames) – trained by Israeli military advisors.[47]

The *Dergue*'s offensive of January 1975 made Eritrean youth a primary target. This campaign of terror caused the largest influx of recruits to both liberation fronts which had, by this time, formally announced the end of the civil war. These new recruits changed the composition of the rank-and-file fighters of both the liberation armies. Urban youth, workers, professionals, and especially women became more visible.

It was in this period that the EPLF demonstrated the organizational efficiency and discipline which distinguished it from the ELF. Its cadres engaged in a reform of the land system with community leaders, established learning centers, and held public sessions to inform the population of the EPLF's goals and intentions.[48] Its medical units also established numerous clinics and sent mobile personnel into outlying areas deprived of any medical care.[49] The policy of *res'kha me'khaal* (self-reliance) was implemented in the liberated zones supplying the population with necessary provisions. The EPLF continued to expand its power base by mobilizing the population in the newly liberated areas. It inherited and adapted to its own use most of the Ethiopian government's military arsenals and transformed its guerrilla units into a conventional army.[50]

By the end of 1977, while the *Dergue* was engaged in war with Somalia, the EPLF and ELF armies captured three-quarters of Eritrea. Liberated zones were placed under the fronts' administration which coordinated military campaigns to hold Asmara under siege. Ethiopia's precarious hold over the capital city and the port cities of Massawa and Assab was maintained by the infusion of new arms, advisors, and support from the Soviet Union.[51] In 1978, faced with a massive Ethiopian offensive strengthened by Soviet aid, the liberation fronts were forced to withdraw from their expanded bases and regroup. Although the aim of the nationalists had been frustrated primarily by Ethiopia's reinvigorated military capability and foreign assistance, the lack of unity between the fronts also contributed to the rebels' inability to counter the hegemon's exercise of power.[52]

The ELF in disarray

In addition to the reinforcement of its military arsenal, Ethiopia conducted a vigorous diplomatic campaign to isolate the Eritrean nationalists from their former allies. It succeeded in wooing away countries which formerly had supported the Eritrean struggle for independence, including the People's Democratic Republic of Yemen (PDRY), Cuba, and Libya.[53] The *Dergue*'s commitment to unity was emphasized by highlighting the Eritrean nationalists' fragmentation. This led historian Haggai Erlich to announce a premature obituary of the Eritrean struggle in 1978.

The story of the Eritrean conflict has been a contemporary replay of a local historical theme.... while the inhabitants of the Ethiopian heartland became militarily united under an ambitious autocrat in the face of challenge, the inhabitants of the peripheral coastal areas fell victim to disunity and decentralist tendencies resulting in military and political weakness ... Eritrean victory may realistically be excluded as a future possibility.[54]

Although the two fronts had signed an agreement to coordinate their activities against the Ethiopian hegemon, distrust continued to undermine the relationship. The loss of their bases and the process by which certain zones were evacuated led to recriminations. Both the ELF and the EPLF accused each other's leadership of sabotage in areas where the Ethiopian armies penetrated the defensive lines.

The question of unity between the two fronts remained a central issue of debate among Eritrean nationalists. From 1976 to 1980, years during which the combatants of both organizations had opportunities to interact and cooperate, the need for unity and the different approaches of the fronts led to a grass-roots movement for a change of leadership within the ELF. For the second time in its history the ELF was criticized by reformists within its ranks for its practice of patronage politics, corrupt leadership, lack of ideological clarity, and its undermining of the EPLF.

By 1976, a clandestine reformist group emerged, the Eritrean Democratic Movement (EDM), with the aim of democratizing the ELF. Its origins lay in the opposition to the ELF's declaration of war on the secessionist PLF in 1972. The EDM did not advocate secession but called for organizational changes. They were immediately labelled as *Falool* (anarchists) by the ELF leadership.[55] When EDM leaders attempted to create a forum for dialogue with the leadership, some were executed or imprisoned by the ELF.[56] Some EDM reformists left the ELF and joined the ranks of the EPLF while others became political refugees in the Sudan, Europe, and in the United States.[57]

The end result was that by 1980, with its organizational structure and policies still mired in personalism, patronage, and power struggles, the ELF was well on its way to decline. Although weakened by power struggles at the helm and dissent from below the ELF continued to compete with the EPLF in the military arena at the cost of deflecting the goal of the nationalist struggle. The EPLF viewed the unilateral withdrawal of the ELF Brigade from the northeastern Sahel front as an abrogation of the joint agreement between the two fronts.[58] ELF efforts to retain a diplomatic edge over the EPLF by conducting separate talks with the Soviet Union (involved heavily on the side of the *Dergue*) while both fronts were withdrawing from their bases merely fuelled the EPLF's suspicions of the ELF. The EPLF's response was to launch a counter-offensive that pushed the ELF armed units out of Eritrean territory and into the Sudan. The lightning attack on the ELF secured the EPLF's supremacy in the Eritrean military arena. 1980 witnessed the end of a decade of inter-Eritrean conflict: civil war (1970–1974), uneasy coexistence (1975–1978), and intermittent hostilities (1979–1980).

The ELF's exit from the military arena did not solve the political fragmentation of the Eritrean nationalists but it opened a new chapter in Eritrea's political history, breaking the stalemate of internal military conflict and ushering in a period of reconciliation of the various groups within the EPLF. A dissident group, the ELF–Central Committee merged with the EPLF in 1987. A radical offshoot of the EDM, calling itself the Eritrean Democratic Movement for the Liberation of Eritrea (EDMLE), also surfaced in the late 1980s.[59] A segment of the EDM, led by Heruy Tedla (a former member of the ELF leadership) joined the EPLF in 1990.[60]

The 1960s and 1970s reflected the growth of a defiant but fragmented nationalism in the Eritrean arena. The ELF's politics of exclusion and patronage, and a fissiparous organizational structure which encouraged ethno-religious fragmentation proved unequal to the dual task of constructing a cohesive effective organization and the struggle to liberate Eritrea from Ethiopian hegemony.

The ELF's organizational weakness and factional leadership drained the nationalists' strength which gradually became dissipated in inter-group rivalries. The absence of a common political platform and a cohesive military strategy gave the Ethiopian hegemon ample opportunity to capitalize on the nationalists' weaknesses. Yet, despite these glaring and costly deficiencies, the ELF's role as a defiant resistance movement against Ethiopian hegemony should not be dismissed.

Even for those sovereign nations invested with regional and international recognition, the construction of a single national identity based on consensus was a gradual process marked by parallel inter-elite power struggles and bloody conflicts.[61] The ELF's defiant nationalism was challenged by the

EPLF's radical, secular nationalism. This rivalry erupted into civil war first in the periods 1972–1974 and 1978–1981. Between 1961 and 1981, the endemic fragmentation of Eritrean nationalism underwent continuous transformation, ultimately coalescing under the radical mobilization of the EPLF, which successfully transcended parochial divisions and narrow agendas.

The 1980s witnessed a qualitative transformation of the Eritrean struggle demonstrated by the emergence of the EPLF as the only organization capable of transcending internal cleavages while challenging the hegemon in both the military and diplomatic arena. In chapter 8 we will examine this maturation of Eritrean nationalism under the EPLF and the quest for legitimacy in the regional and international order. The evolution of the EPLF, from a small band of dissidents in the 1970s to a radical survivor and innovator in the 1980s, a successful liberator overseeing Eritrea's transition to independence and the country's provisional government in the 1990s, requires a detailed study of the maturation of Eritrean nationalism in the course of thirty years of armed struggle.

8   The EPLF's quest for legitimacy

Introduction

The EPLF emerged as the most enduring and articulate interlocutor of Eritrean nationalism in the third decade of the armed struggle. From the outset, the EPLF's goals reflected those of the ELM in its emphasis on a secular nationalism and its youthful membership.

The struggle for Eritrean nationhood was waged on two levels. The first level entailed the military campaigns to evict an Ethiopian occupying army supported by various allies. The second level dealt with the equally arduous struggle to construct a Pan-Eritrean political agenda. In the three decades of resistance to Ethiopian hegemony, the priority accorded to armed struggle and to the building of an army resulted in a military stalemate. The social and political struggle to construct a nation out of the numerous ethnic and confessional groups met with more success. By the mid-1980s the EPLF could boast of an impressive record of mobilizing the various ethnic groups and classes (including Eritrean women) into a single nationalist force united around a single goal: liberation.

The EPLF's early emphasis on the gradual construction of a national identity was based on the identification of Eritrea as an integral part of the African colonial experience. The EPLF's repudiation of ELF patronage politics characterized by internal ethno-religious chauvinism was accompanied by an unequivocal rejection of any pretensions to Pan-Islamic or Pan-Arab tenets.

The young EPLF reformers of the 1970s, like those of the ELM in the 1950s, gave priority to the idea of a secular nationalism and emphasized education and culture as vehicles for political mobilization. In contrast to the ELF, they continued the ELM's policy of rejecting confessional-based programmes. The significant point of departure from the ELM's earlier focus on secular nationalism was the development within the EPLF of a clear political agenda emphasizing anti-colonialism, and opposition to American imperialism and Zionism.

The EPLF's ideological stand can be described as a selective, pragmatic (even eclectic), application of Marxist philosophy adapted to the particular context of Eritrea's nationalist liberation struggle.[1] This fusion of Eritrean nationalism and populist Marxism developed as a response to the Ethio-American alliance which supported Ethiopia's hegemonic claims against the Eritrean nationalists. The EPLF's programs and congresses, replete with "leftist" rhetoric stopped short of official declarations of a future Marxist–Leninist state. Nor was the formation of a vanguard political party given priority during the armed struggle.[2] Yet the EPLF's organizational structure and policies continued to reflect a strong Marxist influence evident in the language employed in the organization's documents and in the strict adherence to the tenets of democratic centralism.

The EPLF's quest for regional and international legitimacy underwent three phases. The first phase, during the first stage of the organization's development between 1969 and 1975, was characterized by demands for redress of Ethiopian violations of Eritrean rights. The EPLF emphasized Eritrea's African identity and rejected the ELF's policy of assimilation into the Pan-Arab sphere, so defining the fundamental parameters within which the struggle for Eritrean nationhood was played out. However, limited opportunities to garner regional support often forced the EPLF to forge alliances with Arab or unpopular African regimes. This diplomatic expedient aroused old fears of Arabization and balkanization. The second phase, 1976–1981, reflected a radicalization of the EPLF's ideology and organizational structure. It was during this period that the rival ELF, which had figured more prominently in Arab circles, was finally eliminated. Diplomatically, it was also a period of isolation due to Ethiopia's alliance with the Soviet Union, especially after the military campaigns which forced the EPLF's strategic withdrawal. In the third phase, 1982–1991, the EPLF launched coordinated political and military campaigns to erode the Addis Ababa regime's legitimacy. The EPLF began a series of diplomatic efforts to attain support and recognition from Ethiopian opposition groups, African countries, and international and regional organizations. The reformulation of its diplomatic strategies after 1980 was also accompanied by a shift from a military to a juridically sanctioned political solution, such as the demand for a UN-sponsored referendum.[3]

Flexibility, discipline, pragmatism, and innovation are the key characteristics distinguishing the EPLF from other Eritrean resistance groups. Its strength can be attributed to its capacity to learn from the lessons of the past. The first lesson was the polarization of Eritrean society along religious lines, which had facilitated Ethiopian incursions into the political fabric of the ex-colony in the late 1940s. The second was the need for effective organizational structure and a disciplined army, the absence of which had contributed to the ELM's swift demise in 1965. The third lesson was the deleterious effect of patronage politics and personalism, features that characterized the ELF's leadership for two decades until its demise in 1981. The fourth lesson was Ethiopia's active diplomatic campaigns which barred the Eritrean liberation movements from access to the regional and international orders which might have facilitated attainment of support and legitimacy.

The EPLF's successful military and political campaigns in 1988 broke the stalemate that had reigned since 1978. The point of departure came with the battle of Afabet and the subsequent capture of the port city of Massawa in 1990. Politically, the coordination of EPLF activities with Ethiopian opposition movements served to precipitate the erosion of the *Dergue*. The EPLF's ability to maintain an effective military and organizational capability enabled it to establish regional alliances and initiate diplomatic challenges in the international arena. This visible weakening of Ethiopia's diplomatic capabilities developed in the wake of increasing superpower ambivalence towards the *Dergue* whose legitimacy was also being challenged actively within Ethiopia.

The end of the Cold War led to unprecedented changes in superpower relations and loosened the hegemon's guaranteed support network. The gradual transformation of the EPLF from a guerrilla army to a significant political as well as a military actor in the Horn was also reflected in its efforts to acquire legitimacy by emphasizing the *Dergue*'s violation of human rights, the use of chemical and cluster bombs, using famine as a political weapon, and the violation of Eritrea's right to self-determination.

The appeal to international justice

The first group which attempted to internationalize the Eritrean conflict comprised the former party politicians in exile who formed the nucleus of the ELF. They called on the UN to exercise its responsibility after the abrogation of the Eritrean–Ethiopian federation.

We deem it to be the duty of the World Organization, as the supreme authority in this matter, to kindly look into the case with promptness as a safeguard to human rights emphasized in its resolution by sending a Commission of Inquiry into Eritrea and allowing the Eritreans at least a referendum, in conformity with the context of its resolutions.[4]

The grievances were directed at Emperor Haile Selassie, described as a "dictator, who had to satisfy at all costs his boundless and insane ambitions."[5] This description, in stark contrast to the prevailing carefully crafted image of a benevolent monarch,[6] did not find a receptive audience until 1974 when the imperial regime was deposed. These first-generation nationalists regarded the failure of the federation as a conspiracy of "the

Anglo-Ethiopian imperialists [who] mobilized fully their diplomatic resources ... in order to achieve at the United Nations what they could not get in Eritrea."[7] In the post-1945 international order, where Ethiopia had forged powerful alliances and disseminated its regime of truth, such grievances were ignored or dismissed as unfounded allegations. Despite the validity of Eritrean demands for redress and overwhelming evidence of Ethiopian violations these early advocates failed to achieve their minimum demand – the right to vote in a referendum.

The UN's inability or unwillingness to shoulder what the nationalists presumed to be its duty led the ELF, whose leadership included those nationalists who lobbied for UN action,[8] to focus their efforts on the neighboring Arab countries. Cultural affinity and shared religion were emphasized in the quest for recognition.[9] Although this approach was successful in acquiring limited military support, Ethiopia effectively countered with a rhetorical offensive built around the "Arabization of the Red Sea" thesis. As the detailed discussion in the previous chapter demonstrates, the ELF's relations with the Arab world resulted in the further marginalization of the Eritrean question. The ELF's close links with the Palestinian Liberation Organization (Fatah) and its adoption of "terrorist" tactics such as hijacking and kidnapping generated American and Israeli support for Ethiopia. In the African political arena, the Eritrean–Arab liaison thus served to feed old fears and hostilities.

The EPLF scrupulously avoided confessional or ethnically based organizational structures and affiliations. The EPLF's initial mobilization efforts adopted an ideological framework that utilized Marxist organizational techniques.[10] In this case, the enemy was identified as the feudal Ethiopian empire and its Western allies. The first manifesto issued by the PLF in 1971, *Neh'nan Elamaa'nan* (Our Struggle and its Goals) explained the reasons which led to the new organization's secession from the ELF: the lack of a clear political line and patronage politics based on ethno-religious chauvinism. The manifesto emphasized that:

... we are freedom fighters and not crusaders ... we are Eritreans and not Arabs ... Our stand is neither ethnic nor sectarian.[11]

This manifesto listed a summary of the PLF's objectives:
1 to liberate [Eritreans] from Ethiopian oppression through armed struggle;
2 to create a society free of economic and political oppression;
3 to build an agriculturally, economically and educationally developed country;
4 to establish a united Eritrean Front (*Hibur Ertrawi selfi*)[12] with no distinction as to religion, ethnic affiliation or sex;

5 to establish close solidarity with all progressive peoples in the world, especially those in Africa, Asia and Latin America;

6 to combat world imperialism led by the United States;

7 to erase Israeli Zionism.[13]

The radicalization of the EPLF and the adoption of a Marxist philosophy and mobilization techniques were evident as early as 1975. The EPLF's general political education manual identifies the enemies of the Eritrean revolution as Ethiopian colonialism and its supporters: imperialist America and Zionist Israel.[14] In these early documents the EPLF stressed the difference between *Na'tznet*, interpreted as the freedom of the flag, and *Harnet*, defined as the liberation from economic as well as political exploitation inherent in the world capitalist system controlled by imperialism. Following this logic, the EPLF political education manual taught that Ethiopia herself was a neo-colony of American imperialism, and that the capitalist countries in Western Europe and North America were free but not liberated. By contrast, people of communist countries like the USSR, China, and Eastern Europe were considered free as well as liberated.[15] Democratic centralism was emphasized as a blueprint for the establishment of a well-organized and disciplined struggle and as a safeguard against factionalism and anarchy.[16] The EPLF's emphasis on discipline and organization, features that distinguished it from other Eritrean liberation movements, was well established as early as 1975.

Externally, the early PLF (*Hizbawi Haltat Harnet Ertra*) established relations with the radical regimes of the Middle East from 1971 to 1975 through the ELF–PLF Foreign Mission headed by Osman Saleh Sabbe. Ostracized by the OAU member states and lacking any international support, Eritrean nationalists turned to the only remaining source of military and financial support: the Middle East. However, these links to the Arab world proved to be more a liability than an asset to the Eritrean cause because they were interpreted as a continuation of the "Arab" and "balkanization" threat to Ethiopia and Africa. In order to counter the prevailing assumptions skillfully exploited by Ethiopia to isolate the Eritreans from African support, the Foreign Mission attempted to allay African fears.

Unity cannot be achieved by massacres ... We would like our African brothers to know that we are not against unity but we have been occupied by a neighboring country. How can, for example, Tanzania occupy Uganda or Kenya occupy Somalia in the name of African unity? It is unthinkable in our case also. Eritrea is not part of Ethiopia and we are not Ethiopians. *We are an African country colonised by another* ... As a liberation movement we have the right to ask for arms from anywhere: Africa, Europe, and the Arab world ... The Ethiopians are exploiting the tune which was played by imperialists to create a schism between Africans and Arabs.[17]

During 1975 the Foreign Mission pursued an active African campaign which sought assistance from regimes that were either opposed to the status quo maintained by the OAU or considered disreputable by the majority of member states. Among these was the notorious regime of Idi Amin Dada of Uganda, Said Barre's irredentist Somali Democratic Republic, and obscure Pan-Africanist groups.[18] It could be argued that the first efforts to gain credibility for the Eritrean cause met with failure not only because of the prevailing pro-Ethiopian stance but was due also to the choice of Eritrean allies. Although constrained by the hegemon's powerful role in the OAU, the Foreign Mission's efforts probably did more harm than good by providing the Ethiopian regime with more grist for its denunciation of the Eritreans as a destabilizing force in Africa. Externally, Osman S. Sabbe's diplomatic brokering failed to obtain even minimum African support to raise the Eritrean question in the OAU's agenda.

Internally, the tactical alliance between the ELF–PLF Foreign Mission and the PLF broke down due to the PLF's insistence on centralized coordination between the aims of the fighters in the field and the diplomats in the foreign relations office. In 1975 the PLF denounced Sabbe and formally dissociated itself from Sabbe's Foreign Mission.[19] Sabbe formally reorganized the ELF–PLF as a splinter group, taking with him most of the Arab support. Arab patronage remained closely linked with the ELF–PLF. After disengaging itself from Sabbe and the Foreign Mission, the PLF was left isolated from any external financial support or diplomatic agency.

The ELF–PLF's list of supporters certainly did not endear the Eritrean cause to the rest of the world. In fact, it marginalized the Eritrean cause as a peripheral Arab interest, lending credence to Ethiopia's accusations of an Arab-supported conspiracy. Within Eritrea, the organization's affiliation with the Arab world led to tensions between nationalists who emphasized their African identity and those advocating membership in the Pan-Arab sphere by virtue of religious beliefs and cultural interaction.

The period from 1969 to 1975 was one of internal fragmentation. By 1975 the ELF faced two other rival organizations, the PLF and the ELF–PLF. The latest splinter organization, led by Sabbe, had the most negative impact on the nationalists' quest for recognition. Sabbe's defection from the PLF led to further isolation of the PLF, which was deprived of any source of support. It was this period of isolation, 1975–1977, that gave rise to the PLF's emphasis on self-reliance and inward-oriented development and the transformation from a mobile guerrilla army into what would become the EPLF.

Lessons of the past: structural and ideological reconfiguration

In the second stage of its development (1976–1981), the EPLF focused on its internal organizational structure. The First Organizational Congress of the EPLF was held on January 31, 1977. This was based on a reassessment of the first seven years of its existence. John Markakis notes:

The National Democratic Programme adopted by the Congress represented a distillation of the ideological convictions that had led the founders of the EPLF earlier to leave the ELF, their experience with the realities of Eritrean society and the nationalist struggle.[20]

The fusion of Afro-Marxist philosophy with secular nationalist aspirations characterized the EPLF's method of constructing a cohesive front from 1971 to 1987.[21] In 1977, the EPLF officially announced its National Democratic Program (NDP) and its eleven objectives:

1 Establish a people's democratic state.
2 Build an independent, self-reliant, and planned national economy.
3 Develop culture, education, technology, and public health.
4 Safeguard social rights (emphasizing workers' and women's rights).
5 Ensure the equality and consolidate the unity of nationalities.
6 Build a strong people's army.
7 Respect of freedom of religion and faith.
8 Provide humane treatment to prisoners of war and encourage the desertion of Eritrean soldiers serving the enemy.
9 Protect the rights of Eritreans residing abroad.
10 Respect the rights of foreigners residing in Eritrea.
11 Pursue a foreign policy of peace and non-alignment.[22]

The 1977 Congress formalized the existing structure of the EPLF. It elected forty-three members to the Central Committee (thirty-seven permanent and six alternate). The Central Committee, in turn, elected Ramadan Mohamed Nur as General Secretary and Issaias Afeworki as Vice-General Secretary, as well as a Politburo made up of eleven members.[23] The new leadership was balanced between Christians and Moslem members.

This Congress emphasized the need for economic self-reliance and a planned economy, objectives that were implemented after the military victories of 1977–1978. Culture and education as vehicles for mobilization and construction of a pluralist Eritrean national identity were stressed. A new educational program was envisioned to provide "proper dissemination of, respect for, and development of the history of Eritrea and its people."[24] The 1977 NDP was also significant for its inclusion of women's rights, especially since women were not recognized as voting citizens in the 1952 Constitution of Eritrea which stipulated that only males twenty-one years of age or over could vote.[25]

The opportunity to implement the objectives arrived with the necessity of administering the liberated zones in 1977–1978. The EPLF needed to strengthen its links with the countryside and still push through reforms while fighting the Ethiopian occupation army. Past history demonstrated the imperatives to resolve social, ethnic, and religious divisions and to mobilize an inclusive rather than an exclusive society.

Thus, it was a pragmatic assessment of the EPLF's organizational needs that led to a series of reforms launched as part of the liberation struggle. Land reforms were enacted which changed the traditional land tenure. Unlike the ELF, which depended largely on the population for its subsistence, the EPLF's land reforms enabled it to "nationalize" tracts of land to feed its personnel. Some lands formerly administered by absentee landlords or evacuated by fleeing Ethiopian military administrators were distributed to landless peasants, while others were retained for use by the EPLF's medical units and feeding centers.[26] Meanwhile the religious prohibitions against women's ownership of land or leadership roles were eliminated.[27] Political participation was instituted via the EPLF's people's assemblies, women's associations, and peasants' associations.

These reforms faced opposition from adherents to entrenched traditional values governing ethnic, class, and gender relations. But the very success of the reforms, particularly the support gained in the countryside, more than matched that of the dissenters. The few opposition demonstrations mounted by religious landed elites were countered by the beneficiaries of the EPLF's policies, who launched even larger demonstrations against elite interests and in favor of the reforms.[28]

External relations seem to have been relegated to a secondary status in light of the military campaigns that brought the liberation armies to the threshold of victory during 1977–1978.[29] By July 1978 the Ethiopian army, supported by the Soviet Union and allies, managed to recapture key towns forcing the EPLF to withdraw to its base in the Sahel in northern Eritrea.

From 1978 to 1980, the *Dergue* launched five offensives aimed at providing a "final solution" to the Eritrean problem.[30] Nevertheless, the EPLF, which actively promoted the rights of marginalized segments of Eritrean societies (peasants, workers and women), continued to implement its policies in education, health, and social reform. The ranks of the EPLF had grown rapidly with the influx of new recruits who joined the organization after it withdrew from liberated zones. The emphasis on a self-reliant economy was put into practice by innovative use of limited resources and technology to ensure the maintenance and survival of the EPLF and its growing constituents.[31] During this period of military withdrawal the EPLF developed even more innovative ways of ensuring survival while simultaneously preparing for future offensives.

The EPLF's ideological affinity for Marxism became untenable after 1978 when the Soviet bloc openly sided with the Ethiopian regime. The EPLF withdrew and retrenched to reformulate its military and political strategies. What ensued was a reiteration of Eritrean nationalism gradually stripped of strident anti-imperialism, anti-fascism, and anti-Zionist polemics. In 1980, the EPLF issued a call for a referendum as a mechanism to facilitate a political solution. This referendum demanded that the Eritrean people be allowed to vote for three alternatives (1) autonomy; (2) federation; (3) independence. The emphasis on the right of self-determination became sharply evident as the EPLF slowly but gradually began to emerge as a political actor as well as a military vehicle for liberation.

Between 1977 and 1980 more than twenty meetings between the EPLF and the ELF's leadership (the Revolutionary Council) were held to bring about a consensus between the two fronts. However, the ultimate goal of organizational unity failed due to their irreconcilable perspectives. The ELF's organizational leadership was still operating on the basis of ethnic and religious affiliations. The old patronage system that led to the EPLF's separation was still intact, along with its inherent problems of organizational inefficiency and fragmented nationalism.

In 1981, two decades of inter-Eritrean military rivalry came to an abrupt and violent end when the EPLF routed the ELF units and became the sole liberation organization within Eritrea. From this point onwards, the EPLF began to function as a military and political organization that focused both on the armed struggle as a vehicle for liberation and political campaigns to attain regional and international legitimacy.

The lessons of the past began to crystalize as the EPLF focused on the politico-diplomatic imperatives of attaining legitimacy. In contrast to the past, when it was only in a position to respond to the hegemon's or the rival ELF's initiatives, the EPLF began an active political campaign of coalition-building with Ethiopian groups which opposed the *Dergue*'s regime.[32] By the 1980s coordinated EPLF activities and Ethiopian armed opposition groups began to engage the Ethiopian military on various fronts.[33] This drained Ethiopia's manpower and resources in the face of another cycle of crippling famine and drought in the mid-1980s.[34] The unification of these various Ethiopian fronts under one umbrella organization – the Ethiopian People's Revolutionary Democratic Front (EPRDF) – coincided with increasing superpower ambivalence toward supporting the Menghistu regime in its various offensives. In addition to domestic opposition to the policies of the *Dergue*, the famine highlighted the erosion of the post-imperial regime's legitimacy in the international arena.

In the first and second stages, the EPLF emphasized organizational efficiency, military discipline, and a self-reliant economy. In light of the imperatives of survival the EPLF was constrained from devoting its scarce material and human resources to diplomatic campaigns. More importantly, it took two decades for the EPLF to match the hegemon's military prowess in the field, because of Ethiopia's maintenance of a superior material edge through transnational patronage. This imbalance in size and resources was balanced by the EPLF's superior organizational efficiency, innovative coordination of guerrilla and conventional military tactics, and committed fighters.

The new discourse: diplomatic and military offensives

Having consolidated its position within Eritrea, the EPLF next turned its attention to political campaigns to attain regional and international legitimacy. Diplomatically, EPLF lobbying campaigns became less reactive and adversarial and more interactive and conciliatory. Militarily, EPLF forces combined both guerrilla and conventional tactics to counter major Ethiopian offensives and mounted successful offensives of their own. Politically, the EPLF consolidated its alliances with dissident groups such as the Tigrayan People's Liberation Front (TPLF) and the Oromo Liberation Front (OLF) within Ethiopia in an effort to erode the legitimacy of the regime on its own doorstep. In a significant departure from its earlier strategies, the EPLF also embarked on an unprecedented formulation of a concrete plan of governance, involving a multi-party system and a mixed economy.

These changes were publicized at the EPLF's Second Congress in 1987. Central features of the Congress were the unification of ELF (Central Command) with the EPLF, major changes within its organizational structure, shifts in foreign relations, and strategies adopted for the establishment of a pluralist Eritrea.[35] The National Democratic Program of 1987 was a revision of the 1977 program, with a significant alteration to the highly centralized structure of the earlier decade. Some of the new provisions included development of a multi-party system, a mixed economy, and the inclusion of Eritrean expatriates. Anti-American imperialist and anti-Zionist rhetoric, and solidarity with international revolutionary movements, emphases that featured so highly in the past, were markedly absent in 1987.[36]

Diplomatically, the political naivety and ideological tenor of earlier EPLF discourse were discarded and replaced by historically sustainable juridical claims which used the precedents of the western Sahara and Namibian cases to press for long-overdue legitimacy.[37] A parallel campaign to lobby for support for Eritrean self-determination in Africa was initiated by the EPLF in the mid-1980s.[38]

The new approach emphasized the existence of a unified Eritrean nation, Ethiopia's illegal occupation of Eritrea, and the need for a positive superpower role. The political discourse of the EPLF reflected the shift from defiant to conciliatory nationalist rhetoric. In a memorandum to the UN in 1987, the EPLF demonstrated a new diplomatic *savoir-faire*:

You will forgive us for reminding you that the legal and moral order which underlies what is called modern civilization is something which we all as a community cannot take for granted ... *The United Nations (and the United States) bear an historic responsibility ... for Eritrea's mis-shaped destiny.* And *we hereby remind the OAU* and its member governments of their duty *to include the Eritrean question* in their agenda as they did those of Namibia and Western Sahara ... *As the Eritrean war emerges from the shadow of isolation and oblivion to which Ethiopian diplomacy had consigned it*, more is being known about its nature, history, and legal basis.[39]

The professionalization of the EPLF's public relations produced a rhetorical medium through which the Eritrean question could be addressed outside the Ethiopian regime of truth. This opened new possibilities for international efforts such as the unofficial talks mediated by former US President Jimmy Carter in 1989 and official negotiations hosted by the US government in 1991.[40] Notwithstanding these breakthroughs, Ethiopia's adroit responses continued to stymie the EPLF's efforts to achieve a political solution.[41]

The EPLF's reformulation of its diplomatic strategy from one of reaction to the hegemon's initiatives to one of interaction as a recognized political actor was made feasible by its increasing military capability. Beginning in 1984 and strengthened by its earlier gains from the first five offensives,[42] the Eritrean People's Liberation Army (EPLA) scored a series of military victories recapturing areas controlled by the Ethiopian army.[43] By 1988, the EPLA had developed into a conventional army utilizing tanks and other weaponry captured from Ethiopian garrisons. Its refined tactics and strategies demonstrated an impressive capacity to utilize guerrilla as well as conventional tactics.[44]

In 1988 the EPLF scored its most impressive victory at the Battle of Afabet. The overall visibility of the conflict was enhanced through increased media exposure following the EPLF's victory.[45] The deteriorating condition of the Ethiopian military figured prominently in US Congressional hearings on Ethiopian famine held in April 1988, at which the EPLF success at Afabet was specifically mentioned.[46] EPLF Secretary-General Issaias Afeworki also invoked the victory at Afabet in his Chatham House address of October 27, 1988.[47]

The EPLA scored yet another significant military victory with the capture of Massawa on February 10, 1990.[48] Ethiopia's attempt to recapture the city included indiscriminate napalm bombing, a tactic which shocked the international community and triggered a superficial but visible media investigation of the "civilian victims" of the "forgotten war" in the Horn.[49] The international media's attention to the destruction of Massawa also gave credence to the EPLF's accusations of the *Dergue*'s atrocities toward civilians and violation of human rights, although the *Dergue* continued to deny such accusations. The *Dergue*'s ambassador in Geneva, Konjit Sinegiorgis, "flatly denied her government's bombing of Massawa, even as people saw video-tapes [sic] of the bombing in a room next door."[50]

Diplomatic and military efforts to erode the regional and international legitimacy of the *Dergue* were augmented by coordinated political campaigns to forge alliances with opposition movements within Ethiopia. Existing links, such as that with the TPLF, were expanded in subsequent years through the EPLF's provision of military training, transportation, and other logistical support for several dissident organizations.[51] The primary success of this initiative was to bring the Eritrean case before the Ethiopian people, eroding both civilian support and Ethiopian military morale. Militarily, these alliances facilitated coordinated offensives against Ethiopian forces on multiple fronts.[52]

The EPLF's alliance with the Ethiopian People's Revolutionary Democratic Front (EPRDF) was based on the latter's recognition of the Eritrean demand for self-determination and a mutual conviction of the need to rid Ethiopia of the Menghistu regime.

The EPLF bases its relationship with Ethiopian movements on the following principles: recognition of the right to self-determination of "Ethiopian" nationalities, recognition of the national and multi-national organizations, formation of an anti-colonial and national democratic solidarity front and all-sided cooperation. On the part of Ethiopian organizations the EPLF asks that they recognize the just and legitimate anti-colonial struggle of the Eritrean people and that they be willing to participate in the solidarity front.[53]

The EPLF's insistence that Ethiopian opposition groups recognize the Eritrean case as one of Ethiopian colonialism produced an enormous amount of theoretical disagreement.[54] Nevertheless, despite lengthy, and at times acrimonious, debates, alliances were maintained with the stronger groups in a pragmatic farsighted strategy on the part of the EPLF to pre-empt any successor regime from continuing Ethiopia's hegemonic domination of Eritrea.

The EPLF's alliance with the EPRDF led to the coordination of attacks against Menghistu's armies. Both organizations benefited from this alliance. The EPLF was able to concentrate on capturing the capital city of Asmara and the EPRDF obtained logistical support and reinforcements for the capture of Addis Ababa. By the end of May 1991, the guerrilla armies emerged victorious and were the main participants in peace talks and ceasefire negotiations in London. The new compromise proposed by both superpowers and publicized by the US government was based on resuscitating the idea of a federal solution.[55] This may have been little more than old hegemonic wine in a new bottle; nonetheless, it was significant that the EPLF was even included in the tasting.

The EPLF's flexibility, discipline, pragmatism, and innovation produced organizational and military capabilities which in the 1990s rivalled those of the hegemon. Diplomatically, the emergence of an Eritrean political discourse capable of taking the initiative rather than just reacting to the hegemon (and other forces) succeeded in breaking its isolation. Militarily, the EPLA superceded Ethiopian armed forces through effective battlefield tactics and organizational skills. Economically, the EPLF's policy of self-reliance established a firm basis for independent survival. In addition, its control of geostrategic areas of the Red Sea coastal strip facilitated the final takeover of Asmara and Assab on May 24–25, 1991. The EPLF's evolution from the constrained politics of a guerrilla organization to the pragmatism of a provisional government enhanced its standing in the regional and international communities. Thus the EPLF demonstrated military, economic, geostrategic, and diplomatic capabilities which broke the stalemate that had characterized the conflict for three decades. After securing the borders and evacuating Ethiopian military personnel from Eritrea the EPLF demonstrated its newly acquired diplomatic acumen by announcing a two-year waiting period followed by a referendum asking the Eritrean people for their decision on independence. The Eritrean quest for legitimacy finally captured regional and international attention with the maturation of diplomatic skills, military sophistication, and a demonstration of economic viability.

9   Building the Eritrean polity

Ertra, Ertra, Ertra	(Eritrea, Eritrea, Eritrea
B'aal dema Indalkese Tedemsisu	Her enemy decimated and
Meswa'eta b'Harnet Tedebisu	Her sacrifices vindicated
	by liberation
Mewa'el Nekhisa ab Elama	Steadfast in its goal
T'emerti Tsin'aaat Koinu Sema	Symbolizing endurance
Ertra Iza Haben Wutsu'aat	Eritrea, the pride of its
	oppressed people
Ameskira Hakhi Kemz'ewet	Proved that the truth
	prevails
Ertra, Ertra	Eritrea, Eritrea
Ab Alem Tchebit'ato	It holds its rightful
G'bue Kibra	place in the world.)[1]

The demise of Ethiopian hegemony

After thirty years of armed struggle, the loss of countless civilian lives, and a casualty toll of 65,000 EPLA fighters[2] the struggle against Ethiopian hegemony ended with an Eritrean military and political victory.[3] Three events marked the demise of Ethiopia's regional hegemony in May 1991: Menghistu Hailemariam's flight to Zimbabwe on May 21, the EPLF's liberation of Asmara on May 24, and the EPRDF's takeover of Addis Ababa on May 28. The EPLF's victory and its total liberation of Eritrea altered dramatically the political and military balance of the Horn.[4] The long-standing demand for Eritrean self-determination was endorsed by the new Transitional Government of Ethiopia (TGE) as the first building block of mutual coexistence between the Eritreans and their new Ethiopian partners.[5] After declaring the formation of a provisional government and its intention to hold a referendum in Eritrea within two years, the EPLF quickly and efficiently replaced the Ethiopian bureaucrats who had occupied the key sectors of the civil service.[6] All EPLF members volunteered to work without pay until a referendum on independence was held to decide the future of the country.[7] EPLF personnel and technical teams repaired damaged roads and built new ones. They established new schools and clinics in areas neglected during the war. They organized rural communities in preparation for the planting season and launched new projects to reforest areas depleted by soil erosion.[8] They revised the educational curriculum for elementary and secondary schools,[9] and worked as reporters and journalists for the newly established newspaper.[10] The policy of self-reliance that had served the liberation front so well during the war years continued to enable the Eritrean nationalists to determine the priorities of post-war reconstruction without being dependent on external forces.

While Eritrea progressed towards rehabilitating its economy and society at a "snail's pace"[11] relations with neighboring Ethiopia underwent a dramatic transformation. The mutual needs and interests of the former rivals were emphasized and priority was given to normalizing relations between the two countries. Eritrean–Ethiopian relations during the interim period (May 1991–April 1993) were based on cooperation and interdependence, thus disproving both the Pan-Ethiopian and Cold War skeptics. Leaders of the Ethiopian and Eritrean governments publicly reaffirmed that the transition to democracy and economic development of their respective countries depended on maintaining regional stability.[12] Assab was declared a free port and Massawa was opened as a free transit port for goods heading for Ethiopia. Ethiopia's need for access to the sea, which had been a major justification for its control over Eritrea, was met without recourse to violence. The Ethiopian official currency, the *Birr*, was used in both Eritrea and Ethiopia. Other agreements were signed regarding trade and communications. Telephone communications were restored on May 26, 1992 after a four-year interruption.[13]

In September 1992, after sending a delegation to visit Eritrea, the OAU announced that it would participate in the referendum as an observer, and in December the UN General Assembly passed Resolution 47/114 authorizing the establishment of a United Nations Observer Mission to Verify the Referendum in Eritrea (UNOVER).[14] The TGE reaffirmed its support for the Eritreans' demand for self-determination and its willingness to abide by the results of the referendum. In a clear indication of the new cooperation between the two countries, the Ethiopian Foreign Minister expressed his hope that

developing economic, trade, and social relations between the two peoples based on mutual trust and benefit will be a trail blazer for an economic and social integration in the Horn of Africa sub-region which we hope to see materialize in the not too distant future.[15]

During the transitional period the basis for the new relations of cooperation was based on a realization of the economic interdependence of the two countries. However, both interim governments, freed from the constraints of dictatorship and external rivalry, took steps to ensure long-term benefits for their respective peoples. The end of Cold War politics and superpower rivalry, which had favored Ethiopian interests over those of Eritrea, also equalized the balance of power between the two countries. Domestically, the majority of the population of both countries, suffering from the effects of war, endorsed the new leaderships' emphasis on peaceful dialogue to further economic and social integration based on mutual respect. With the demise of Ethiopian hegemony over Eritrea the antagonistic and confrontational relations of three decades came to an end. Internationally and regionally, the demand of the Eritrean people for self-determination was no longer an isolated case viewed as a dangerous precedent, but one of many cases which highlighted the need for a reassessment of international and regional norms and rules governing the modes of conflict resolution in the post-World War II era. The demise of Ethiopian hegemony inaugurated a new era of interdependence and cooperation between the two countries. National resources and the energies of citizens were finally freed from the imperatives of war and channelled towards the exercise of self-determination and popular participation in the choice of a national identity.

Eritrea in transition: the birth of a new nation

In the domestic arena, the two-year period of transition was a time of fundamental change for Eritrean society. The Provisional Government of Eritrea (PGE) promulgated new laws of citizenship, conducted civic education, and introduced the rule of law. Among the first legal decrees issued by the PGE was the Eritrean Nationality Proclamation no. 21/1992 which clearly outlined the criteria for Eritrean citizenship based on birth, naturalization, adoption, and marriage.[16] In contrast to the customs of Eritrea's patriarchal society, which gave more importance to a father's origin, the PGE declared that "any person born to a father or a mother of Eritrean origin in Eritrea or abroad is an Eritrean national by birth."[17] The proclamation also dealt with the delicate issue of the rights of long-term settlers who could not claim nationality by birth.[18] Naturalization applied to persons who were not of Eritrean origin but who lived in Eritrea from 1934 until 1951 or who lived in Eritrea for a period of ten years from 1952 onwards.[19] All eligible persons were required to apply for a certificate of nationality from the Secretary of Internal Affairs, thus making the official acquisition of an Eritrean identity a matter of choice rather than birth right. This proclamation enabled the PGE to conduct a census of the eligible voters residing inside Eritrea as well as abroad.

In October 1992, the Eritrean Referendum Commission announced that out of a total population of 3.5 million, 1.8 million eligible voters had registered (a third of whom lived either in refugee camps in the Sudan or abroad).[20] Unlike the 1952 elections, women and naturalized citizens were allowed to vote, provided they met the required criteria. The alternatives of federation, autonomy, or independence that the EPLF had demanded in the 1980s were replaced with a simple "yes" or "no" vote for independence. Proclamation no. 22/1992, issued by the PGE on April 7, 1992 featured only one question:

The Referendum Ballot shall be worded as follows:
Place an X or other mark in one box:
Do you approve Eritrea to become an independent
sovereign state?
    Yes   No[21]

The UN, OAU, and numerous organizations and countries were invited to participate as observers.[22] Recalling Eritrea's past experience with the UN and the intervention of external powers during decolonization the PGE sent a memorandum to the UN, reprinted in the weekly Eritrean newspapers:

The Eritrean people ... have always called for the UN to observe and legitimate its right to self-determination by holding a referendum within two years. The PGE in order to avoid any misunderstanding or a repetition of past errors would like to bring attention to the following: (1) The right to self-determination will be exercised by the Eritrean people themselves. It is a right that is not given or selected by another group or people. (2) The Eritrean case was a just struggle conducted against a coercive incorporation and not a case of secession. (3) Reasons of "historical imperatives," "outlets to the sea," "international or regional interests," are unjust, unacceptable, unfounded and irrelevant to the Eritrean case.[23]

In addition to the UN, OAU, and the Arab League, the list of 536 observers included representatives from the USA, UK, Ethiopia, Egypt, Russia, Yemen, Sudan, Tunisia, and regional and international non-governmental organizations (NGOs).[24]

The Eritrean referendum of April 23–25, 1993 was a watershed in modern Eritrea's history. Eritreans queued in disciplined lines with registration cards in hand at the 1,010 polling stations in an atmosphere charged with festive excitement. The capital city, towns, and villages were decorated with hundreds of green, red, and blue EPLF flags and the formerly banned UN flag of olive branches on a background of sky blue. Posters urging people to vote were plastered on walls, shops, and fences. The cost of the referendum was estimated at a little over $4.5 million contributed by the UN, donor countries, and Eritreans in the diaspora. The logistics of hosting foreign observers, transporting them to the polling stations, and providing personnel for each station were organized by the Referendum Commission and hundreds of civilian volunteers.[25]

Organizationally, the occasion was a carefully planned event which demonstrated the PGE/EPLF's efficiency, pragmatism, and high degree of popular legitimacy. All eligible voters were registered by mid-December. From December until April civic education about voting procedures was conducted in all regions using the local languages. Despite the fact that the majority of the population had no prior experience of voting, the Referendum Commission's efforts to educate the population proved to be successful.[26] The 99.8 percent vote for independence, announced on April 27, 1993, dispelled any doubts about the wishes of the population.[27]

Eritrean independence was finally legitimized by the United Nations, the OAU, and the members of the international community. On April 27, 1993, the UN Special Commissioner, Samir Sanbar, formally announced the referendum to be free and fair.

I have the honor in my capacity as Special Representative of the Secretary-General for UNOVER, to certify that, on the whole, the referendum process in Eritrea can be considered to have been free and fair at every stage, and that it has been conducted to my satisfaction.[28]

The eighteen-man OAU observer mission led by H. E. Papa Louis Fall from Senegal also declared that

the manner in which polling was conducted in Eritrea was generally free, fair and devoid of significant irregularities ... [The] observer team was particularly impressed with the high degree of enthusiasm, discipline and maturity exhibited by the Eritrean electorate and people in view of the warm reception they extended to the OAU team in spite of previous misconceptions and misunderstanding.[29]

With international and regional recognition of Eritrean aspirations of independence the quest for one's own nation and a separate political identity were realized. The verification of the referendum as a free and fair exercise of self-determination by the UN and the OAU removed the last barrier to sovereign nationhood.

Having achieved external legitimacy the PGE moved swiftly towards preparations for a formal declaration of independence and the institutionalization of the structures of government. The Central Committee of the EPLF held its seventh meeting on May 11–12, 1993 to discuss the formation of the first government of independent Eritrea.[30] On May 19, 1993, Proclamation no. 37/1993 was issued announcing the establishment of a four-year transitional government. The government consisted of fourteen ministries, five authorities, three commissions, two departments, and a Civil Service Office.[31] This decree delineated the structure and scope of authority of the new government made up of: a legislative body, the National Assembly (*Hagerawi Baito*); an executive body, the Council of State (*Bet Mikhri Menghisti*); and a Judiciary (*Ferdawi Akal*). The transitional government was a hybrid between a presidential and parliamentary system in which the legislative and executive bodies were inextricably linked due to the fact that its officials held dual membership in both sectors of government. The President held a dual position as the Chairman of the National Assembly and Chief Executive of the Council of State. The judiciary was the only body that exercised autonomy.

The National Assembly functioned as the highest legislative body in the new government. It was empowered to formulate internal and external policies and to select the president of the nation. The National Assembly was made up of 138 people consisting of 78 members of the Central Committee of the EPLF, 30 elected officials from the provincial assemblies, and 30 citizens (10 of whom were women) appointed by the Central Committee of the EPLF.[32]

The Council of State constituted the highest executive body, and reported to the National Assembly. The 25-member body was chaired by the President of the nation and was responsible for political, economic, and social policies and their implementation.[33] The President, as head of state and commander-in-chief appointed ministers, heads of offices, and special commissions.

The judiciary (*Ferdawi Akal*) is autonomous from both the National Assembly and the Council of State. This body is entrusted with protecting the rights (*mesel'at*), interests (*rebha'tat*), and freedoms (*natznet'at*) of the government, organizations, associations, and individuals.

The proclamation of a four-year transitional government was accompanied by a decision to postpone the demobilization of EPLF military and civilian personnel. The government had provided housing, food, and shelter for its fighters but economic decisions to develop a budget for salaries had been shelved until independence. Citing the lack of sufficient capital the government announced that EPLF personnel would continue their work as unpaid volunteers. The leadership announced this decision without consulting the majority of the rank-and-file. The 80,000–90,000 members of the EPLF, accustomed to the flow of information channelled through the hierarchical chain of command through seminars and informational meetings were caught by surprise by this decision.

The euphoria and rejoicing in the aftermath of the referendum had raised the expectations of the rank-and-file that with independence their demobilization would usher in a new era of economic security. On the morning of May 20, 1993, a commando unit took over Asmara International Airport in protest. While most of the inhabitants of the capital city went about their routine tasks unaware of the protest, the President, Issaias Afeworki, met with the rebels to hear their views. By early afternoon, young fighters carrying kalashnikovs took over key government offices and Asmara's residents woke up to the fact that a protest was underway. Not a single shot was fired during these tense hours when a call was put out for all EPLF members to gather for a meeting between the President, the rebels, and rank-and-file members at the soccer stadium at 8:00 p.m. The protest (*Adma Tegadelti*) was limited to Asmara and did not elicit similar actions from the armed units stationed in other parts of Eritrea. After a frank debate during which the dissidents expressed their anger and dismay at the government's unilateral decision, which they perceived as the beginning of unegalitarian practices of the leadership, the assembly disbanded peacefully. The next day, the President addressed the nation on radio and television announcing that immediate steps would be taken to reduce the size of the army, to convene the Third Congress of the EPLF, proceed with demobilization, and initiate salary scales.[34]

The decision to remain as unpaid volunteers taken by the seventh meeting of the Central Committee, was based on the fact that this country did not have the sufficient economic resources. That it was not found acceptable by those *tegadelti* whose impoverished families were reduced to begging is a natural and acceptable response . . . Yesterday's protest, leaving aside its manifestation, was a reflection of this country's primary problem . . . It is only natural for human beings to react.[35]

The President also responded to some social and administrative grievances which had given rise to accusations of corruption and unegalitarianism against government officials.

Our tradition of egalitarianism and solidarity enabled us to achieve our goals. During the armed struggle there was no gap between leaders and fighters. [Since liberation] this tradition had partially changed . . . but efforts have not stopped to put a stop to some leaders who had acted improperly . . . Although such excesses have not been predominant, they gave rise to grievances among the fighters . . . Be that as it may, the procedure of expressing grievances was illegal. The mob-like expression of dissidence was an embarrassment to the dignity and pride of this country as well as its fighters.[36]

The President further stated that the protest provided an important lesson for the government, its fighters, and people and concluded with an appeal to uphold the EPLF's tradition of patriotism, solidarity, and collective welfare which ensured the survival of the organization and attainment of independence. The leadership's prompt response to the dissidents, its willingness to address their economic, social, and political grievances demonstrated a continuation of the EPLF's pragmatism and flexibility.

Eritrea's first post-independence government came into existence conscious of the dangers of unmet economic needs and unfulfilled promises. The peaceful resolution of this protest, rather than casting a shadow on independence celebrations, provided an important lesson on the need for strengthening state–society relations.[37]

On Monday, May 24, 1993, independent Eritrea's new flag was hoisted at a celebration rally attended by heads of state and international dignitaries. Among them was the Ethiopian President Meles Zenawi, who congratulated the Eritrean people on their independence and expressed his hope that "the wounds of the past will be healed."[38] Fifty-two years after its decolonization and thirty-two years after the beginning of its armed struggle Eritrea emerged as a sovereign, independent state.

To build the Eritrean polity

Independent Eritrea faces multiple challenges of economic, social, and political reconstruction. Although future generations will continue to feel the after-effects of the long war, Eritreans have emerged with a strong sense of nationalism which binds the different ethnic and religious groups as citizens. What Trevaskis described as a "conglomerate of different communities" has, after thirty years of war, fused into a single people. While Italian colonialism can be credited for demarcating modern Eritrea's boundaries, Ethiopian hegemonic domination was the principal contributing factor in the construction of a separate Eritrean political identity.

Eritreans finally achieved their quest for a country of their own. They proved to the outside world that they can coexist and cooperate with their larger neighbor if the relationship is based on consent and consensus rather than coercion. The needs of both countries – Ethiopia's access to the sea and Eritrea's need for a stable trading and financial partner – were achieved through negotiation and bilateral agreements. The first independent government of Eritrea also emphasized the importance of solidarity between the peoples of both countries and announced that it is cooperating with the Ethiopian government to enable the "free movements of people and harmonization of immigration laws."[39] These new relations of economic interdependence and social reconciliation became possible because Eritrea and Ethiopia treated each other as equals. The end of the Cold War also decreased the possibility of external intervention, which could have favored one side over the other.

The new nation faces immense problems of reconstruction. During the interim period while the country prepared for the referendum, investments and international economic assistance were delayed.[40] External assistance was also not forthcoming because of the government's insistence on dictating the terms of aid and prioritizing projects dealing with food security, land reform, education, and social justice. Prior to independence a proposed aid package of $26 million tied to free-market reforms was rejected by the Eritrean government due to a "misunderstanding" over priorities and a clash of attitudes. After a series of meetings compromises were reached and aid started to flow from the USAID, the European Community, and the World Bank.[41]

The long years of war and the absence of the rule of law had created a socio-economic system based on patronage and bribery. The government faced problems of corruption, inflation, a thriving black market, and unequal development of urban and rural areas.[42] New laws intended to correct these problems were drafted and put into effect immediately. The leadership appealed to the population for support in these efforts to eliminate poverty and inequality, and create a better life for all citizens.

The development of a country can be measured by the even growth of all sectors of society. It is not only unjust but also backward when only the elite enjoys life while the majority of consumers struggle to survive. The [government] ... calls on everyone to cooperate in implementing the guidelines and proclamations.[43]

On the eve of independence, the government raised the salaries of the civil service in recognition of the high cost of living. The liberalization of the economy necessitated the lifting of state control over the local economy while at the same time trying to curb excessive prices by merchants and petty traders. Maintaining a balance between a gradual opening of the economy and protecting the rights of consumers and suppliers resulted in a cautious move towards privatization. In order to avoid the dangers of an unfettered free market system, economic dependency, and uneven develop-ment without scaring off investors the government revised the guidelines and laws dealing with both local and foreign companies.[44]

Nevertheless, Eritrea's natural resources, such as natural gas, oil, gold and copper deposits, fisheries, and tourism, provided the new nation with a strong position from which to dictate its terms of investment. The prospects of oil deposits along the Eritrean coast, confirmed by new geological studies, led to exploratory talks between Eritrean and multinational companies in 1992.[45] Mobil Oil was the first to establish a branch office in Asmara with Shell, Agip and Total, following suit.[46] Two of the first decrees after the declaration of independence were Proclamation no. 40/1993 dealing with the regulation of oil exploration and Proclamation no. 41/1993 concerning revenue collection from oil exploration activities.[47] Maintaining a balance between the government's policy of self-reliance and attracting international investors will be essential to the integration of the previously isolated Eritrea's economy and its national reconstruction.

The importance of striking a balance between Eritrean national interests and the international economic community was stressed during the new nation's participation at the meeting of the UN Economic and Social Council in July 1993. President Issaias Afeworki stressed the need for a convergence of interests between donors and recipients.

What is required, and what has been conspicuously lacking, is international assistance commensurate with the needs of the country ... The aspect that needs elaboration perhaps is the impact of assistance on recipient communities: whether it inspires or dampens their creativity and self-respect? what mechanisms and instruments can be developed to inhibit mentalities and attitudes of permanent dependence?

Our government believes that all assistance granted or disbursed must include in-built mechanisms of sustainability with a view of [generating], at least partially, the funds for other development projects...[48]

These views reflected a maturation of Eritrea's policy of self-reliance and a willingness to come to terms with the new nation's need for integration in the world economic system. Its potential for a viable economy – assessed as too poor and weak by the UN in 1950 – has certainly been reversed in the 1990s. The uncertainties of whether the new nation and its former guerrilla leaders could demonstrate the necessary flexibility and operate as functional members of the international economic system were dispelled in the early months of its existence. Eritrea's future success will depend on how it develops its economic capabilities and allocates its resources to meet the demands of its population.

Jackson and Rosberg noted in 1982 that at independence almost all African countries were endowed with the juridical attributes of statehood without, however, also having in place the empirical reality that undergirds it.[49] In effect they received the institutions and structures of government, but without the benefit of the mass civic loyalty and sense of political community that could animate the state and create the nation-state. That latter task, of building national civic cultures, has preoccupied the post-colonial African states during the past thirty years and, sad to say, thus far it has been accomplished with only partial success. Eritrea represents another, perhaps unique, case of African state-building.

The referendum of April 1993, which gave Eritrea its independence, was conducted from the "empirical" base of a mature nationalism and a strong sense of political community nurtured during the thirty years' war with its imperial neighbor. The new state also emerged with a dedicated leadership group, the experience of running a "parallel polity" under fire, and the rudiments of an administrative cadre drawn both from the military contingents and the supporting services of the "parallel polity." All this is at least as much, and perhaps more, than was true of other African states, such as Algeria, Mozambique, Angola, Zimbabwe, and Guinea-Bissau as they emerged from "wars of national liberation." But is it enough of a foundation on which to build the new Eritrean polity? Perhaps, but given the mixed bag of experience,[50] for good and for ill, of modern Africa, it is worth devoting some sober reflection to some of the daunting political problems facing the new Eritrean regime.

Of these problems, the institutional one deserves close attention. Given the disarray, the inefficiency, and the often corrupt nature of the administrative infrastructure left behind by the Ethiopians in the main towns, the Eritreans confront a mixed blessing: on the one hand, they can simply sweep away the old institutions and rebuild with brand new ones, but on the other hand they must literally create (or recreate) institutional memories, the minutiae of administrative regulation, the hierarchies of bureaucratic responsibilities, and learn, and learn quickly, the dynamics and machineries of meeting public needs with official responses. As the events of May 20, 1993 demonstrated, unfulfilled promises and unmet expectations can lead either to active confrontation or a gradual disengagement of the society from its government. If Eritreans are to succeed in establishing a pluralist and democratic system of government a great deal will depend on crafting mechanisms of accountability, maintaining open channels of communication between the leadership and its constituents, decentralizing the various bodies of government, and ensuring a system of checks and balances.

Another set of problems, although less visible than those involving institution-building, is equally challenging. At issue are the imperatives of moving from a war economy to one based on peace; of shifting minds, energies, and attitudes from resistance to reconstruction; of giving "empirical" reality to the ideological concepts of the struggle. In effect, what will be needed is a new covenant between the Eritrean people and the state based on the reciprocities of civic obligation and not on the need to survive in the face of a common enemy. Of course, there is no standard list that defines this problematic: its content is situationally defined. In the Eritrean case, the following questions, at least, will have to be answered.

First, given the general commitment to democracy, can the Eritrean leadership develop a *modus operandi* that combines its efficient mobilizing capability with the flexibility necessary for the tasks of governance? In order for democracy to succeed Eritreans *must be socialized not merely mobilized* to democratic values. In the past, the EPLF's success was based on a hierarchical chain of command and its ability to impose discipline in the pursuit of a collective goal of independence. The maintenance of the political unity forged among Eritreans of different ethnic communities, religious affiliations, and ideological orientations during the liberation struggle requires tolerance. Democracy – a messy business, at best – requires that individual rights, liberties, diverse opinions, and interests be taken into consideration simultaneously with the collective good. If the government of Eritrea does not succumb to the temptation to overvalue order and stability and thus curb the sphere of political participation, the population can be socialized to live with the happy uncertainties of democracy.

Secondly, is there, or can there be found, an ideology appropriate to national construction, one that can define the transition from the liberation struggle to the formation of an Eritrean polity? The most difficult task facing the future Eritrean government will be to harmonize the private and public spheres, giving each its due in the new democratic environment. During the war years and the interim period from 1991 to 1993, the private sphere was subordinated to the attainment of the larger common good: independence. The country's economic survival and reconstruction of the war-shattered economy were made possible because of such collective endeavors and discipline. Having achieved independence and shouldered the burdens of governance a balance must be struck so that both the public good and individual needs can be maintained and the gains of the past can be perpetuated. In this task, both the people and the state will have to constantly reaffirm and revise the basis of interaction between the governing institutions and the governed.

Thirdly, given the past history of fratricidal conflict within the Eritrean political camp, can the present leadership capitalize on its current unity to devise ways by which internal differences can be contained and/or institutionalized, rather than erupting in violence? Bold and innovative steps need to be taken by the post-independence government in order to ensure that war is not used as a substitute for political dialogue. Protecting the constitutional rights of all citizens without discrimination on the basis of ethnicity, religion, or gender is a fundamental step towards the creation of a unity based on diversity. Future governments need to be careful not to fall into the self-destructive trap of most new African governments, i.e. curtailing the democratic rights of the opposition in the name of eliminating threats to "national security." The government of independent Eritrea prohibits the formation of "political parties based on religion, ethnicity, region, province ... and those with direct or indirect linkages to political forces abroad."[51] It has also taken the time and expended efforts in educating its people about the dangers of religious fundamentalism and ethnic chauvinism. At the outset of 1993 it appeared that the new government was successful in establishing the basis for a relatively inclusive political system which included former opponents. Members of defunct liberation fronts such as the ELF, ELF–PLF, EDM, and other organizations which had been in exile joined the new government as members of the *Baitó* (Assembly) and civil service. It set up the legal framework for a pluralist system that utilized both traditional social customs and modern laws.[52] It took steps to ensure that the population was informed about the nature and functioning of the new political framework.[53] The more challenging task will be to keep it going.

Finally, how can political pluralism be maintained? Successful pluralist polities which maintain self-conscious social groups in tolerant accommodation to each other are rare in modern Africa. The potential for a democratic Eritrean polity exists. It will be up to both the government of Eritrea and its people to ensure that the lessons of the past have not been in vain.

Notes

INTRODUCTION

1 "A room of one's own. A country of one's own. A century in which one was not a guest." These lines, which echo Virginia Woolf, come from the gifted Somali novelist Nuruddin Farah, in *Sardines* (Saint Paul, MN: Greywolf Press 1992, 3rd edn.), 4. Although they were written about his own land Farah's imagery is uncannily apt for the Eritrean quest of a nation, which began with inhabiting a space free from alien rule and later developed into a formidable challenge to domination by its more powerful neighbor to the south.

1 THE ERITREAN QUESTION IN PERSPECTIVE

1 Donald N. Levine, *Greater Ethiopia: The Evolution of a Multiethnic Society* (Chicago: University of Chicago Press, 1974), 26.
2 Levine, *Greater Ethiopia*, 46.
3 Haggai Erlich, *Ethiopia and the Challenge of Independence* (Boulder: Lynne Rienner Publishers, 1986), 2.
4 Erlich, *Challenge of Independence*, 20.
5 Erlich, *Challenge of Independence*, ix.
6 Christopher Clapham, *Transformation and Continuity in Revolutionary Ethiopia* (Cambridge: Cambridge University Press, 1988), 206.
7 Clapham, *Transformation and Continuity*, 207.
8 Clapham, *Transformation and Continuity*, 209–210.
9 Clapham, *Transformation and Continuity*, 207.
10 John H. Spencer, *Ethiopia at Bay: A Personal Account of the Haile Selassie Years* (Algonac: Reference Publications Inc., 1987), 257.
11 Spencer, *Ethiopia at Bay*, 318.
12 Spencer, *Ethiopia at Bay*, 319.
13 Paul B. Henze, "Eritrea," in Michael Radu (ed.), *The New Insurgencies: Anticommunist Guerrillas in the Third World* (New Brunswick: Transaction Publishers, 1990), 121.
14 Henze, "Eritrea," in Radu, *New Insurgencies*, 95.
15 Paul B. Henze, "Eritrea: The Economic Challenge," presented at a conference of Eritreans for Peace and Democracy, Baltimore, MD, November 3–4, 1990, 3 (emphasis mine).
16 John H. Spencer, in the US Government's *Ethiopia and the Horn of Africa: Hearings Before the Subcommittee on African Affairs of the Ninety-Fourth Congress, Second Session on US Relations with Ethiopia and the Horn of Africa*, August 4–6, 1976 (Washington, DC: Government Printing Office 1976), 13.

17 Haggai Erlich, *The Struggle Over Eritrea, 1962–1978: War and Revolution in the Horn of Africa* (Stanford: Hoover Institution Press, 1983), 55.
18 Ruth Iyob, "Reassessing Ethiopia's Claim to Uniqueness," *Africa Today*, 36: 3–4 (1989), 129.
19 This position is also held by the EPLF.
20 Bereket Habteselassie, *Eritrea and the United Nations* (Trenton, NJ: Red Sea Press Inc., 1989), 54.
21 Roy Pateman, *Eritrea: Even the Stones Are Burning* (Trenton, NJ: Red Sea Press Inc., 1990), 8.
22 Pateman, *Stones Are Burning*, 8.
23 Pateman, *Stones Are Burning*, 22–23.
24 A. M. Babu, "Eritrea: Its Present is the Remote Future of Others," in *Eritrea: The Way Forward: Proceedings of a Conference on Eritrea*, November 9, 1985, organized by the United Nations Association (UNA–UK, May 1986), 56.
25 A. M. Babu, "The Eritrean Question in the Context of African Conflicts and Superpower Rivalries," in Lionel Cliffe and Basil Davidson (eds.), *The Long Struggle of Eritrea for Independence and Constructive Peace* (Trenton, NJ: Red Sea Press Inc., 1988), 50.
26 Babu, "Eritrean Question," 49–50.
27 *Ibid.*
28 *Ibid.*
29 Edmond J. Keller, *Revolutionary Ethiopia: From Empire to People's Republic* (Bloomington: Indiana University Press, 1988), 150.
30 Keller, *Revolutionary Ethiopia*, 2.
31 Lionel Cliffe, "The Eritrean Liberation Struggle in Comparative Perspective," in Lionel Cliffe and Basil Davidson (eds.), *The Long Struggle of Eritrea for Independence and Constructive Peace* (Trenton, NJ: Red Sea Press Inc., 1988), 89.
32 Cliffe, "Eritrean Liberation," 89.
33 Cliffe, "Eritrean Liberation," 96.
34 John Markakis, *National and Class Conflict in the Horn of Africa* (Cambridge: Cambridge University Press, 1987), 104.
35 Richard Leonard, "Popular Participation in Liberation and Revolution," in Lionel Cliffe and Basil Davidson (eds.), *The Long Struggle of Eritrea for Independence and Constructive Peace* (Trenton, NJ: Red Sea Press Inc., 1988), ch. 6.
36 Michael Chege, "Conflict in the Horn of Africa," in Emmanuel Hansen (ed.), *Africa: Perspectives on Peace and Development* (London: The United Nations University, 1987), 96.
37 Georges Nzongola-Ntalaja, "The National Question and the Crisis of Instability in Africa," in Emmanuel Hansen (ed.), *Africa: Perspectives on Peace and Development*, 78.
38 Nzongola-Ntalaja, "National Question," 79.
39 It should be remembered that the Axumite empire's legacy had been appropriated by Ethiopian chroniclers and given currency by Africanists who equated Axum with modern Ethiopia. Myth and historical facts were later combined to refer to Ethiopian national history.
40 Hedley Bull, *The Anarchical Society: A Study of Order in World Politics* (London: Macmillan Publishers, 1977), 215–216 (emphasis mine).

41 Immanuel Wallerstein, *The Politics of the World-Economy: The States, the Movements and the Civilizations* (Cambridge: Cambridge University Press, 1984), 38.
42 T. J. Jackson Lears, "The Concept of Cultural Hegemony: Problems and Possibilities," *The American Historical Review*, 90: 3 (June 1985), 572.
43 Michel Foucault, *The Order of Things: An Archeology of the Human Sciences* (New York: Vintage Books, 1973).
44 Quintin Hoare and Geoffrey Nowell Smith (eds.), *Selections from the Prison Notebooks of Antonio Gramsci* (New York: International Publishers, 1971), 210–246.
45 For a concise analysis of the Gramscian contribution to and departure from orthodox Marxism see Stephen Gill, *American Hegemony and the Trilateral Commission* (Cambridge: Cambridge University Press, 1990), 41–46.
46 Walter L. Adamson, *Hegemony and Revolution: A Study of Antonio Gramsci's Political and Cultural Theory* (Berkeley: University of California Press, 1980), 169–201.
47 René Lemarchand, *The Green and the Black: Qadhafi's Policies in Africa* (Bloomington: Indiana University Press, 1988), 167.
48 Lemarchand, *The Green and the Black*, 169.
49 *Ibid.*
50 The Foucauldian concept of a "regime of truth" is discussed in detail in the next section.
51 South African hegemony is an illustration of how its autarkic economic development, abundant geostrategic resources, and military superiority enabled it, for an extended period, to defy regional and international norms.
52 Bull, *The Anarchical Society*, 201.
53 Lemarchand, *The Green and the Black*, 169.
54 Lemarchand, *The Green and the Black*, 168.
55 Although Israel's economic assets do not compare with those of South Africa, its role as gatekeeper of Western "democracy" in the struggle to contain "communism" has provided it with patronage linkages to the US. Israel was also able to convince US policy makers that it was indispensable as a strategic asset to contain Soviet influence in the area. Another crucial asset has been the "guilt factor," which has enabled Israel to draw upon the victimization of its peoples by Hitler's regime. Out of this relationship Israel has garnered both the military and economic wherewithal to develop and sustain its regional hegemony in the Middle East.
56 Barry Smart, *Michel Foucault* (London: Tavistock Publications, 1985), 67–68.
57 I am indebted to William Hughes, University of California–Davis, for the long hours of discussion on the "regime of truth" as the "decoding of history and the encoding of reality."
58 Levine, *Greater Ethiopia*, 1–11. See also Peter Schwab, *Haile Selassie I: Ethiopia's Lion of Judah* (Chicago: Nelson-Hall Inc., 1979), 10–12.
59 See for example E. Sylvia Pankhurst, *Eritrea on the Eve: The Past and the Future of Italy's "First-Born" Colony, Ethiopia's Ancient Sea Province* (Essex: Lalibela House, 1952); E. Sylvia and Richard K. P. Pankhurst, *Ethiopia and Eritrea: The Last Phase of the Reunion Struggle 1941–1952* (Essex: Lalibela House, 1953); Patrick Gilkes, *The Dying Lion: Feudalism and Modernization in Ethiopia* (New York: St. Martin's Press, 1975); Spencer, *Ethiopia At Bay*.

2 REGIONAL HEGEMONY IN THE POST-WORLD WAR II ORDER

1 Cited in John Ellis, *The Social History of the Machine Gun* (New York: Pantheon Books, 1970), 70.

2 Reprinted in Leroy A. Bennet, *International Organizations: Principles and Issues* (Englewood Cliffs, NJ: Prentice-Hall, 1988), 455–456.

3 N. D. White, *The United Nations and the Maintenance of International Peace and Security* (Manchester: Manchester University Press, 1990).

4 Bennet, *International Organizations*, 139. Bennet argues that the lessons of the failures of the League of Nations to effectively apply sanctions to aggressor nations (such as Japan after its invasion of Manchuria in 1931, Germany upon its reoccupation of the Rhineland in 1936, and Italy after its invasion of Ethiopia in 1935) was due to "a failure of national will on part of the League members and non-members."

5 Non-state actors or groups such as the Frente Popular para la Liberación de Saguia el-Hamra y Rio de Oro (POLISARIO), South-West Africa People's Organization (SWAPO) and the Palestine Liberation Organization (PLO), due to a high degree of regional legitimacy and sponsorship of their respective regional organizations (OAU and Arab League) have acquired observer status. For an extended discussion on this theme, see Richard Mansbach, *The Web of World Politics: Non-State Actors in the Global System* (Englewood Cliffs, NJ: Prentice-Hall, 1976).

6 Ian Clark, *The Hierarchy of States: Reform and Resistance in the International Order* (Cambridge: Cambridge University Press, 1989), 29.

7 Christopher C. Shoemaker and John Spanier, *Patron–Client State Relationships: Multilateral Crises in the Nuclear Age* (New York: Praeger Publishers, 1984), 10–15.

8 Hedley Bull (ed.), *Intervention in World Politics* (Oxford: Clarendon Press, 1984).

9 General Assembly Resolution 1514 (XV), UNGAOR Supplement (no. 16), 66–67, UN Document A/4684, 1960. The resolution was adopted by a vote of 89 in favor and no opposition with 9 abstentions from the USA, UK, France, Belgium, Portugal, Spain, South Africa, Australia, and the Dominican Republic.

10 This section clearly states that a member "which has persistently violated the principles contained in the present Charter may be expelled from the Organization by the General Assembly upon the recommendation of the Security Council." This section has never been invoked, much less used against a member state.

11 UN General Assembly Resolution 2625 (XXV) UNGAOR Supplement (no. 28), 121–123, UN Document A/8028, 1970 (emphasis mine).

12 Jan F. Triska (ed.), *Dominant States and Subordinate States: The United States in Latin America and the Soviet Union in Eastern Europe* (Durham: Duke University Press, 1986).

13 John W. Holmes, "The Way of the World," *International Journal*, 35: 2 (Spring 1980), 217.

14 Ian Brownlie (ed.), *Basic Documents on African Affairs* (Oxford: Oxford University Press, 1971), 2.

15 Rupert Emerson, "The Problem of Identity, Selfhood and Image in the New Nations: The Situation in Africa," *Comparative Politics*, 1: 3 (April 1969), 297.

16 Basil Davidson, *The Black Star: A View of the Life and Times of Kwame Nkrumah*, (Boulder: Westview Press, rev. edn., 1989), 84.

17 Brownlie, *Basic Documents*, 2.

18 Emerson, "Problems of Identity," 298.

19 James Mayall, "Self-determination and the OAU," in I. M. Lewis, (ed.), *Nationalism and Self-Determination in the Horn of Africa* (London: Ithaca Press, 1983), 80–85.

20 The first phase, 1940s–1950s, was concerned with the attainment of nationhood and emphasized the right of African peoples to determine their political destiny. The second, 1960s to present, I would argue, was preoccupied with fending off any centrifugal challenges (ethnic, religious, territorial) to the recognized states.

21 These provisions are cited in Yassin El-Ayouty and I. William Zartman (eds.), *The OAU after Twenty Years* (New York: Praeger Publishers, 1984), 358. That primacy, as Gerhard Von Glahn, *Law Among Nations* (New York: Macmillan Press, 1986) points out is reinforced in UN General Assembly Resolution 1564, 1960: "The true interpretation, however, was laid down ... in the 1960 Declaration on the granting of Independence to Colonial Countries and Peoples, in which the General Assembly endorsed the idea that 'any attempt aimed at the partial or total disruption of the national unity and the territorial integrity of a country is incompatible with the purposes and principles of the Charter of the United Nations,'" 219.

22 Brownlie, *Basic Documents*, 3.

23 See "Declaration to the Colonial Peoples," Section IV, at the Pan-African Congress, Manchester, 1945, cited in Colin Legum, *Pan-Africanism: A Short Political Guide* (New York: Praeger Publishers, 1962), 137.

24 See I. M. Lewis, "Pre- and Post-Colonial Forms of Polity in Africa," in Lewis (ed.), *Nationalism and Self-determination*, 74.

25 The Ethiopian–Eritrean federation was terminated officially on November 12, 1962. The Eritrean Liberation Movement (ELM), with headquarters in Port Sudan, and the Eritrean Liberation Front (ELF), with offices in Cairo, were already in existence.

26 Gino Naldi, *The Organisation of African Unity: An Analysis of its Role* (London: Mansell Publishing Ltd., 1989), 5.

27 Jon Woronoff, *Organizing African Unity* (Metuchen, NJ: Scarecrow Press Inc., 1970), 624.

28 Robert H. Jackson, "Negative Sovereignty in sub-Saharan Africa," *Review of International Studies*, 12: 2 (1986), 253.

29 Claude E. Welch jun., "The OAU and International Recognition: Lessons From Uganda," in Yassin El-Ayouti and I. M. Zartman (eds.), *The Organization of African Unity after Ten Years: Comparative Perspectives* (New York: Praeger Publishers, 1975), 115.

30 The Brazzaville group included Cameroon, Central African Republic, Chad, Congo (Brazzaville), Dahomey, Gabon, Ivory Coast, Niger, Mauritania, Madagascar, Senegal, and Upper Volta.

31 This group met in Casablanca, January 3–7, 1961, to map out a campaign against colonialism and neo-colonialism as a counter to the Brazzaville group. The Casablanca group was led by Ghana, Algeria, Guinea, and Egypt.

32 This group included Ethiopia, Liberia, Nigeria, Sierra Leone, Somalia, and Togo.
33 See Introduction in Lewis (ed.), *Nationalism and Self-determination*, 4.
34 Edmond J. Keller, "The Politics of State Survival: Continuity and Change in Ethiopian Foreign Policy," *Annals*, 489 (January 1987), 77–83.
35 It was only after Emperor Haile Selassie had been deposed in 1974 that inequalities inherent in the Ethiopian empire were discussed in African circles or the international media. For an example of post-1974 works on the emperor see Ryszard Kapuscinski, *The Emperor: Downfall of an Autocrat* (New York: Vintage Books, 1984), 108–151. An OAU delegation led by Pascal Gayama, Deputy Secretary General of the OAU, visited Eritrea in September 1992. Interviewed by a reporter Gayama admitted that the organization "was well aware that there was war in Eritrea for 30 years. But we never heard the Eritrean case being raised in the OAU sessions." *Hadas Ertra* "Interview with OAU Representative" (September 23, 1992).
36 For an example of such approaches to the study of Ethiopia see Erlich, *Challenge of Independence*.
37 Ethiopia's hegemony extended to the states and territories that constitute the Horn (Eritrea, Somalia, Djibouti) and to an extent over the Sudan.
38 Harold G. Marcus, *Ethiopia, Great Britian, and the United States 1941–1974: The Politics of Empire* (Berkeley: University of California Press, 1983), 48.
39 The term "dominance" in this context refers to states that use brute force to impose their will on weaker states. It is qualitatively different from hegemony (both regional and international) wherein additional prerequisites such as legitimacy and diplomatic effectiveness are required. As used here, it is an extrapolation of David Abernathy's treatment of dominance and superpower hegemony. For further discussion see Triska (ed.), *Dominant States*, 103–124.
40 Keller, *Revolutionary Ethiopia*, 2.
41 For further discussion on the failure of democracy in post-independence Africa see Richard Sklar, "Democracy in Africa," in Patrick Chabal (ed.), *Political Domination in Africa: Reflections on the Limits of Power* (Cambridge: Cambridge University Press, 1986), 18.
42 Ethiopia's claims to both Eritrea and the Ogaden were sanctioned by the region and facilitated by international military and economic support. Its claims to Djibouti, though, were contested by France which pre-empted its absorption. The historical timing of the decolonization of these areas confirms the "time-bound" application of self-determination in the African political and diplomatic arena.
43 An excellent example of the economist interpretation is found in Robert Gilpin, *The Political Economy of International Relations* (Princeton: Princeton University Press, 1987), 72. Although this particular phrase is used to describe economic regimes and hegemons in the global market economy, its theoretical usefulness can be extended to the political context. In Ethiopia's case, portrayal of the Eritrean and Ogadeni demands for self-determination as ethnic secessionism was viewed as the harbinger of continental fragmentation. The fear of balkanization served as a common political cause uniting the heads of new states.
44 Donald Pettersen, "US Policy in the Horn of Africa, Ethiopia Abandoned? An

American Perspective," *International Affairs*, 62: 4 (Autumn 1986), 627–645. See also Robert Patman, *The Soviet Union and the Horn* (Cambridge: Cambridge University Press, 1990), 150–190.

45 Ironically, it also helped create a radical intelligentsia that was instrumental in the eventual overthrow of the imperial regime and the substitution of Soviet for US largess. See Randi Ronning Balsvik, *Haile Selassie's Students: The Intellectual and Social Background to Revolution, 1952–1977* (East Lansing, MI: Michigan State University, 1985), 93–102; John Markakis and Nega Ayele, *Class and Revolution in Ethiopia* (Trenton, NJ: Red Sea Press Inc. 1986), 77–101; Richard Greenfield, *Ethiopia: A New Political History* (New York: Praeger Publishers Inc., 1965).

46 Jack Shepherd, *The Politics of Starvation* (New York: Carnegie Endowment for International Peace, 1975); James McCaan *From Poverty to Famine in Northeastern Ethiopia: A Rural History, 1900–1935* (Philadelphia: University of Pennsylvania Press, 1987); Kurt Jansson et al., *The Ethiopian Famine* (London: Zed Press, 1987).

47 Mesfin Woldemariam, *Rural Vulnerability to Famine in Ethiopia, 1958–1977* (London: Intermediate Technology Publications, 1986); Peter Gill, *A Year in the Death of Africa: Politics, Bureaucracy, and the Famine* (London: Grafton Books, 1986); Dawit Wolde Giorgis, *Red Tears: War, Famine and Revolution in Ethiopia* (Trenton, NJ: Red Sea Press Inc., 1989).

48 James F. Keeley, "Towards a Foucauldian Analysis of International Regimes," *International Organization*, 44: 1 (Winter 1990), 91.

49 Dayle Spencer et al., "Closing the Mediation Gap: The Ethiopia/Eritrea Experience," *Security Dialogue*, 3:23 (1992), 89–98; Hizkias Assefa, "The Challenge of Mediation in Internal Wars: Reflections on the INN Experience in the Ethiopian/Eritrean Conflict," *Security Dialogue*, 3:23 (1992), 101–106.

50 Although Cohen was to reverse his opinions after the EPLF's military victory on May 25, 1991 the imperative of Ethiopian "unity" remained a constant factor. See Herman J. Cohen, "Statement by Herman J. Cohen, Assistant Secretary of State for African Affairs before the Subcommittee on Africa of the Foreign Affairs Committee and the International Task Force of the Select Committee on Hunger," February 28, 1990, 7.

51 *Hadas Ertra*, "*Hiburant Mengstat America N'Mesreh Referendum Z'wuel Wefeya Ghera*," no. 48 (February 13, 1993).

52 *Hadas Ertra*, "*Baito Tzet'a n'Abalnet Ertra ab Wedeb Hiburat HageratDdegifu*," no. 78 (June 29, 1993).

53 *Hadas Ertra*, "*Bandera Ertra ab Wudeb Hadnet Africa Tesekila*" (June 9, 1993).

54 OAU, President Issaias Afeworki, "Address to the OAU Summit," Cairo, Egypt, June 28, 1993.

3 ERITREA AND THE AFRICAN ORDER

1 C. Conti Rossini, *Proverbi Tradizionali e Canzoni Tigrini* (Italia: Amboglio Airoldi, 1942), 305. Rossini's translation from Tigrigna to Italian reflects the Tigrigna use of the term red snake: "*Dope che il serpente rosso ha morso; per quanto cerchi, non si trova il suo rimedio*." By contrast, the English translations have substituted "white" for the original "red" snake attributed to Bahta

Hagos. See Tekeste Negash, *No Medicine for the Bite of a White Snake: Notes on Nationalism and Resistance in Eritrea, 1890–1940* (Uppsala: Reprocentralen HSC, 1986), 1; and Richard Caulk, "'Black Snake, White Snake': Bahta Hagos and his Revolt against Italian Overrule in Eritrea, 1894," in Donald Crummey (ed.), *Banditry, Rebellion and Social Protest in Africa* (London: James Currey Ltd., 1986).

2 Keshi Tekhle Woldeab wrote a letter calling for *"Harnet b' Hibret"* (liberation through unity), as a process for Eritrea's decolonization, *Nai Ertra Semunawi Gazeta* (May 21, 1949).

3 Letter to the Ministers of Foreign Affairs of Great Britain, United States of America, and France from Woldu Ghebremeskel, President of the Union with Ethiopia Society, Foreign Office, FO 371/63175 128279 (Asmara, June 15, 1946).

4 The term "Pan-African" was first introduced by a Trinidadian, Henry Sylvester-Williams, who convened the first Pan-African Conference held at Westminister Hall, London in 1900. It was later revived by Dr. William Edward Burghardt Dubois who convened the first Pan-African Congress in 1919. For details see Adekeunle Ajala, *Pan-Africanism: Evolution, Progress and Prospects* (New York: St. Martin's Press, 1974), 4.

5 Locksley Edmondson, "Pan-Africanism and the International System: Challenges and Opportunities," in W. Ofuatey-Kodjoe (ed.), *Pan-Africanism: New Descriptions in Strategy* (Lanham: University Press of America, 1986), 287.

6 An interesting analog can be drawn with Pan-Slavism in Central Europe. See Aleksa Djilas, *The Contested Country: Yugoslav Unity and Communist Revolution, 1919–1953* (Cambridge: Cambridge University Press, 1991), 27.

7 Bill Freund, *The Making of Contemporary Africa: The Development of African Society Since 1800* (Bloomington: Indiana University Press, 1984), 118–121. See also Richard Sandbrook, *The Politics of Africa's Economic Stagnation* (Cambridge: Cambridge University Press, 1985), 42–62.

8 The phrase "things fall apart" has been used by poets, novelists, and social scientists to indicate the disintegration of a way of life. It gained currency among Africanists with the publication of Chinua Achebe's celebrated novel, *Things Fall Apart*, about a pre-colonial West African village's encounter with the Europeans. The title was borrowed from the first stanza of a poem entitled "The Second Coming" by William Butler Yeats published in 1921: "Things fall apart; the center cannot hold; mere anarchy is loosed upon the world; the blood dimmed tide is loosed; and everywhere the ceremony of innocence is drowned." The phrase has also been used by social scientists to capture the political and socio-economic deterioration of modern African politics. See Dennis Austin, "Things Fall Apart?" *Orbis*, 25:4 (Winter 1982), 925–946.

9 Patrick Manning, *Slavery and African Life: Occidental, Oriental, and African Slave Trades* (Cambridge: Cambridge University Press, 1990), 25.

10 Colin Legum, "Pan-Africanism and Communism," in Sven Hamrell and Carl Gosta Widstrand (eds.), *The Soviet Bloc, China and Africa* (Uppsala: Scandinavian Institute of African Studies, 1964), 9.

11 S. Neil MacFarlane, *Superpower Rivalry and 3rd World Radicalism: The Ideas of National Liberation* (London: Croom Helm, 1985), 112.

12 George Padmore, *Pan-Africanism or Communism* (New York: Doubleday & Co., 1971), 65–82.

13 Ali A. Mazrui and Michael Tidy, *Nationalism and New States in Africa* (Nairobi: Heinemann Educational Books, 1984), 6–7.

14 T. R. Makonnen was originally from what was then known as British Guyana and had considerable influence in the Pan-Africanist movement, and especially with Nkrumah, who gave him a job in the African Bureau in Accra. For details see Legum, *Pan-Africanism*, 27–31. The self-styled "Ras Makonnen" worked together with E. Sylvia Pankhurst in supporting Ethiopia's claims to Eritrea. For further details see Kenneth King (ed.), *Ras Makonnen: Pan-Africanism From Within* (Oxford: Oxford University Press, 1973), 159–160.

15 Nnamdi Azikwe, *Renascent Africa* (London: Frank Cass and Co., 1937), 163.

16 Horace Campbell, *Rasta and Resistance: From Marcus Garvey to Walter Rodney* (Trenton, NJ: Africa World Press, 1987), 47–50. See 227–229 for specific reference to Eritrea.

17 EPLF, "*Africa Ketek'lebelu Zigba'e Amaratzi Fetah,*" *Dimtzi Hafash* (Eritrea: EPLF radio broadcasts, July 14–20, 1990), 1.

18 Margery Perham, *The Colonial Reckoning: The End of Imperial Rule in Africa in the Light of British Experience* (New York: Alfred Knopf, 1962), 51–52.

19 The first goal of the OAU in Article II of the Charter is "To promote the unity and solidarity of the African States." Brownlie, *Basic Documents*, 3.

20 *Ibid.*

21 The term *balkanization* was first used to refer to Africa by Leopold Senghor but was quickly adapted by various African leaders and officials. It should be noted that in the 1960s the term was used to refer to various movements, such as the secessionists of Katanga, the proponents of independence in Mauritania and Togo, and the disintegration of the Mali Federation. For details see Legum, *Pan-Africanism*, 119–121. In Ethiopia the Amharic term "*tegentaai*" was used to refer to Eritrean "secessionists" who would bring about the disintegration/ balkanization of the continent.

22 Hugh Seton-Watson, *Nations and States: An Enquiry into the Origins of Nations and the Politics of Nationalism* (London: Methuen & Co., 1977), 340–341.

23 Victor Le Vine and Timothy Luke, *The Arab-African Connection: Political and Economic Realities* (Boulder: Westview Press, 1979), 1. See also Ayre Oded, *Africa and the Middle East Conflict* (Boulder: Lynne Rienner Publishers, 1987), 82–88.

24 The ELF attempted to dissociate itself from this categorization by denying that it was "a purely Muslim movement" in 1969 at the Islamic Summit Conference. See Pateman, *Stones Are Burning*, 99.

25 Pateman, *Stones are Burning*, 96–97.

26 Bernard Schechterman, "Horn of Africa Liberation Movements," *Middle East Review*, 19: 1 (Fall 1986), 47–57.

27 *Ethiopian Herald*, "Ethiopia's Commitment to African Unity, Solidarity" (May 26, 1988), 10.

28 Hans J. Morgenthau "International Organization and Foreign Policy," in *Foundations of World Organization: A Political and Cultural Appraisal* (New York: Harper & Brothers, 1952), 378–379. The author was referring to membership in international organizations such as the UN but his argument is equally applicable to the OAU and other regional and international organizations established since this publication.

29 Edward Said "Figures, Configurations and Transfigurations," *Race & Class,*

32: 1 (July–September 1990), 8. Said's point is equally applicable to regional as well as superpower hegemony.

30 It should be noted that in the two major Eritrean languages, Tigrigna and Tigre, there is no specific expression for "colonialism." They use the term "*meg'zaat*" in Tigre and "*megz'aati* or *g'zaat*" in Tigrigna. This term was used in the expressions "*gz'aat Turki*" to describe Turkish occupation and rule, "*megz'aati Tilian*" of Italian colonialism, and lastly "*meg'zaati Etiopia*" to refer to Ethiopian occupation and rule. In contrast, Ethiopia's official language, Amharic, differentiates "*g'zat*" (rule) from "*kign-g'zat*" (settler colonialism) which describes Ethiopian imperial rule over the southern peoples such as the Oromos. The operative words and concepts from the Eritrean nationalist perspective seem to suggest that military occupation, and the presence of alien peoples imposing their rule constitute *meg'zaati*, which they equate with "colonialism" in the English language.

31 This situation is in contrast with that of the POLISARIO, established as recently as 1973, which has the full diplomatic and military backing of the Maghreb hegemony – Algeria. The role of Algerian support for Western Sahara's bid for sovereignty should not be underestimated. For details see Paula Oliver, *Sahara: Drama de una Decolonizacion, 1960–1987* (Mallorca, Spain: Miquel Font Editor, 1987), 231–234; John P. Entelis, *Algeria: The Revolution Institutionalized* (Boulder: Westview Press, 1986), 181–192; and *Algeria News Report* (Washington, DC: The Embassy of the Democratic and Popular Republic of Algeria), November 15, 1977–December 15, 1980.

32 Crawford Young, "Self-Determination Revisited: Has Decolonization Closed the Question?" presented at the International Conference on the Conflict in the Horn of Africa, Madrid, Spain, September 12–14, 1989, 28. I am grateful to the author for granting me permission to cite from this work.

33 James Mayall, *Nationalism and International Society* (Cambridge: Cambridge University Press, 1990), 123–124.

34 Mayall, "Self-Determination," in Lewis (ed.), 80.

35 Richard Cox, *Pan-Africanism in Practice: PAFMECA 1958–1964* (London: Oxford University Press, 1964), 17.

36 Cox, *Pan-Africanism in Practice*, 17.

37 The Cairo resolution of respecting colonial borders, if applied strictly, would justify the Ogaden borders demarcated by the British and that of Eritrea by the Italians.

38 ELF–PLF, *United Nations Documents on Eritrea* (Tripoli, Arab Libyan Republic: ELF–PLF Foreign Mission, 1971), 3–4.

39 EPLF, "*Ze'yelo Degef Hagerat Arab n' Sowra Ertra*," *Sagem* 2: 8 (August 1990), 14–16.

40 EPLF, *Neh'naan Elamaa'nan* (November 1971), 14.

41 Zaki Laidi, *The Superpowers in Africa: The Constraints of a Rivalry, 1960–1990* (Chicago: University of Chicago Press, 1990), 127–130.

4   THE ORIGINS OF THE ERITREAN CONFLICT

1 G. K. N. Trevaskis, *Eritrea: A Colony in Transition, 1941–52* (London: Oxford University Press, 1960), 18. See also British Military Administration, *The First*

to be Freed: The Record of British Military Administration in Eritrea and Somalia, 1941–1943 (London: His Majesty's Stationery Office, 1944).

2 J. C. Gray and L. Silberman, *The Fate of Italy's Colonies: A Report to the Fabian Colonial Bureau* (London: Fabian Publications Ltd., July 1948), 24–26.

3 Nicolo Ponde, "*La Razza e l'Impero*," in *Gazetta del Popolo* (Milano, June 7, 1936). See also James Dugan and Laurence Lafore, *Days of Emperor and the Clown: The Italo-Ethiopian War, 1935–1936* (New York: Doubleday & Co., 1973), 326.

4 Stephen H. Longrigg, British Military Administration, *Half-Yearly Report by the Military Administrator on the Occupied Enemy Territory of Eritrea: From the Period 1st January to 30th June 1942* (Asmara: Eritrea, July 29, 1942), 6–7.

5 Empire of Ethiopia, *Eritrea and Benadir (Italian Somaliland)* (Addis Ababa: Ethiopian Press and Information Department, 1945).

6 For details see *Report of the Four Powers Commission of Investigation, Former Italian Colonies.* Vol. i, *Report on Eritrea* (1948), 96–105. These figures are difficult to verify in the absence of accurate census figures and the indirect polling methods used at that time.

7 The Ogaden, although ceded to Ethiopia by the British in 1897, was inhabited by transhumant and nomadic Somalis who often needed to cross international boundaries in search of grazing and water for their stock. For details see Marcus, *Ethiopia, Great Britain, and the United States*, 41.

8 Marcus, 79–87.

9 For details on the debates concerning the three Italian colonies by the Big Four see Okbazghi Yohannes, *Eritrea: A Pawn in World Politics* (Gainesville: University of Florida Press, 1991), 51–125.

10 UN *Report of the United Nations Commission for Eritrea* (Lake Success, New York 1950). See Section 1, Annex XI, paragraph 3, p. 1.

11 UN *Report* (1950), 1.

12 UN *Report* (1950), 3.

13 UN *Report* (1950), Section C of resolution 289 A (IV), Paragraph 1, 3.

14 UN *Report* (1950), Section C of resolution 289 A (IV), Paragraphs 2(a) and 2(b), 3.

15 UN *Report* (1950). For a complete list of witnesses and party representatives who met with the Commission see Annex 17, 119–127.

16 It is interesting to note that while the Commission lists the majority of party officials who met privately and publicly to give their testimonies and statements, the key figure of Ato Woldeab Woldemariam is conspicuous in its absence among the witnesses. Ato Woldeab, who as editor of the *Eritrean Weekly Gazette* had participated in many of the debates and was one of the founders of the MFHE, later an advocate of independence in the LPP, the Intellectual Party of Eritrea, and later the Independent Party of Eritrea, is not referred to directly. Rather, the Commission's annex lists three documents with his name and party affiliation through a third party as "Information from the Administering Authority regarding statement by Mr. Woldemariam of the Independent Eritrea Party." See UN *Report* (1950), Annex 16, 97–98.

17 See "Interview with Ato Woldeab Woldemariam," *Hadas Ertra* (May 24, 1991).

18 *Mahber Fikri Hager Ertra* is literally translated from Tigrigna to English as "Association of Love of the Country of Eritrea." *Mahber* is a word that

originally meant "Association" and after 1946 was adopted to describe "political parties" as well as "political associations." Throughout this work, the initials MFHE will be used to refer to this first political association.

19 "Formal" party politics were not "officially" permitted by the BMA until October 1946 after the Four Power Commission (FPC) decided to investigate Eritreans' choice of a future political system. See Trevaskis, *Eritrea*, 68–69. See also Jordan Gebre-Medhin, *Peasants and Nationalism in Eritrea: A Critique of Ethiopian Studies*, (Trenton, NJ: Red Sea Press Inc., 1989), 73–78; Lloyd S. Ellingson, "Eritrea: Separatism and Irredentism, 1941–1985" (PhD dissertation, Michigan State University, 1986), 39–41.

20 Gebremeskel Woldu was a Catholic from the highlands, Woldeab Woldemariam a Protestant of Tigrayan parentage but a long-time resident in Asmara, and Ibrahim Sultan a Moslem from the lowlands. For detailed biographical information see Giuseppe Puglisi, *Chi'e dell'Eritrea? Dizionario Biografico* (Asmara: Agenzia Regina, 1952).

21 On voluntary associations see Immanuel Wallerstein, "Voluntary Associations," in James S. Coleman and Carl Rosberg jun., (eds.), *Political Parties and National Integration in Tropical Africa* (Berkeley: University of California Press, 1964), 334.

22 Wallerstein, "Voluntary Associations," 334.

23 James S. Coleman, "Nationalism in Tropical Africa," *American Political Science Review*, 48: 2 (June 1954), 405.

24 Coleman, "Nationalism in Tropical Africa," 412.

25 Coleman, "Nationalism in Tropical Africa," 404.

26 Gebre-Medhin, *Peasants and Nationalism*, 80.

27 Trevaskis, *Eritrea*, 52.

28 James S. Coleman, *Nigeria: Background to Nationalism* (Berkeley: University of California Press, 1960), 414

29 Woldeab Woldemariam made these events public in his series of published articles, "*Ertra n'men?*" in the *Nai Ertra Semunawi Gazeta*, no. 242 (May 7, 1947) through which he responded to the UP's allegations of opportunism and implied ineligibility to speak as an Eritrean patriot. He stated "From 1941–1944 ... we worked for *Mahber Fikri Hager* loyally and defended it without seeking praise or official positions ... In 1945 my colleagues and I established another party and began our [clandestine] political activities. We proposed a UN trusteeship for 15 years which we regarded as beneficial to both ... Eritrea and Ethiopia and Eritreans. ... The 15-year trusteeship would have benefited Ethiopia which would have had the chance to rebuild after the war. It would have benefited Eritreans because it would have enabled the young nation and its people to coalesce its political thoughts."

30 Tigrai refers to the territory which separated Eritrea and Ethiopia. It is also the seat of the ancient Axumite kingdom and the capital of Ethiopia under Emperor Yohannes before Menelik established a new capital at Addis Ababa. The population of Tigrai consists of Tigrigna and Amharic speakers. Tigrai should not be confused with Tigre, the population of lowland Eritrea and the main language throughout the coastal and lowlands of Eritrea.

31 See Trevaskis' interpretation of the highland society's reaction to the leadership of Ras Tesemma Asberom of Akele Guzai in his *Eritrea*, 63–73.

32 See letter by Seyoum Maascio, Secretary-General of *Mahber Ertra n'Ertrawian*, in response to Tedla Bairu, Secretary-General of the Unionist Party, which states that one of the goals of that party was "to incorporate *Tigrigna* speakers such as *Tselemti, Welkait*, and *Tzegde*." Seyoum Maascio further argued that "it is not just that Eritreans and Tigryans whose history, language and culture is recognized internationally should be forced to be subordinated without the right to express opinion" (author's translation). For details see *Nai Ertra Semunawi Gazeta*, no. 248 (June 4, 1947).

33 Stephen H. Longrigg, *A Short History of Eritrea* (Westport, CT: Greenwood Press Publishers, 1945), 174–175; Trevaskis, *Eritrea*, 62–74.

34 Trevaskis explains the BMA's decision to retain Italian personnel as a pragmatic choice due to Britain's other colonial obligation: "By ill chance the British had to undertake this difficult Eritrean commitment at a time of military reversals and embarrassments in the Middle and East," Trevaskis, *Eritrea*, 18. But this "pragmatic" solution was interpreted by the Eritreans as a betrayal of Britain's role as a liberator and led to "doubts" of its "impartiality." Combined with incursions from Ethiopia, the BMA's use of Moslem Sudanese Defense Forces to keep order in Eritrea, and the dismal state of the economy worsened by the BMA's decision to levy more taxes, led to the rise of sectional parties.

35 Lloyd S. Ellingson, "The Emergence of Political Parties in Eritrea, 1941–1950," *Journal of African History*, 18: 2 (1977), 261–281.

36 The *Nabtab* are the ruling caste of the Beni Amer confederacy. For details see S. F. Nadel, *Races and Tribes of Eritrea* (Asmara: British Military Administration, Eritrea, January 1944).

37 See Brigadier J. M. Benoy's public address to the assembly of chiefs and representatives of the people published in the *Nai Ertra Semunawi Gazeta*, no. 217 (October 24, 1946).

38 Interview with Ato Woldeab Woldemariam, August 3, 1990, Rome, Italy. This interview was conducted in Tigrigna and translated into English by the author.

39 Gebremeskel Woldu, who had arranged for the *Waa'la* to be held at Bet Ghiorghis, was accused of "going soft" on unification with Ethiopia. He refuted this charge in a series of articles in the unionist newspaper *Ethiopia*. For specific details, see "*Itfrah Mentini Be'inte Ze'haleweke T'hamem*," *Ethiopia*, no. 79 (October 31, 1948).

40 Interview with Ato Woldeab Woldemariam, August 3, 1990, Rome, Italy.

41 These discussions were reprinted in the *Nai Ertra Semunawi Gazeta* in detail. For more information see no. 222 (November 26, 1946) and no. 223 (December 3, 1946).

42 *Ibid.*

43 See "Notice to Readers from Major Lane," *Nai Ertra Semunawi Gazeta* (December 11, 1946).

44 In order to avoid confusion the English translations of the various Eritrean parties under which they registered with the administering authority, the BMA, will be used. The official documents and newspapers of the period 1946–1950 use various names. The UP's officials used various names, such as *Mahber Hibret Ertra ms Ethiopia – Hanti Ethiopia* which translates literally as "Party of Union of Eritrea with Ethiopia – One Ethiopia." A shortened version, *Mahber Andinet*, which used the Amharic word *andinet* for "oneness" or "union" rather than the

Tigrigna *hibret* is also found in the Tigrigna language weekly *Nai Ertra Semunawi Gazeta* published by the BMA. This should not be confused with the youth section of the UP which called itself *Mahber Andinet* and spearheaded the terrorist activities of the UP and was banned in 1949. Since the original *Mahber Fikri Hager Ertra (MFHE)* was never dissolved officially, the UP, at times, also used the name *Mahber Fikri Hager – Ertra ms Ethiopia* (Patriotic Association of Eritrea – Union with Ethiopia). It should be noted that the Unionist Party or UP refers to the supporters of unconditional union led by Ato Tedla Bairu and Abune Markos and established on December 4, 1946. The Moslem League is also known by its Arabic name, *El Rabita El Islamiya*. The Liberal Progressive Party (LPP), which underwent various permutations is also known by its Tigrigna name of *Ertra n'Ertrawian* (Eritrea for Eritreans). It was at times also referred to as *Mahber Harnet 'n Limaa't Ertra – Ertra n'Ertrawian* (Liberation and Development Party of Eritrea). By 1949, it was registered as *Mahber Natznet'n Limaat'n Ertra* (Freedom and Development Party of Eritrea) which became shortened to *Mahber Natznet Ertra*. It is referred to as the LPP only by the foreign press and in the reports by the UN Commission of Inquiry which used translators. In most cases it was referred to as *Ertra n'Ertrawian* by most inhabitants.

45 Trevaskis, *Eritrea*, 74.
46 *Nai Ertra Semunawi Gazeta*, "*Mahber Fikri Hager nai Ertra: (Ertra m's Ethiopia)*" (January 9, 1947).
47 *Nai Ertra Semunawi Gazeta*, "*Mahber netzanet Ertra: Ertra n'Ertrawian*," no. 234 (February 27, 1947).
48 *Nai Ertra Semunawi Gazeta*, no. 234 (February 27, 1947).
49 *Nai Ertra Semunawi Gazeta*, no. 234 (March 18, 1947).
50 Ibrahim Sultan, "*El Rabita El Islamiya*," *Nai Ertra Semunawi Gazeta* (December 11, 1946).
51 Gebremeskel Woldu, "*Itabane E'gzi'o Wuste Mensut*," *Nai Ertra Semunawi Gazeta* (April 21, 1947). Unlike the debate between Tedla Bairu and Woldeab Woldemariam (which deteriorated into personal insults) Gebremeskel Woldu, who understood the ways and history of the Eritrean public, admonished the new UP leadership which had fallen under the domination of Tedla Bairu, the Church, and the Ethiopian empire without resorting to personal attacks. His demotion from the organization that he founded and worked for for five years and his shattered ideals of a unifying "love of country" (*Fikri Hager*) are reflected in the traditional lament (*ehh!*) that concluded his statement.
52 *Nai Ertra Semunawi Gazeta* (July 10, 1947).
53 Ibrahim Sultan, "Response to the Editor regarding Ato Tedla Bairu's statement regarding the Moslem League," *Nai Ertra Semunawi Gazeta*, no. 230 (January 29, 1947). Ibrahim Sultan pointed out that "The ML has been established and recognized by its members and does not require legitimation by *Mahber Fikri Hager – Ertra m's Ethiopia*. It should be noted that the *MFHE (UP)* [was] not authorized to judge the validity of political parties." Seyoum Maascio, Secretary-General of the LPP, responded to Tedla Bairu's statement, casting aspersions on the goals of the LPP. Seyoum Maascio objected to the use of "violent language" used by the UP leader and admonished him that "to think . . . that unity with Ethiopia is better [than independence] was foolishness and madness." See *Nai Ertra Semunawi Gazeta*, no. 248 (June 4, 1947).

54 Mohammed Kadi, "*Mahber Hibret Ertra m's Ethiopia – Miswaa'e*," *Nai Ertra Semunawi Gazeta*, no. 249 (June 12, 1947).

55 "Political Conditions in Eritrea," *Nai Ertra Semunawi Gazeta*, (August 16, 1947). The author of this article stated that "the Moslem League is considering a 10-year trusteeship under Italy! . . . How can anyone want to go back to being called a '*brutto nero?*'"

56 Ellingson, "Eritrea: Separatism and Irredentism," 72–80.

57 *Nai Ertra Semunawi Gazeta*, no. 249 (April 3, 1949).

58 F. G. Drew, British Military Administration, *Eritrea: Annual Report for 1949* (Asmara, December 31, 1949), 5.

59 The banned Eritrean newspapers were: *Ethiopia*, published by the UP; *Sout Arrabita al Islamiya al Eritrea*, published by the ML; *Natznet Ertra*, published by the LPP. The banned Italian newspapers were: *Giornale dell'Eritrea; Lunedi del Medio Oriente; Eritrea Nuova;* and *Il Lavoro*. For more details see F. G. Drew, BMA, *Eritrea: Annual Report for 1949*, 55–56.

60 Drew, *Eritrea*, 5.

61 Drew, *Eritrea*, 6.

62 Drew, *Eritrea*, 3.

63 Gebremeskei Woldu, in *Nai Ertra Semunawi Gazeta* (April 21, 1947).

64 UN *Report* (1950), 3.

65 F. G. Drew, BMA, *Eritrea: Annual Report for 1949*, 2.

66 Drew, *Eritrea*, 6.

67 "*Me'merekta Selfi Natznet Ertra,*" *Nai Ertra Semunawi Gazeta, no. 308* (July 28, 1949).

68 *Ibid.*

69 Woldeab Woldemariam's leadership of the IEP is mentioned very briefly in the *Report of the United Nations Commission For Eritrea*, Supplement no. 8 (A/ 1285), Paragraph 193, 30. See also *Nai Ertra, Semunawi Gazeta* (April 4, 1950).

70 For details see F. G. Drew, BMA, *Eritrea: Annual Report for 1949*, 6. See also UN *Report* (1950), 17.

71 Ellingson, "The Emergence of Political Parties in Eritrea," 278.

72 UN *Report* (1950), 17.

73 *Nai Ertra Semunawi Gazeta* (February 22, 1950).

74 For details on the political assassinations and *shifta* activities see F. G. Drew, BMA, *Eritrea: Annual Report for 1950* (Asmara, December 31 1950), 10–30.

75 UN *Report* (1950), 5.

76 Although Woldeab Woldemariam was the President of the Independent Eritrea Party (IEP) which joined the Bloc in 1950, any direct communication between him and the Commission is not listed. There are three references to him sent to the Commission by the BA listed as "Information from the Administering Authority regarding statement by Mr. Woldemariam of the Independent Eritrea Party." See UN *Report* (1950), Annex 16, 97–98. Annex 17 of the same document lists 17 witnesses of the IEP which met with the Commission from February 24 to March 23, 1950. The witnesses for the IEP consisted of representatives from the highlands, lowlands, coastal areas, Asmara, and major towns.

77 See *Nai Ertra Semunawi Gazeta* (April 4, 1950) for details on the attempted assassination.

78 *Ibid.*

79 For details see "Summary findings on the wishes of the people," UN *Report* (1950), 21. Paragraphs 132–133, 135.
80 UN *Report* (1950), 25. Paragraphs 165 and 172.
81 UN *Report* (1950), 25. Paragraph 170.
82 UN *Report* (1950), 26. Paragraph 171.
83 UN *Report* (1950), 24. Paragraph 160 (emphasis mine).
84 UN *Report* (1950), 29. Paragraph 190. The memorandum stresses the fact that the British preference for partition of Eritrea as a solution and the Bevin–Sforza plan were agreed to by the UP in November 1949.
85 UN *Report* (1950), 33. Paragraph 227.
86 UN *Report* (1950), 31. Paragraph 205.
87 UN *Report* (1950), 32. Paragraph 214.
88 UN *Report* (1950), 35. Paragraph 265 (emphasis mine). It should be noted that the Guatemalan–Pakistani representatives categorically rejected the return of Italian trusteeship and the annexation of Moslem-inhabited lands to the Sudan. Their emphasis on the right of the Eritrean people to exercise self-determination seems to be borne out by their arguments.
89 Ibid., UN *Report* (1950), 36. Paragraph 276.
90 The "minorities" mentioned by the Guatemalan and Pakistani representatives refer to Italian, Arab, Jewish, Sudanese, and Greek communities then residing in Eritrea.

5 THE FEDERATION YEARS: 1952–1962

1 Trevaskis, *Eritrea*, 129–130.
2 Spencer, *Ethiopia at Bay*, 233–240.
3 For details see United Nations, "Text of Resolution 390 A(V) adopted on December 2, 1950 by the General Assembly of the United Nations," *The Final Report of the United Nations Commission in Eritrea*, General Assembly, Official Records: Seventh Session, Supplement no. 15 (A/2188), New York, 1952, 74–75.
4 UN *Final Report* (1952), 2
5 *Ibid.*, 2.
6 The Ethiopian government demanded that its representative be empowered to nominate and/or approve the head of the Eritrean government, to veto laws passed by the Eritrean Assembly, and to confirm the appointment of judges. The UN Commissioner considered these demands to be violations of the autonomy granted to Eritrea by the UN and after numerous meetings and correspondence limited the Ethiopian representative of the emperor to certain official functions. For more details see UN *Final Report* (1952), 8–9.
7 UN *Final Report* (1952), 9. Paragraph 102.
8 Professional associations included the Eritrean Chamber of Commerce, Eritrean Employees Association of the BA, and the Asmara University Circle. For more details see UN *Final Report* (1952), 12–17.
9 UN *Final Report* (1952), 12. Paragraph 132.
10 Others who did not attend the hearings but submitted written documents were representatives of the Greek and Sudanese communities. UN *Final Report* (1952), 13–14. Paragraphs 141 and 145.
11 UN *Final Report* (1952), 14–15. Paragraphs 155–157.

12 UN *Final Report* (1952), 19–20. Paragraph 201 (emphasis mine).

13 UN *Final Report* (1952), 21. Paragraph 220.

14 For details see Trevaskis, *Eritrea*, 118–120.

15 UN *Final Report* (1952), 36. Paragraphs 407–408.

16 UN *Final Report* (1952), 37. Paragraphs 415–416.

17 Tedla Bairu was elected by 49 votes to 11 with 2 abstentions and 4 spoiled papers; Ali Radai was elected by 48 votes to 17 with 1 abstention. See UN *Final Report* (1952), 37. Paragraph 424.

18 Anze Matienzo, "Speech to the Eritrean National Assembly," *Nai Ertra Semunawi Gazeta*, 8 (May 8, 1952).

19 UN *Final Report* (1952), 42–46.

20 *Ibid.*

21 UN *Final Report* (1952), 74.

22 Wolde Giorgis, *Red Tears*, 80–81.

23 *Ibid.*

24 Constitution of Eritrea, adopted by the Eritrean Assembly on July 10, 1952 and ratified on September 11, 1952 by the emperor of Ethiopia.

25 Constitution of Eritrea, 1952.

26 This newspaper was a weekly published in Tigrigna, Italian, and Arabic which began circulation in 1952. See *Andinet'n Me'belnaan*, no. 12 (May 25, 1952).

27 Foreign Service despatch, from Edward W. Clark, American Consul, no. 775a. 21/6–1953 (June 10, 1953).

28 Thomas J. Farer, *War Clouds on the Horn of Africa* (Washington, DC: Carnegie Endowment for International Peace, 1976), 24.

29 Constitution of Eritrea (1952).

30 ELF–PLF *United Nations Documents*, 48–49.

31 For details see Foreign Service Despatch from George C. Moore, American Consul, Asmara, to the Department of State, Washington DC, USA, no. 775.00/6–2058 (June 20, 1958).

32 *Ibid.*

33 This is a verse of a Tigrigna song from the late 1950s which was popular in the *Bet-Shahi* (tea-houses) and *Inda Suwa* (beer-houses) of Asmara.

34 Tekie Fessehatzion, "Eritrea: From Federation to Annexation, 1952–1962" (Washington DC: Eritreans for Peace and Democracy, Working Paper no. 2, March 1990), 41.

35 A telegram informing the US Secretary of State that Eritrean exiles in Cairo had requested entry visas to the USA to address the UN was cabled on April 21, 1959. See Foreign Service Despatch, no. 775a.c/4–2159.

36 See Foreign Service Despatch from Matthew Looram, American Consul, Asmara to Department of State, Washington DC, USA, no. 775a.00/6–1561, June 15, 1961 and 771a/00/8–3061 (August 30, 1961).

37 See Foreign Service Despatch, Matthew Looram, American Consul, Asmara, to Department of State, Washington DC, USA, no. 775a.00/10–261 (October 2, 1961).

38 Foreign Service Despatch, "Assassination Attempt on Melake Selam Dimetros Ghebremariam" from Matthew Looram, American Consul, Asmara, to the Department of State, Washington DC, USA, no. 775.00.00/11–1561 (November 15, 1961).

39 *Ibid.*
40 This was a Tigrigna verse that was popular in 1961 in Asmara.
41 Foreign Service Despatch, Matthew Looram, American Consul to the Department of State, Washington DC, USA, no. 775a.00/5.2562 (May 25, 1962).
42 *Ibid.*
43 Foreign Service Despatch, Thomas R. Byrne, Chargé d'Affaires ad interim, American Embassy, Dar es Salaam, no. 775a.006–562 (June 5, 1962).
44 Foreign Service Despatch, Edward W. Holmes, First Secretary, American Embassy, Addis Ababa, to Department of State, Washington DC, USA, No. 775.00a/6.662 (June 6, 1962).
45 Foreign Service Despatch, "Monthly Summary of Events – June 1962" from Matthew Looram, American Consul, Asmara to the Department of State, Washington DC, USA, No. 775a.00/7462 (July 4, 1962).
46 *Ibid.*
47 *Ibid.*
48 *Ibid.*
49 Foreign Service Despatch, "Eritrean Internal Scene – Ethiopia's Efforts to Bring about Union," Matthew Looram, American Consul to the Department of State, Washington DC, USA, no. 775a.00/7–362 (July 3, 1962).
50 Asfha Woldemichael's speech to the Eritrean Assembly was published the next day, see *Zemen* (November 15, 1962), 1.
51 Habteselassie, *Eritrea and the United Nations*, 40–41.
52 Tekie Fessehatzion documents Ethiopian Foreign Minister Aklilu's threats to Anze Matienzo, whose political future became uncertain with the change of regime in his native Bolivia. For details see Fessehatzion, "Eritrea," 15–16.
53 John Lonsdale, "African Pasts in Africa's Future," *Canadian Journal of African Studies*, 25: 1 (1989).
54 Eric J. Hobsbawm, *The Age of Empire, 1875–1914* (New York: Vintage Books, 1989).

6 SECULAR NATIONALISM: THE CREATIVE RADICALISM OF THE ELM

1 Markakis, *National and Class Conflict*, 107.
2 *Harekat Tahrir Eritrea* is Arabic and its English translation, Eritrean Liberation Movement (ELM), is used to refer to this first organized resistance. After expanding its recruitment activities in the highlands where Tigrigna was spoken it was also known as *Mahber Shew'ate.*
3 Markakis, *National and Class Conflict*, 106.
4 For further details see Tim Niblock, *Class and Power in the Sudan: The Dynamics of Sudanese Politics, 1898–1985* (New York: State University of New York Press, 1987), 163–183.
5 John Markakis, "The Nationalist Revolution in Eritrea," *Journal of Modern African Studies*, 26:1 (March 1988), 55.
6 School teachers such as Woldeab Woldemariam and Osman Saleh Sabbe played a key role in the early development of Eritrean opposition.
7 Stefano Poscia, *Eritrea: Colonia Tradita* (Rome: Edizioni Associate, 1989), 69–70.

8 Markakis, *National and Class Conflict*, 106–107.
9 The establishment of the ELM eight months after the brutal suppression of the general workers' strike on March 10, 1958 provided a propitious outlet for unemployed workers, alienated civil servants, and students in urban areas.
10 Poscia, *Eritrea: Colonia Tradita*, 70.
11 *Ibid.*
12 This song was an adaptation from the late 1800s when Imbi'ale Woldu (Ras Woldemichael of Hamsien) chose to ally himself with the Ethiopian empire led by Yohannes IV rather than continue to fight. He was promptly imprisoned and Ras Alula of Tigray consolidated his hold over the highlands of Eritrea. The significance of this song was that it highlighted the role of the elite nationalists who were repeatedly contained by the empire through cooptation or coercion. See documentation of oral traditions, in Johannes Kolmodin, *Traditions de Tsazzega et Hazzega: Textes Tigrigna, Archives d'Etudes Orientales*, 5:1 (Rome: J. A. Lundell, 1912), 241–244. See also EPLF, *Ertra'n Kalsan'n: Kab Tinti Ksab 1941* (January 1987), 34–37.
13 The ELM leaders were influenced by the 1958 bloodless coup which resulted in the Sudanese Army taking over the parliamentary government that had governed the Sudan since its independence in 1956.
14 Interview with Kesete Habtezion, a participant in the student demonstrations of 1960, August 14, 1990, New York, USA.
15 MTA was not the first such organization. The first was the *Mahber M'mhiash Hagerawi Bahli* (Association for the Improvement and Preservation of National Culture), established in the late 1950s by two singers, Tewolde Redda and T'Kabo Woldemariam. For details see Poscia, *Eritrea: Colonia Tradita*, 88.
16 This was in reference to the American broadcasts from the Kagnew Station and the Amharic language broadcasts from Radio Ethiopia.
17 The term *shigey* refers to the lighted torch used by young people in New Year festivities as well as the torch of freedom. This song was popularized by Tewolde Redda in the 1960s and came to signify the denial of freedom to Eritreans.
18 This song reiterated the negative consequences of Moslem–Christian rivalry exacerbated by Ethiopian intervention in Eritrean affairs in the 1940s, which resulted in the fragmentation of political parties. The singer, Ateweberhand Segid, was imprisoned and tortured by Ethiopian authorities which resulted in the loss of an eye.
19 Markakis, *National and Class Conflict*, 197.
20 *Hadas Ertra*, "Interview with Abu Tyara," no. 57 (March 14, 1992).
21 For an excellent example of the continuity of these nationalist symbols, see the EPLF's 1987 Bologna Congress, attended by Woldeab Woldemariam and Ibrahim Sultan, where Tewolde Redda, Al-Amin Abdeletif, and other MTA singers performed the songs from the 1960s.
22 *Hadas Ertra*, "Clandestine Struggle: The ELM," no. 98 (August 5, 1992).
23 Markakis, *National and Class Conflict*, 108.
24 Scholars have differed on Awate's role as a leader in the Eritrean liberation struggle: Markakis claims that the first shots were "fired neither by the ELM nor the ELF" while Poscia argues that Awate, a Beni Amer, opted to join the ELF which was recruiting members through a fellow Beni Amer – Idris M. Adem. See Poscia, *Eritrea: Colonia Tradita*, 80.

25 Idris M. Adem held that the Eritrean Christians had delivered the country to Ethiopian control and therefore could not be trusted with key roles in the independence movement being envisaged in the second bid for nationhood.
26 Markakis, *National and Class Conflict*, 109.
27 Poscia, *Eritrea: Colonia Tradita*, 83.
28 Different figures are given of the casualties suffered by the ELM's first and final ill-fated dispatch by both Poscia and Markakis. Poscia asserts that only approximately ten ELM fighters survived while the rest were killed, thus putting the figure up to forty. (See Poscia, *Eritrea Colonia Tradita*, 83.) The author states that "*Solo una decina di combattenti del Mle riescono sfuggire all'agguato; tutti altri vengono uccisi.*" Markakis on the other hand states that "ELF units surrounded the [ELM] group at Ela Tada ... killing six of its members in the process." Markakis' figures would then place the casualty figures to below ten killed. For more details see Markakis, *National and Class Conflict*, 109.
29 Dejach Asrate Kassa had played a key role in putting down the aborted Ethiopian coup against the emperor in December 1960. He was appointed by the emperor as the Governor General of the province in 1964 and promoted to *Ras* in 1966. The aristocrat proved adept at manipulating the perennial Christian fears and endemic land conflicts to create an Eritrean force, Commandos 101, trained by Israeli military advisors and supplied by the Ethio-American mutual assistance agreements. The ELF's connection to the Arab world was used to strengthen Ethiopian forces, forge new alliances with Israel, and divide the Eritrean population which feared Moslem dominance.
30 Poscia, *Eritrea: Colonia Tradita*, 86–87. This account was corroborated by personal interviews with several participants between 1986 and 1989 in Rome, USA, and Eritrea.
31 Markakis, "Nationalist Revolution," 52 (emphasis mine).

7 DEFIANT NATIONALISM: THE ELF AND THE EPLF, 1961–1981

1 The "Arabization" of the Red Sea as a threat to Ethiopia's sovereignty popularized by Haile Selassie was also continued by the post-imperial regime. As recently as November 1988, the Ethiopian leader stated accusingly "some Arab countries are investing more of their oil wealth in subversive acts against Ethiopia than they do in their own constructive development," "Menghistu Hailemariam: Interview Granted to the *New York Times*" (Addis Ababa, November 26, 1988), 20. See also Ethiopian Ministry of Information Press Department, *Historical Truth About Eritrea* (Addis Ababa, July 1988).
2 The portrayal of the Eritrean struggle as a dual (Communist and Arab) threat has been a dominant feature of analyses. For further details see *Ethiopia and the Horn of Africa: Hearings before the Subcommittee on African Affairs of the Ninety-Fourth Congress, Second Session*; George Shepherd jun., *The Trampled Grass: Tributary States and Self-Reliance in the Indian Ocean Zone of Peace* (New York: Praeger Publishers, 1987), 68–70 and 80–83; Haggai Erlich, "The Soviet Union and Ethiopia: The Misreading of *Politica Sciona* and *Politica Tigrina*," and Paul B. Henze, "The Soviet Impact on African Political Dynamics," in Dennis L. Bark (ed.), *The Red Orchestra: The Case of Africa, Volume II*

(Stanford: Hoover Institution Press, 1988) 130–133 and 40–43, respectively; and Gilkes, *Dying Lion*, 196–203.

3 Fernando Lopez-Alves, "Political Crises, Strategic Choices, and Terrorism: The Rise and Fall of the Uruguyan Tupamaros," *Journal of Terrorism and Political Violence*, 3: 1 (Fall 1989), 217–226.

4 *Shifta* is the term used to refer to bandits. Although the Ethiopian government(s) use the term to refer to the Eritrean nationalists in its Amharic version – *wenbedye* – its use has become narrower in the modern era. For more information refer to Eric J. Hobsbawm, *Primitive Rebels: Studies in Archaic Forms of Social Movements in the 19th and 20th Centuries* (New York: W. W. Norton & Co. Inc., 1959), 16; Eric J. Hobsbawm, *Bandits* (New York: Pantheon Books, rev. edn. 1981), 12–15; and Crummey (ed.), *Banditry, Rebellion and Social Protest*, 133–167.

5 The first political exile was Woldeab Woldemariam, founder of the Liberal Progressive Party and editor of the Tigrigna language *The Eritrean Weekly News*, in the 1940s. He arrived in Cairo in 1954.

6 One of these who had contacts with the political exiles was Abdelkarim al-Khattabi, a Moroccan exile who had fought against the French. He is said to have advised the early ELF members to adapt the Algerian *Wilaya* system which was used by the Algerian Front de Libération Nationale.

7 Oded, *Africa and the Middle East Conflict*, 82. See also Bernard Lewis, *Race and Slavery in the Middle East: An Historical Enquiry* (New York: Oxford University Press, 1990), 22–25; and Manning, *Slavery and African Life*, 50–53.

8 Interview with Andeab Gebremeskel, former EDM leader, May 4, 1991, Los Angeles, California, USA.

9 ELF, "We Are Part and Parcel of the International Workers' Movement," *Eritrean Revolution* 1:6, October 1976–April 1977 (Beirut, Lebanon: ELF Foreign Information Center, 1977), 13.

10 Henze, "Eritrea" in Radu, *New Insurgencies*, 102.

11 Poscia, *Eritrea: Colonia Tradita*, 84. The Cairo triumvirate included Idris M. Adem, Idris O. Glawdewos, and Osman Saleh Sabbe.

12 Osman Saleh Sabbe was a native of Hirgigo in the Samhar area. This zone was regarded by many as part of his constituency.

13 Recent works have been more systematic about the actual events that led to the demise of the ELM. For the most detailed account of the ELM, which includes interviews of former ELM members, see Poscia, *Eritrea: Colonia Tradita*, 69–83; and Markakis, *National and Class Conflict*, 104–109.

14 In Zone 3 cattle raids on the Christian Tsenadegle further aggravated the perennial conflict over grazing disputes with the Saho. The large number of Saho recruits of this zone was regarded as ominous by the population who viewed them as "Moslem" armies.

15 Richard Sherman, *Eritrea: The Unfinished Revolution* (New York: Praeger Publishers, 1980), 75–76.

16 Pateman, *Stones Are Burning*, 118.

17 One of the most notable was Woldai Kahsai, the leader of Zone 5 (referred to as the "Christian" zone). The incident which led to this significant defection was the knifing of twenty-seven Christian fighters by the Vice-Commander Mohamed Eshal. See also "*Neh'nan Elamaa'nan*" (the first manifesto of the

EPLF), November 1971, 10.

18 Such published accounts appeared in newspapers almost daily in the Amharic *Addis Zemen* and the Tigrigna *Hibret* between 1967 and 1968.

19 Tedla Bairu joined the Supreme Council after leaving his last post as the Ethiopian Ambassador to Sweden.

20 Poscia, *Eritrea: Colonia Tradita*, 98–99.

21 The first of these rectification meetings was held on July 25, 1968 and was attended by all zone commanders. At the second meeting, which came to be known as the Anseba Conference, on September 10, 1968 representatives of the first and second zones were absent. This was followed by the Adobha Conference, August 10–12, 1969, which instituted structural changes that replaced the Cairo-based leadership with the establishment of a new leadership based inside Eritrea. For more details see Poscia, *Eritrea: Colonia Tradita*, 102–110.

22 EPLF, *Hafeshawi Politicawi T'mherti N'Tegadelti* (General Political Education for Fighters) (Eritrea: EPLF, 1975), 41–43.

23 *Hadas Ertra*, "Interview with Tegadalaai Ghidei Ghebremdhin Hagos," no. 59 (March 21, 1992).

24 Osman S. Sabbe and Woldeab Woldemariam had both condemned the extreme actions of the General Command. Sabbe had been the first to issue the invitation to fighters to join him in creating a new organization.

25 This organization of splinter groups adopted the name *Hizbawi Hailat Harnet Ertra* or Eritrean People's Liberation *Forces*. The term "Tripartite Unity" is applied here to avoid confusion with the *Hizbawi Ginbar Harnet Ertra*, or Eritrean People's Liberation Front.

26 The nine members were: Mohammed Ali Umaro, Abu Tyara (Mohamed Omar), Omar Damer, Mesfin Hagos, Ali Osman, M'aasho Embaye, Mohamed Osman, Mohamed Said Alamin, and Mehari Debessai.

27 EPLF, *Hafeshawi Politicawi Temherti: 1 Kifli, Tikimiti 1978* (General Political Education, Part I, October 1978) (Boston: Asmara Printing Company, 1980), 96.

28 ELF, *Eritrea: The National Democratic Revolution versus Ethiopian Expansionism* (Beirut: ELF Foreign Information Center, 1979), 53–54.

29 The PLF's organizational first charter reflected the leftist orientation of the PLF. The program concluded with a call for all nationalists to struggle for an Eritrean society free from exploitation and affirmed its solidarity with the "progressive" peoples of the world. EPLF, *Neh'nan Elamaa'nan* (Eritrea: *Hizbawi Hailat Harnet Ertra*, November 1971), 17.

30 This was the first time that any official mention was made of a struggle to eradicate the patriarchal social structures that placed Eritrean women in a subordinate position to men.

31 The first joint committee of the three organizations was the one formed in Beirut in charge of equitable distribution of resources channelled by the External Mission of the ELF–PLF.

32 The term *Menkaa'e*, a Tigrigna word has a double meaning. The first meaning refers to a bat. See EPLF, *Dictionary: English–Tigrigna–Arabic* (Rome: RICE, 1985), 48. The equation of bats to the clandestine opposition is said to have indicated nocturnal activities such as secret meetings held in secret or darkness. Its second meaning, is a slang term used to refer to "left-handed" persons, which could be interpreted as an indication of leftist orientations.

33 The *Menkaa'e* group included members of the EPLF leadership such as Tewolde
   Eyob, Yohannes Sebhatu, and Mussie Tesfamichael. Recruits to this group
   included military leaders such as Solomon Woldemariam who later turned
   against the *Menkaa'e* leadership. For more information see Poscia, *Eritrea:*
   Colonia Tradita, 134–137.

34 This was in reference to the fact that key positions had been held by Abrha
   Tewolde, former commander of Zone 5. Other members included Kidane Kiflu,
   coordinator of the ELF clandestine cells assassinated in Kassala, and Asmerom
   Ghereghziher and Tewolde Eyob who were from the above mentioned two
   regions. The omission of the fact that Issaias Afeworki originated from the
   Hamasien region and had indisputably held a leadership role remains a
   curiosity. See Poscia, *Eritrea: Colonia Tradita*, 136–137.

35 See EPLF publication *A'enawi Minkiskas nai 1973* (The Destructive Movement
   of 1973) (Eritrea: EPLF, 1973), 1–83.

36 Stefano Poscia notes that the circumstances surrounding the elimination of the
   Menkaa'e constitutes a period in the EPLF full of "question marks" which will
   remain unanswered until some of its former members decide to speak about
   their experiences openly. Poscia, *Etritrea: Colonia Tradita*, 135.

37 For more information, refer to the recent publications on the Ethiopian
   Revolution: Keller, *Revolutionary Ethiopia*; Clapham, *Transformation and*
   Continuity; and John W. Harbeson, *The Ethiopian Transformation: The Quest*
   for the Post-Imperial State (Boulder: Westview Press, 1988).

38 Clapham, *Transformation and Continuity*, 42.

39 Keller, *Revolutionary Ethiopia*, 193 (emphasis mine).

40 Clapham, *Transformation and Continuity*, 42.

41 René Lefort, *Ethiopia: The Heretical Revolution?* (London: Zed Press, 1983), 72.

42 Henze, "Eritrea" in Radu, *New Insurgencies*, 108; and Poscia, *Eritrea: Colonia*
   Tradita, 145.

43 Markakis, *National and Class Conflict*, 137.

44 An exceptionally bloody clash which lasted several days occurred eighteen
   kilometers from Asmara between ELF units stationed at *Woki D'ba* and EPLF
   units stationed at *Zagher*.

45 Lefort, *Heretical Revolution*, 73.

46 The first stage of the revolution was hailed as unique by some Western analysts
   because there was no bloodshed. A popular refrain of a song, "*Alem'nem Dem*
   Ethiopia Tikdem," symbolized the "bloodless stage."

47 Pateman, *Stones Are Burning*, 101.

48 François Houtart, "Social Aspects of the Eritrean Revolution," *Eritrean*
   Symposium (London: January 12–13, 1979). Richard Sherman asserts that the
   EPLF was a "sociopolitical innovator, while the ELF often follow[ed] the EPLF
   in a revised form sometime thereafter" (Sherman, *Unfinished Revolution*, 51).
   For more information on the EPLF's programs of reforestation and environ-
   mentally conscious policies see Scott Jones, "Environment and Development in
   Eritrea," *Africa Today*, 38: 2 (1991), 33–60.

49 The EPLF holds in its ranks a very well trained core of Eritrean medical doctors
   and specialists who joined the Front after 1975. For specific information on the
   EPLF's medical achievements see Afeworki Abraham and Haile Debas (eds.),
   Eritrean Medical Journal, 2: 2 (October 1984), 1–61.

50 Roy Pateman, "The Eritrean War," *Armed Forces and Society* 17: 1, Transac-

tion Periodicals Consortium (Fall 1990), 87–90.

51 Pettersen, "US Policy," 627–645; Edmond J. Keller, "United States Foreign Policy on the Horn of Africa: Policymaking with Blinders On," in Gerald Bender, James S. Coleman, and Richard S. Sklar (eds.), *African Crises Areas* (Berkeley: University of California Press, 1985), 184–190; and Richard J. Payne, *Opportunities and Dangers of Soviet–Cuban Expansion: Toward a Pragmatic US Policy* (New York: State University of New York, 1988), 29–32.

52 Erlich, *Struggle Over Eritrea*, 85–96.

53 The PDRY and Cuba actively supported the *Dergue*'s diplomatic as well as military initiatives while Libya provided material support. Only Syria and Algeria remained steadfast in their support of the Eritrean cause. On the role of the PDRY see Fred Halliday, *Revolution and Foreign Policy: The Case of South Yemen, 1968–1987* (Cambridge: Cambridge University Press, 1990), 172–174, 240.

54 Erlich, *Struggle Over Eritrea*, 119.

55 The term *Falool* in its original use in Tigrigna was used to indicate "free" or "uninhibited/unconstrained" behavior. The ELF's leadership used it as a synonym for anarchist. Although the EDM never exhibited the abolition of all kinds of leadership, they were quite clear on the need for the ousting of the ELF leadership. But it would be incorrect to view them as anarchists in the conventionally accepted sense of the word.

56 EDM, *Political Statement of the Provisional Central Committee (PCC), Eritrean Democratic Movement (EDM) on the Presentation of Our Revolution* (Kassala, Sudan, October 1, 1983).

57 Interview with Andeab Gebremeskel, former EDM leader, Los Angeles, California, USA, May 4, 1991.

58 EPLF, *Political Report and National Democratic Programme, Adopted at the Second and Unity Congress of the Eritrean People's Liberation Front and the Eritrean Liberation Front (Central Committee)* (Eritrea: March 19, 1987), 65.

59 The EDMLE, also known in Tigrigna as *DeMHaE* claimed that it had a fighting force of 3,000 stationed in Adi Grat, Tigray, Ethiopia. See *Democraciawi Men'kis'kas Harnet Ertra: Temekuro DMHaE* (The Democratic Movement for the Liberation of Eritrea) (July 1989). For more details on EDMLE and the Eritrean Toilers' Emancipation League (ETEL) see ETEL, *Mae'bel Shekalay* 1: 1 (September 1990), 1–9.

60 EPLF, "*EDM ms EPLF Tetzenbiru*," *Sagem*, 2:11 (November 1990).

61 One only need look at the post-colonial African experience of endemic conflicts arising out of the demands by various segments in the multiethnic and linguistic societies whose interests are felt to be neglected by autocratic regimes or single party systems. The Biafran and Katangan experiences are only two examples.

8   THE EPLF'S QUEST FOR LEGITIMACY

1 EPLF documents, proclamations, and training manuals for fighters of the 1970s reflect adaptation of radical Latin American experiences drawn from the *Tupamaros* of Uruguay, Fidel Castro's Cuba, Vietnam, the Bolshevik model of the USSR, and Mao Zedong's People's Republic of China.

2 There are no primary documents available to substantiate the existence of a

"party" within the EPLF. But the existence of the "Eritrean People's Revolutionary Party" is discussed by Tesfatsion Medhanie, *Eritrea: Dynamics of a National Question* (Amsterdam: B. R. Gruner, 1986), 66. An "Eritrean Socialist Party" (*Nai Ertra Mahbernetawi Selfi [EMaS]*), within the EPLF is discussed by EDMLE publications. For details see ETEL, *Mae'bel Shekalay*, 1.

3 EPLF, *"Referendum: Enko Agebab n'Nebari Fetah,"* *Sagem*, 2:6 (June 1990), 3–6.

4 ELF–PLF, *Eritrea: A Victim of UN Decision and of Ethiopian Aggression. Appeal of the Eritrean People to the 26th Session of the General Assembly* (New York, December 3, 1971), 71.

5 ELF–PLF, *Eritrea: A Victim of UN Decision*, 4.

6 John H. Spencer, "Haile Selassie: Triumph and Tragedy," *Orbis*, 18: 4 (Winter 1975), 1129–1137.

7 ELF–PLF, *Eritrea: A Victim of UN Decision*, 14.

8 These included Woldeab Woldemariam, Osman S. Sabbe, and Taha Mohamed Nur, who were signatories to the published appeal to the UN in 1971.

9 Osman Saleh Sabbe, *The History of Eritrea*, trans. Muhammad Fawaz Al Azein (Beirut: Dar Al-Masirah, 1974), 31–51.

10 EPLF, *Neh'naan Elamaa'nan* (author's translation throughout).

11 EPLF, *Neh'naan Elamaa'nan*, 19–22.

12 It is interesting to note that at this stage, this early PLF document did not distinguish between the connotation of front and party. In the Tigrigna version of the original manifesto the term *selfi* refers to a front and not to the later use of "party." The English language version published in 1973 translates the term *selfi* as a "National United Front." For more details see Eritreans for Liberation in North America (EFLNA), *Liberation*, 2: 3 (March 1973), 23.

13 *Ibid.*

14 EPLF, *Hafeshawi Politicawi T'mherti*, 18. The declared opposition to "Israeli Zionism" can best be understood not as evidence of Arab affiliation so much as a response to Israel's training of Ethiopian military personnel, especially the notorious Commandos 101.

15 EPLF, *Hafeshawi Politicawi T'mherti*, 60.

16 EPLF, *Hafeshawi Politicawi T'mherti*, 78–79.

17 Mohamed Said Nawud, "Eritrean Struggle is a National Liberation Movement," reprint of interview from *Africa Magazine*, 44 (April 1975), 7–13.

18 ELF–PLF, "OAU Must Do Something to Stop Ethiopian Crimes in Eritrea: Eritrean Liberation Front Demands Formation of an African Commission of Inquiry on Eritrea," *The Eritrean Review*, 26 (July 1975), 1–5.

19 Bereket Habteselassie, *Conflict and Intervention in the Horn of Africa* (New York: Monthly Review Press, 1980), 69–70. See also EPLF, *Hafeshawi Politicawi Temherti*, 123.

20 Markakis, *National and Class Conflict*, 143–144.

21 Although the term "Afro-Marxist" has been used to refer to regimes or states, it does not exclude national liberation movements. Keller includes the Movimiento Popular de Libertação de Angola (MPLA) and Frente de Libertação de Moçambique (FRELIMO) as the antecedents of the Afro-Marxist regimes. Keller describes them as "hybrids with both Leninist and populist traits. The most well-articulate among them grew out of national liberation movements."

The EPLF, too, exhibited this hybrid trait, combining populist nationalism with Marxist organization structures. But unlike the MPLA or FRELIMO, although it upheld the universal goals of Marxism–Leninism of "eliminating exploitation of man by man," it refrained from embracing it as an official ideology. Moreover, while the MPLA and FRELIMO leadership promoted the existence of a Communist Party, there is no evidence that such an organ existed in the EPLF. For further discussion on the nature of Afro-Marxist regimes and their antecedents see Edmond J. Keller and Donald Rothchild (eds.), *Afro-Marxist Regimes: Ideology and Public Policy* (Boulder: Lynne Rienner Publishers, 1987), 1–21, and Crawford Young, *Ideology and Development in Africa* (New Haven: Yale University Press, 1982), 22–96.

22 EPLF, *Kedamay Wudbawi Guba'e nai Hizbawi Hailtat Harnet Ertra* (First EPLF Organizational Congress) January 31, 1977, 1–5. For the English version see Sherman, *Unfinished Revolution*, 166–174.

23 The members of the Politburo included Sebhat Efrem, Petros Solomon, Al Amin Mohamed Said, Haile Woldetensae, Ibrahim Afa, Mesfin Hagos, Ali Said Mohamed Said Barre, Mahmoud Sherifo, Ukbe Abraha, and Berhane Gebregzabher. For further details, see Poscia, *Eritrea: Colonia Tradita*, 306.

24 EPLF, *Objectives of the National Democratic Programme: First Organizational Congress* (Eritrea, January 31, 1977).

25 "Constitution of Eritrea," in UN *Final Report* (1952), 76–89.

26 James Firebrace and Stuart Holland, *Never Kneel Down: Drought, Development and Liberation in Eritrea* (Nottingham, England: Bertrand Russell House, 1984), 35–38.

27 Amrit Wilson, *Women and the Eritrean Revolution: The Challenge Road* (Trenton, NJ: Red Sea Press Inc., 1991), 72–73.

28 Firebrace and Holland, *Never Kneel Down*, 36.

29 For details on the development of an effective military capability of the EPLF and the evolution of a disciplined army – the Eritrean People's Liberation Army (EPLA) – see Pateman, "Eritrean War," 81–98. For more information on the military victories of the EPLA, see EPLF, *Political Report and National Democratic Program*, 112.

30 The first offensive (*kedamai werrar*) was launched in July–August 1978; the second offensive (*kal'ai werrar*) in November 1978; the third (*sal'sai werrar*) in January–February 1979; the fourth (*rab'ai werrar*) in March–April, 1979; the fifth offensive (*hamushai werrar*) in July 1979. The other major offensives were the sixth (*shadu'shai [keih kokhob] werrar*) in February –June, 1982; the seventh offensive (*shabu'ai [sela'hta] werrar*) in March–August, 1983 and the eight offensive (*shamunai [bahri negash] werrar*) in October–December 1985. For detailed accounts see EPLF, "*Hamed D'bae Nadew Keme'i Nei'ru?*" *Sagem*, 11 (April 1988), 8.

31 For more information on the EPLF's economic, health, and educational policies see Firebrace and Holland, *Never Kneel Down*, 29–41.

32 The EPLF established relations with the Ethiopian People's Revolutionary Party (EPRP) in 1970 which were terminated in 1977 due to the EPRP's rejection of the Eritrean right to self-determination. A splinter group from the EPRP, the Ethiopian People's Democratic Movement (EPDM), has continued to have ties with the EPLF. Relations with the Tigray People's Liberation Front

(TPLF) began in 1976, deteriorated sharply in 1986 and were re-established some time in 1988. Other organizations with whom the EPLF has relations are the Western Somali Liberation Front (WSLF), Sidama Liberation Front (SLF), Afar Liberation Front (ALF) and MEISON (All-Ethiopia Socialist Movement). For more information see EPLF, *Political Report and National Democratic Program*, 146–150.

33 Pateman, *Stones Are Burning*, 125.

34 For details on the impact of famine and drought in the 1980s see Wolde Giorgis, *Red Tears*; Jansson et al., *The Ethiopian Famine*; and Robert D. Kaplan, *Surrender or Starve: The Wars Behind the Famine* (Boulder: Westview Press, 1988).

35 The ELF (Central Command) was a splinter group from the defunct ELF. For more details about the unification and merger see EPLF, "*Abnetawi Hadnet*," *Fitzametat* no. 120 (September 1987), 1–2.

36 EPLF, *Political Report and National Democratic Program*, 166–169.

37 Gebre Hiwet Tesfagiorgis, *Eritrea: A Case of Self-Determination* (Washington, DC: Eritreans for Peace and Democracy), Working Paper no. 1 (January 1990).

38 EPLF delegates to various African countries in the mid-1980s visited Malagasy, Uganda, Kenya, Tanzania, Senegal, Ivory Coast, Guinea-Bissau, Mozambique, Sudan, Somalia, Egypt, Algeria, Libya, Morocco, and Tunisia. See also EPLF, "*Kalsi Ab Meda Diplomacy*," *Sagem*, no. 1 (July 1987), 13–14.

39 EPLF, *Memorandum to the 42nd Regular Sessions of the United Nations General Assembly* (New York: October 1987), 5–7.

40 The March 1991 talks were held in Washington, DC. The EPLF delegation was led by Issaias Afeworki and the Ethiopian government was led by Ashagre Yigletu. No progress was made on either side.

41 These included Ethiopia's agreeing to participate in the peace talks but later refusing to permit UN participation by invoking the principle of non-intervention in internal affairs of sovereign states.

42 A unique account of the Red Star Campaign can be found in an Amharic-language novel, *Oromai* (Addis Ababa: Kuraz Publishing Agency, 1983) by the Ethiopian novelist Be'aalu Ghirma. The author, utilizing fictitious names to camouflage government officials, succeeds in providing an accurate and compelling account of the events surrounding the failure of this campaign. For information on the economic expenditures of the Red Star Campaign see Keller, *Revolutionary Ethiopia*, 208–210. For details on the EPLA's response, see Pateman, *Stones Are Burning*, 137–138. For a reassessment from the Ethiopian perspective see Wolde Giorgis, *Red Tears*.

43 Richard Leonard, "Popular Participation," in Cliffe and Davidson, *Long Struggle*, 110.

44 Pateman notes that by 1988 the EPLA had amassed over 200 tanks and armored vehicles and a fleet of fast attack speedboats. The EPLA was already "better equipped than any other African conventional army except those of Angola, Egypt, Ethiopia, Mozambique, Nigeria and South Africa." Pateman, *Stones Are Burning*, 121.

45 Mary Battiata, "Ethiopian Rebels Claim Huge Victory: 3-Day Battle Seen as Part of New Strategy," *Washington Post* (March 24, 1988); "All For the War Front Vows Mengistu", *Africa Analysis*, 45 (April 1988); "Ethiopia: The

diplomatic battle", *Africa Confidential* (November 18, 1988), 4–6; Lily Butler, "Who is Winning in Eritrea?", *New Africa* (December 1988), 68–70.

46 US Government, *Human Rights and Food Aid in Ethiopia. Hearing before the Subcommittee on Human Rights and International Organizations and the Subcommittee on Africa of the Committee of Representatives, 100th Congress, Second Session* (Washington DC, April 21, 1988), 10.

47 "Speech Delivered at Chatham House" (Issaias Afeworki's speech on October 27, 1988, reprinted in the EPLF's *Adulis*, November 1988).

48 Colin Legum, "After Menghistu, What?" *New Africa* (July 1990), 23; Clifford Krauss, "Ethiopia Talks to Resume under US Leadership," *The New York Times* (January 11, 1991); Reid G. Miller, "Civilians Become Victims in Fight for Important City," Associated Press, reprinted in *Adulis*, 8: 5, (May 1990); "The End for Mengistu," *Foreign Report*, 212, (May 24, 1990), 7; *Africa Watch* (24 July 1990); "Eritrea's Fate Hinges on Battle for Massawa," *Arab News* (February 24, 1990).

49 Reid G. Miller, "Civilians Become Victims". American television gave an unprecedented coverage of the bombing of Massawa in its late night program *Nightline* which was also made available for sale to the public. See "War in Eritrea," MPI Home Video Presentation, ABC News Production, no. 052990.

50 EPLF, *Eritrea Challenge*, no. 9 (October 1990), 5.

51 The opposition movements include EPDM, WSLF, OLF, ALF, MEISON (All-Ethiopian Socialist Movement), and SLF.

52 *FBIS*, AFR-88–094, May 16, 1988, 1; Colin Legum, "Menghistu's Dilemma," *New African* (June 1990), 23; Michael A. Hiltzik, "Briefing Paper: Ethiopian Rebels Making Gains; "Regime Fading", *Los Angeles Times*, April 19, 1991, H/4.

53 EPLF, *Political Report and National Democratic Program*, 146–147.

54 EPLF's relations with the Ethiopian opposition were characterized by heavily polemical debates and points of disagreement concerning strategic versus tactical alliance. Relations with the EPRP were terminated earlier in 1976 and new links were forged with the EPDM, which recognized the right of the Eritreans to self-determination. The EPLF's longest relationship with the TPLF (since 1976) was broken off temporarily in 1986 but vigorously resumed some time in 1988. For more information see EPLF, *Political Report and National Democratic Program*, and TPLF, *Gemgam: Kh'alsi Hizbi Ertra: Kabei Na'bei* (April 1986), 42–91 (translation mine).

55 Clifford Krauss, "2 Conflicting Plans for Peace Offered in Ethiopia Talks," *The New York Times* (February 24, 1991), 7. Visitors to Asmara after its liberation by the EPLF on May 24, 1991 report that the idea of a second federation with Ethiopia was not a popular option. (Conversation with Dr. Tekie Fessehatzion, August 4, 1991.)

9 BUILDING THE ERITREAN POLITY

1 For a full text of the Eritrean national anthem see *Hadas Ertra*, no. 76 (May 22, 1993), 8.

2 In 1991 the EPLF casualty figure was estimated at 50,000. In 1993, a revised figure of 65,000 was announced in the media, radio, and government publications.

3 *Hadas Ertra*, "Excerpts from the Town Meeting of Secretary-General Issaias Afeworki with the people of Asmara on May 17," no. 76 (May 20, 1992).

4 *Hadas Ertra*, "*Carta Kerni Africa z'leweta Hamushte Me'aaltitat*", Year 1: no. 69 (author's translation: "Five Days that Changed the Map of the Horn of Africa") (April 25, 1992). See also "Ethiopia: New Government, New Map," *Africa Confidential*, 32: 22 (November 8, 1991), 7.

5 TGE, *Principles of Cooperation Between the Transitional Government of Ethiopia and the Provisional Government of Eritrea* (Addis Ababa, Ethiopia, 1991). See also "*Ye'Ertra Hezb Ye Rasu'n Edel Lemewesen Wusanie Hezb Indiakha'hid Tefekede*," *Addis Zemen* (July 5, 1991), 1.

6 The structure of the provisional government, its various branches, and authority were announced in Proclamation no. 23, 1992. For details see PGE, *Gazeta Awajat Ertra*, 5: 5 (Asmara, May 25, 1992).

7 EPLF fighters held meetings in June 1991 where they agreed to continue working in their various posts without pay until the referendum scheduled for April 1993 was held.

8 *Hadas Ertra*, no. 8, (October 1991).

9 PGE, *Declaration of Policies on Education in Eritrea* (Department of Education, October 2, 1991), 1–7. See also PGE, *Regulations Enacted to Determine the Establishment and Management of Non-Governmental Schools and their Supervision.* (Department of Education, November 1, 1991), 1–9.

10 *Hadas Ertra*, no. 65 (April 11, 1992).

11 This saying was attributed to the EPLF leader, Issaias Afeworki, in response to a question from the public regarding a timetable for the opening up of the economy at the first anniversary of liberation held in Asmara, Eritrea in 1992.

12 In an interview by *Jeune Afrique*, Meles Zenawi stated that Ethiopia wants to encourage Eritrea's transition to democracy. "*L'Erythree s'était engagée dans la bonne voie, celle de la democratisation – et il fallait l'encourager à poursuivre ses efforts en ce sens*," *Jeune Afrique*, 1648 (August 6–12, 1992), 62. Issaias Afeworki also reaffirmed the need for a stable and democratic neighboring Ethiopia. See *Hadas Ertra* (September 11, 1991).

13 Telephone communication had been cut between the two countries since 1988. British Telecom was one of the international companies that contributed to the re-establishment of telecommunication lines in post-war Eritrea. For more information, see *Hadas Ertra*, no. 78 (May 27, 1992), 1.

14 United Nations, UNOVER ERITREA, Department of Public Information, New York, DP1/1334 – March 1993 – 3M. See also United Nations General Assembly, Forty-Seventh Session, Third Committee, Agenda Item 97 (b), A/C.3/47/L.20/Rev.1 (November 10, 1992).

15 Statement by H. E. Seyoum Mesfin, Minister of Foreign Affairs of the Transitional Government of Ethiopia at the Forty-Seventh Session of the United Nations General Assembly (October 5, 1992), 21.

16 PGE, *Eritrean Nationality Proclamation no. 21/1992*, 2/1992, no. 3, Asmara (April 6, 1992), 1–4.

17 PGE, *Eritrean Nationality Proclamation*, 1.

18 The inclusion of nationality by birth and naturalization to include settlers is evidence of diminishing parochialism and the formation of an encompassing national identity transcending ethnic, regional, and linguistic affiliations. It should be noted that disagreements over eligibility of who can participate in

Eritrea's political affairs had led to acrimonious debates (discussed in chapter 4) and fragmentation during the 1940s.

19 PGE, *Eritrean Nationality Proclamation*, 2–3.

20 *Hadas Ertra*, no. 11 (October 7, 1992).

21 PGE, *Eritrean Referendum Proclamation no. 22/1992*, 2/1992, no. 4, Asmara (April 7, 1992), 4.

22 *Hadas Ertra, "Referendum ab Miazia 23–24–25 Ki'kayed Iyu,"* no. 20 (November 7, 1992).

23 *Hadas Ertra*, no. 6 (September 18, 1991).

24 See *Hadas Ertra* no. 102 (August 17 1992); no. 105 (August 29, 1992); no. 9 (September 30, 1992); and no. 14 (October 17, 1992).

25 Author's observations who attended the Eritrean referendum as an independent observer from April 20 to May 30, 1993.

26 For details see Referendum Commission of Eritrea, *"Memrihi N'Admezti"* (Guidelines for Voters), (Department of Information, Asmara, 1993).

27 The final count of the referendum showed that 1,100,260 eligible persons voted yes for independence, 1,822 voted no and 328 votes were invalid. The percentage figures are: 99.805 percent votes for independence; 0.165 percent voted against and 0.030 percent were invalidated due to irregularities. The total number of registered EPLA members was 79,295 which was added to the 861,074 registered civilians. See Referendum Commission of Eritrea, press releases (Asmara, April 22, 1993 and April 27, 1993).

28 United Nations Special Commissioner, UNOVER, April 27, 1993, statement made on radio and television.

29 OAU, "OAU Observer Team Declares Polling in Eritrea Free and Fair," press release no. 2 (Asmara, April 26, 1993).

30 PGE, *"Wusane Shab'aai Mae'kelai Shimagele HGHaE (Hagagi Akal Giziawi Menghisti Ertra)*, "Resolutions of the Seventh Meeting of the Central Committee of the EPLF (May 1993).

31 For a complete list see EPLF "Proclamation on the Structure, Powers and Tasks of the Government of Eritrea," *Hadas Ertra* no. 76 (May 22, 1993).

32 EDLF, "Proclamation."

33 The members of the Council of State consisted of the ministers of: regional administration; defense; internal affairs; justice; foreign affairs; information and culture; finance and development; industry and tourism; agriculture; marine resources; construction; energy, minerals and water resources; education; health; and ten administrators of: Sahel; Barka; Gash and Setit; Seraie; Akeleguzai; Hamasien; Dankalia; Semhar; Senhit; and Asmara.

34 Reported in *Hadas Ertra, "Adma Tegadelti'n Wusanetat Mae'kelai Shimagele's,"* no. 76, (May 22, 1993).

35 "Press Conference of Ato Issaias Afeworki," *Hadas Ertra* no. 78 (May 29, 1993).

36 "Press Conference of Afeworki" (May 29, 1993).

37 In a number of informal conversations regarding the protest and its resolution, the general feeling among fighters was that it constituted an important lesson because it demonstrated that communications between the leadership and its people need to be open and that any excesses or corruption also needed to be discouraged by the people.

38 Reported in *Hadas Ertra*, "President Meles Zenawi's Speech," Special issue, no. 77 (May 27, 1993).

39 Telephone interview with Ato Arefaine Berhe, Minister Counselor and Deputy Head of Mission, Embassy of Eritrea, Washington, DC, August 9, 1993.

40 Saleh, Heba, "Now that the War is Over," *BBC Focus on Africa*, 3:3 (July–September 1992), 49.

41 Hubbell, Stephen, "Eritrea Nascent: The Next Fight for Independence," *The Nation* (May 31, 1993). See also Sarah Gauch, "Eritrea Seeks Industrial Revival," *African Business* (February 1993), 45.

42 Reported in *Hadas Ertra*, "Equal Attention to Urban and Rural Areas," no. 16 (October 23, 1991).

43 Reported in *Hadas Ertra*, no. 70 (April 29, 1992).

44 PGE, *Investment Proclamation, no. 18/1991, Gazette of Eritrean Laws*, 1:4 (Asmara, December 1991).

45 Mahmoud Nagati, "Red Sea Oil Shows Attract Attention to Miocene Salt, Post-Salt Sequence," *Oil and Gas Journal* (December 7, 1992), 46–53.

46 Reported in *Hadas Ertra*, no. 73 (May 9, 1992).

47 PGE, "*Dimtzi Hafash*," radio broadcast, August 3, 1993.

48 United Nations, "Address by H. E. Issaias Afeworki, President of Eritrea to the 1993 Regular Session of the Economic and Social Council," Geneva (July 3, 1993).

49 Robert H. Jackson and Carl G. Rosberg, "Why Africa's Weak States Persist: The Empirical and Juridical in Statehood," *World Politics*, 35:1 (October 1992).

50 For an excellent analysis of the consequence of the legacies of this failure and constraints to democratization see René Lemarchand, "Africa's Troubled Transitions," *Journal of Democracy*, 3:4 (October 1992), 99–108 and René Lemarchand, "Uncivil States and Civil Societies: How Illusion Became Reality," *Journal of Modern African Studies*, 30:2 (June 1992), 177–191.

51 Reported in *Hadas Ertra*, "President Issaias Afeworki Responds to Questions from the People," no. 83 (June 16, 1993).

52 The PGE since 1991 published eight proclamations concerning the re-establishment of laws concerning the civil code, and governing crimes, adjudication, labor and commerce. For details see PGE, *Negarit Gazeta*, 1 (September 15, 1991). Traditional customs governing adjudication and administration were adapted to existing structure of local governments.

53 The PGE used the media (radio, television and newspapers, as well as official publications) to educate the population about civic duties, political parties, modes of popular participation, and voting. In addition, it issued a new series of pamphlets with a special focus on pluralist systems, political parties, and systems of governance which are also used to inform the public. For details see PGE, *State, Government, Party* (Asmara: Department of Media and Culture, December 1992), 1–56.

Bibliography

ARCHIVES

Istituto Italo-Africano, Rome, Italy
Research and Information Center on Eritrea (RICE), Rome, Italy
Research and Information Center on Eritrea (RICE), Asmara, Eritrea

OFFICIAL PUBLICATIONS

British Military Administration. *Eritrea: Annual Report for 1949*. Asmara, December 31, 1949. (F. G. Drew.)
Eritrea: Annual Report for 1950. Asmara, December 31, 1950. (F. G. Drew.)
The First to be Freed: The Record of British Military Administration in Eritrea and Somalia, 1941–1943. London: His Majesty's Stationery Office, 1944.
Half-Yearly Report by the Military Administrator on the Occupied Enemy Territory of Eritrea: From the Period 1st January to 30th June 1942. Asmara, July 29, 1942. (Stephen H. Longrigg.)
Empire of Ethiopia. *Eritrea and Benadir (Italian Somaliland)*. Addis Ababa: Ethiopian Press and Information Department, 1945.
Ethiopian Ministry of Information Press Department. *Historical Truth About Eritrea*. Addis Ababa, July 1988.
"Menghistu Hailemariam: Interview Granted to the *New York Times*." Addis Ababa, November 26, 1988.
Four Powers Commission (FPC). *Report of the Four Power Commission of Investigation, Former Italian Colonies*. Vol. 1, *Report on Eritrea*, 1948.
Gebremeskel, Woldu. Letter to the Ministers of Foreign Affairs of Great Britain, United States of America and France, FO 371/63175 128279, British Public Records. Asmara, June 15, 1946.
Government of Algeria. *Algeria News Report*. Washington DC: The Embassy of the Democratic and Popular Republic of Algeria, November 15, 1977–December 15, 1980.
Organization of African Unity. "OAU Observer Team Declares Polling in Eritrea Free and Fair," press release no. 2. Asmara, April 26, 1993.
President Issaias Afeworki, "Address to the OAU Summit." Cairo, Egypt, June 28, 1993.
Resolutions and Declarations Adopted by the Meetings of the Assembly of Heads of State and Government (1963–1983). Addis Ababa: OAU Secretariat, 1987.
Permanent People's Tribunal. *Advisory Opinion on Eritrea. The Eritrean Case,*

Proceedings of the Permanent People's Tribunal of the International League for the Rights and Liberation of Peoples Session on Eritrea. May 24–26, 1980. Rome, Italy: Research and Information Center, 1984.

Provisional Government of Eritrea. *Declaration of Policies on Education in Eritrea.* Department of Education, Asmara, October 2, 1991.

"Dimtzi Hafash." Radio broadcast, August 3, 1993.

Eritrean Nationality Proclamation no. 21/1992. 2/1992, no. 3, Asmara, April 6, 1992.

Eritrean Referendum Proclamation no. 22/1992. 2/1992, no. 4, Asmara, April 7, 1992.

Gazeta Awajat Ertra, 5:5 1992, Asmara, May 25, 1992.

Investment Proclamation, no. 18/1991, Gazette of Eritrean Laws 1:4, Asmara, December 31, 1991.

Negarit Gazeta, vol. 1. September 15, 1991.

Regulations Enacted to Determine the Establishment and Management of Non-Governmental Schools and their Supervision. Department of Education, Asmara, November 1, 1991.

State, Government, Party. Department of Media and Culture, Asmara, December 1992.

"Wusane Shab'aai Mae'kelai Shimagele, HGHaE (Hagagi Akal Giziawi Menghisti Ertra," "Resolutions of the Seventh Meeting of the Central Committee of the EPLF." May 1993.

Referendum Commission of Eritrea. *"Memrihi N'Admezti"* (Guidelines for Voters). Department of Information, Asmara, 1993.

Press releases, Asmara, April 22 and 27, 1993.

Transitional Government of Ethiopia. Principles of Cooperation Between the Transitional Government of Ethiopia and the Provisional Government of Eritrea. Addis Ababa: Ethiopia, 1991.

Statement by H. E. Seyoum Mesfin, Minister of Foreign Affairs of the Transitional Government of Ethiopia at the Forty-Seventh Session of the United Nations General Assembly. October 5, 1992.

United Nations. "Address by H. E. Issaias Afeworki, President of Eritrea to the 1993 Regular Session of the Economic and Social Council." Geneva, July 3, 1993.

Constitution of Eritrea. 1952. (Found in UN *Final Report,* 1952.)

The Final Report of the United Nations Commission in Eritrea, General Assembly, Official Records: Seventh Session, Supplement no. 15 (A/2188). New York, 1952.

Forty-Seventh Session, Third Committee, Agenda Item 97(b), A/C.3/47/L.20/ Rev.1, November 10, 1992.

General Assembly Resolution 1514 (XV), UNGAOR Supplement (no. 16), UN Document A/4684, 1960.

General Assembly Resolution 2625(XXV), UNGAOR Supplement (no. 28), UN Document A/8028. 1970.

Report of the United Nations Commission for Eritrea, General Assembly, Official Records, Fifth Session, Supplement no. 8 CA/1285. Lake Success, New York, 1950.

Semir Sanbar's Radio Address, UN Special Commissioner. Asmara, Eritrea, April 27, 1993.

UNOVER ERITREA, Department of Public Information, New York, DP1/ 1334 – March 1993 – 3M.

United States Government. *Ethiopia and the Horn of Africa, Hearings Before the Subcommittee on African Affairs of the Ninety-Fourth Congress, Second Session on US Relations with Ethiopia and the Horn of Africa.* Washington, DC: Government Printing Office, August 4–6, 1976.

Foreign Service Despatch (FSD), no. 775a.21/6–1953, June 10, 1953; no. 775.00/ 6.2058, June 20, 1958; no. 775a.c/4–2159, April 21, 1959; no. 775a.00/6–1561, June 15, 1961; no. 771/00/8–3061, August 30, 1961; no. 775a.00/10–261, October 2, 1961; no. 775.00.00/11–1561, November 15, 1961; no. 775a.00/ 5.2562, May 25, 1962; no. 775a.006–562, June 5, 1962; no. 775.00a/6662, June 6, 1962; no. 775a.00/7462, July 4, 1962; no. 775a.00/7–362, July 3, 1962;

Human Rights and Food Aid in Ethiopia. Hearing before the Subcommittee on Human Rights and International Organizations and the Subcommittee on Africa of the Committee of Representatives, 100th Congress, Second Session. Washington, DC: US Government Printing Office, April 21, 1988.

NEWSPAPERS AND PERIODICALS

Addis Zemen, June 18, 1991; July 5, 1991.
Africa Analysis, no. 45, April 15, 1988.
Africa Confidential, November 18, 1988; November 8, 1991.
Africa Magazine, no. 44, April 1975.
African Business, February 1993.
Africa Research Bulletin, October 15, 1989.
Africa Watch, July 24, 1990.
Andinet'n Me'belnaan/Unione e Progresso, no. 12, May 25, 1952.
Arab News, February 24, 1990.
BBC Focus on Africa, vol. 3, no. 3, July–September 1992.
Christian Science Monitor, February 3, 1993.
Economist, March 20, 1993.
Eritrean Medical Journal, vol. 2, no. 2, Octobr 1984.
Ethiopia, no. 79, October 31, 1948.
Ethiopian Herald, May 26, 1988.
Foreign Broadcasting Information System (FBIS), May 16, 1988; October 17, 1989; October 19, 1989; October 24, 1989; November 3, 1989.
Foreign Report, no. 212, May 24, 1990.
Gazetta del Popolo, Milano, June 7, 1936.
Hadas Ertra, May 1991; September 1991; October 1991; March 1992; April 1992; May 1992; August 1992; September 1992; October 1992; November 1992; February 1993; April 1993; May 1993; June 1993; July 1993; August 1993.
Jeune Afrique, no. 1648, August 6–12, 1992.
Los Angeles Times, April 9, 1991; April 19, 1991.
Nai Ertra Semunawi Gazeta, October 1946; November 1946–December 1946; December 1946; January 1947; February 1947; March 1947; April–May 1947; May–June 1947; June–July 1947; August 1947; March 1949; May 1949; July 1949; February 1950; March–April 1950; May 1952.
The Nation, May 31, 1993.
New Africa, December 1988; June 1990; July 1990.

The New York Times, January 11, 1991; February 24, 1991.
Oil and Gas Journal, December 7, 1992.
Washington Post, March 24, 1988.
Zemen, November 15, 1962.

BOOKS AND ARTICLES

Adamson, Walter L. *Hegemony and Revolution: A Study of Antonio Gramsci's Political and Cultural Theory*. Berkeley: University of California Press, 1980.

Ajala, Adekeunle. *Pan-Africanism: Evolution, Progress and Prospects*. New York: St. Martin's Press, 1974.

Assefa, Hizkias. "The Challenge of Mediation in Internal Wars:Reflections on the INN Experience in the Ethiopian/Eritrean Conflict," *Security Dialogue*. 3:23, 1992.

Austin, Dennis. "Things Fall Apart?" *Orbis*, 25:4, Winter 1982.

Azikwe, Nnamdi. *Renascent Africa*. London: Frank Cass and Co., 1937.

Babu, A. M. "Eritrea: Its Present is the Remote Future of Others," in *Eritrea: The Way Forward. Proceedings of a Conference on Eritrea*, organized by the United Nations Association, November 9, 1985. UNA–UK, May 1986.

"The Eritrean Question in the Context of African Conflicts and Superpower Rivalries," in Lionel Cliffe and Basil Davidson (eds.), *The Long Struggle of Eritrea for Independence and Constructive Peace*. Trenton, NJ: Red Sea Press Inc., 1988.

Balsvik, Randi Ronning. *Haile Selassie's Students: The Intellectual and Social Background to Revolution, 1952–1977*. East Lansing, MI: Michigan State University, 1985.

Bender, Gerald J., Coleman, James S., and Sklar, Richard S. (eds.). *African Crises Areas and US Foreign Policy*. Berkeley: University of California Press, 1985.

Bennet, Leroy A. *International Organizations: Principles and Issues*. Englewood Cliffs, NJ: Prentice-Hall, 1988.

Brownlie, Ian (ed.). *Basic Documents on African Affairs*. Oxford: Oxford University Press, 1971.

Bull, Hedley. *The Anarchical Society: A Study of Order in World Politics*. London: Macmillan Publishers, 1977.

(ed.), *Intervention in World Politics*. Oxford: Clarendon Press, 1984.

Butler, Lily. "Who is Winning in Eritrea?" *New Africa*, December 1988.

Campbell, Horace. *Rasta and Resistance: From Marcus Garvey to Walter Rodney*. Trenton, NJ: Africa World Press, 1987.

Caulk, Richard. "'Black Snake, White Snake': Bahta Hagos and his Revolt against Italian Overrule in Eritrea, 1894," in Donald Crummey (ed.). *Banditry, Rebellion and Social Protest in Africa*. London: James Currey Ltd., 1986.

Chege, Michael. "Conflict in the Horn of Africa," in Emmanuel Hansen (ed.), *Africa: Perspectives on Peace and Development*. London: The United Nations University, 1987.

Clapham, Christopher. *Transformation and Continuity in Revolutionary Ethiopia*. Cambridge: Cambridge University Press, 1988.

Clark, Ian. *The Hierarchy of States: Reform and Resistance in the International Order*. Cambridge: Cambridge University Press, 1989.

Cliffe, Lionel. "The Eritrean Liberation Struggle in Comparative Perspective," in

Lionel Cliffe and Basil Davidson (eds.), *The Long Struggle of Eritrea for Independence and Constructive Peace*. Trenton, NJ: Red Sea Press Inc., 1988.

"Forging a Nation: The Eritrean Experience," *Third World Quarterly*, 2:4, October 1989.

Cohen, Herman J. "Statement by Herman J. Cohen, Assistant Secretary of State for African Affairs before the Subcommittee on Africa of the Foreign Affairs Committee and the International Task Force of the Select Committee on Hunger." February 28, 1990.

Coleman, James S. "Nationalism in Tropical Africa," *American Political Science Review*, 48:2, June 1954.

Nigeria: Background to Nationalism. Berkeley: University of California Press, 1960.

Cox, Richard. *Pan-Africanism in Practice: PAFMECA 1958–1964*. London: Oxford University Press, 1964.

Crummey, Donald (ed.), *Banditry, Rebellion and Social Protest in Africa*. London: James Currey Ltd., 1986.

Davidson, Basil. *The Black Star: A View of the Life and Times of Kwame Nkrumah*. Boulder: Westview Press, rev. edn. 1989.

"The Eritrean Question: The Ways Forward," in Lionel Cliffe and Basil Davidson, (eds.). *The Long Struggle of Eritrea for Independence and Constructive Peace*. Trenton, NJ: Red Sea Press Inc., 1988.

Djilas, Aleksa. *The Contested Country: Yugoslav Unity and Communist Revolution, 1919–1953*. Cambridge: Cambridge University Press, 1991.

Dugan, James and Lafore, Laurence. *Days of Emperor and the Clown: The Italo-Ethiopian War, 1935–1936*. New York: Doubleday & Co., 1973.

Edmondson, Locksley. "Pan-Africanism and the International System: Challenges and Opportunities," in W. Ofuatey-Kodjoe (ed.), *Pan Africanism: New Descriptions in Strategy*. Lanham: University Press of America, 1986.

El-Ayouty, Yassin and Zartman, William I. (eds.). *The OAU after Twenty Years*. New York: Praeger Publishers, 1984.

Ellingson, Lloyd S. "The Emergence of Political Parties in Eritrea, 1941–1950," *Journal of African History*, 18:2, 1977.

"Eritrea: Separatism And Irredentism, 1941–1985." Unpublished PhD dissertation, Michigan State University, 1986.

Ellis, John. *The Social History of the Machine Gun*. New York: Pantheon Books, 1970.

Emerson, Rupert. "The Problem of Identity, Selfhood and Image in the New Nations: The Situation in Africa," *Comparative Politics*, 1:3, April 1969.

Entelis, John P. *Algeria: The Revolution Institutionalized*. Boulder: Westview Press, 1986.

Erlich, Haggai. *Ethiopia and the Challenge of Independence*. Boulder: Lynne Rienner Publishers, 1986.

"The Soviet Union and Ethiopia: The Misreading of *Politica Sciona* and *Politica Tigrina*," in Dennis L. Bark (ed.), *The Red Orchestra: The Case of Africa, Volume II*. Stanford: Hoover Institution Press, 1988.

The Struggle Over Eritrea, 1962–1978: War and Revolution in the Horn of Africa. Stanford: Hoover Institution Press, 1983.

Farah, Nuruddin. *Sardines*. Saint Paul, MN: Greywolf Press, 3rd edn., 1992.

Farer, Thomas J. *War Clouds on the Horn of Africa.* Washington, DC: Carnegie Endowment for International Peace, 1976.

Fessehatzion, Tekie. "Eritrea: From Federation to Annexation, 1952–1962." Washington, DC: Eritreans for Peace and Democracy, Working Paper no. 2, March 1990.

Firebrace, James and Holland, Stuart. *Never Kneel Down: Drought, Development and Liberation in Eritrea.* Nottingham, England: Bertrand Russell House, 1984.

Foucault, Michel. *The Order of Things: An Archeology of the Human Sciences.* New York: Vintage Books, 1973.

Freund, Bill. *The Making of Contemporary Africa: The Development of African Society Since 1800.* Bloomington: Indiana University Press, 1984.

Gauch, Sarah. "Eritrea Seeks Industrial Revival," *African Business,* February 1993.

Gebre-Medhin, Jordan. *Peasants and Nationalism in Eritrea: A Critique of Ethiopian Studies.* Trenton, NJ: Red Sea Press Inc., 1989.

Ghirma, Be'aalu. *Oromai.* Addis Ababa: Kuraz Publishing Agency, 1983.

Gilkes, Patrick. *The Dying Lion: Feudalism and Modernization in Ethiopia.* New York: St. Martin's Press, 1975.

Gill, Peter. *A Year in the Death of Africa: Politics, Bureaucracy, and the Famine.* London: Grafton Books, 1986.

Gill, Stephen. *American Hegemony and the Trilateral Commission.* Cambridge: Cambridge University Press, 1990.

Gilpin, Robert. *The Political Economy of International Relations.* Princeton: Princeton University Press, 1987.

Gray, J. C. and Silberman, L. *The Fate of Italy's Colonies: A Report to the Fabian Colonial Bureau.* London: Fabian Publications Ltd., July 1948.

Greenfield, Richard. *Ethiopia: A New Political History.* New York: Praeger Publishers Inc., 1965.

Gunther, John. *Inside Africa.* New York: Harper Brothers, 1963.

Habteselassie, Bereket. *Conflict and Intervention in the Horn of Africa.* New York: Monthly Review Press, 1980.

Eritrea and the United Nations. Trenton, NJ: Red Sea Press Inc., 1989.

Halliday, Fred. *Revolution and Foreign Policy: The Case of South Yemen, 1968–1987.* Cambridge: Cambridge University Press, 1990.

Harbeson, John W. *The Ethiopian Transformation: The Quest for the Post-Imperial State,* Boulder: Westview Press, 1988.

Henze, Paul B. "Eritrea," in Michael Radu (ed.), *The New Insurgencies: Anticommunist Guerrillas in the Third World.* New Brunswick: Transaction Publishers, 1990.

"Eritrea: The Economic Challenge." Presented at a conference of Eritreans for Peace and Democracy, Baltimore, MD, November 3–4, 1990.

"The Soviet Impact on African Political Dynamics," in Dennis L. Bark (ed.), *The Red Orchestra: The Case of Africa, Volume II.* Stanford: Hoover Institution Press, 1988.

Hoare, Quintin and Nowell Smith, Geoffrey (eds.). *Selections from the Prison Notebooks of Antonio Gramsci.* New York: International Publishers, 1971.

Hobsbawm, Eric J. *The Age of Empire, 1875–1914.* New York: Vintage Books, 1989.

Bandits. New York: Pantheon Books, rev. edn., 1981.

Nations and Nationalism Since 1780: Programme, Myth and Reality. Cambridge: Cambridge University Press, 1990.

Primitive Rebels: Studies in Archaic Forms of Social Movements in the 19th and 20th Centuries. New York: W. W. Norton & Co. Inc., 1959.

Hobsbawm, Eric J. and Ranger, Terence (eds.). *The Invention of Tradition*. Cambridge: Cambridge University Press, 1983.

Holmes, John W. "The Way of the World," *International Journal*, Canadian Institute of International Affairs, 35:2, Spring 1980.

Houtart, François. "Social Aspects of the Eritrean Revolution," *Eritrean Symposium*, London, January 12–13, 1979.

Hubbell, Stephen. "Eritrea Nascent: The Next Fight for Independence," *The Nation*, May 31, 1993.

Iyob, Ruth. "Reassessing Ethiopia's Claim to Uniqueness," *Africa Today*, 36: 3–4, 1989.

Jackson, Robert H. "Negative Sovereignty in sub-Saharan Africa," *Review of International Studies*, 12:2, 1986.

Jackson, Robert H. and Rosberg, Carl G. "Why Africa's Weak States Persist: The Empirical and Juridical in Statehood," *World Politics*, 35:1, October 1992.

Jansson, Kurt, Harris, Michael and Penrose, Angela. *The Ethiopian Famine*. London: Zed Press, 1987.

Jones, Scott. "Environment and Development in Eritrea," *Africa Today*, 38:2, 1991.

Kaplan, Robert D. *Surrender or Starve: The Wars Behind the Famine*. Boulder: Westview Press, 1988.

Kapuscinski, Ryszard. *The Emperor: Downfall of an Autocrat*. New York: Vintage Books, 1984.

Keeley, James F. "Towards a Foucauldian Analysis of International Regimes," *International Organization*, 44:1, Winter 1990.

Keller, Edmond J. "The Politics of State Survival: Continuity and Change in Ethiopian Foreign Policy," *Annals*, 489, January 1987.

Revolutionary Ethiopia: From Empire to People's Republic. Bloomington: Indiana University Press, 1988.

"United States Foreign Policy on the Horn of Africa: Policymaking With Blinders On," in Gerald Bender, James S. Coleman, and Richard S. Sklar (eds.), *African Crises Areas and US Foreign Policy*. Berkeley: University of California Press, 1985.

Keller, Edmond J. and Rothchild, Donald (eds.). *Afro-Marxist Regimes: Ideology and Public Policy*. Boulder: Lynne Rienner Publishers, 1987.

Keohane, Robert and Nye, Joseph S. *Power and Interdependence: World Politics in Transition*. Boston: Little and Brown, 1977.

King, Kenneth (ed.). *Ras Makonnen: Pan-Africanism From Within*. Oxford: Oxford University Press, 1973.

Kolmodin, Johannes. *Traditions de Tsazzega et Hazzega: Textes Tigrigna*. Archives d'Etudes Orientales, 5:1. Rome: J. A. Lundell, 1912.

Laidi, Zaki. *The Superpowers in Africa: The Constraints of a Rivalry, 1960–1990*. Chicago: University of Chicago Press, 1990.

Lears, T. J. Jackson. "The Concept of Cultural Hegemony: Problems and Possibilities," *The American Historical Review*, 90:3, June 1985.

Lefort, René. *Ethiopia: The Heretical Revolution?* London: Zed Press, 1983.

Legum, Colin. "After Menghistu, What?" *New Africa*, July 1990.

"Menghistu's Dilemma," *New Africa*, June 1990.

"Pan-Africanism and Communism," in Sven Hamrell and Carl Gosta Widstrand (eds.), *The Soviet Bloc, China and Africa*. Uppsala: Scandinavian Institute of African Studies, 1964.

Pan-Africanism: A Short Political Guide. New York: Praeger Publishers, 1962.

Legum, Colin and Lee, Bill. *The Horn of Africa in Continuing Crisis*. New York: Africana Publishing Company, 1979.

Lemarchand, René. "Africa's Troubled Transitions," *Journal of Democracy*, 3:4, October 1992.

The Green and the Black: Qadhafi's Policies in Africa. Bloomington: Indiana University Press, 1988.

"Uncivil States and Civil Societies: How Illusion Became Reality," *Journal of Modern African Studies*, 30:2, June 1992.

Leonard, Richard. "European Colonization and the Socio-Economic Integration of Eritrea," in *Proceedings of the Permanent People's Tribunal of the International League for the Rights and Liberation of Peoples, Session on Eritrea, Milan, Italy, May 24–26, 1980*. Rome: Research and Information Center on Eritrea, 1984.

"Popular Participation in Liberation and Revolution," in Lionel Cliffe and Basil Davidson (eds.), *The Long Struggle of Eritrea for Independence and Constructive Peace*. Trenton, NJ: Red Sea Press Inc., 1988.

Levine, Donald N. *Greater Ethiopia: The Evolution of a Multiethnic Society*. Chicago: University of Chicago Press, 1974.

Le Vine, Victor and Luke, Timothy. *The Arab-African Connection: Political and Economic Realities*. Boulder: Westview Press, 1979.

Lewis, Bernard. *Race and Slavery in the Middle East: An Historical Enquiry*. New York: Oxford University Press, 1990.

Lewis, I. M. (ed.). *Nationalism and Self-determination in the Horn of Africa*. London: Ithaca Press, 1983.

Longrigg, Stephen H. *A Short History of Eritrea*. Westport, CT: Greenwood Press Publishers, 1945.

Lonsdale, John. "African Pasts in Africa's Future," *Canadian Journal of African Studies*, 25:1, 1989.

Lopez-Alves, Fernando. "Political Crises, Strategic Choices, and Terrorism: The Rise and Fall of the Uruguyan Tupamaros," *Journal of Terrorism and Political Violence*, 3:1, Fall 1989.

MacFarlane, S. Neil. *Superpower Rivalry and 3rd World Radicalism: The Ideas of National Liberation*. London: Croom Helm, 1985.

Manning, Patrick. *Slavery and African Life: Occidental, Oriental, and African Slave Trades*. Cambridge: Cambridge University Press, 1990.

Mansbach, Richard. *The Web of World Politics: Non-State Actors in the Global System*. Englewood Cliffs, NJ: Prentice-Hall, 1976.

Marcus, Harold G. *Ethiopia, Great Britain, and the United States 1941–1974: The Politics of Empire*. Berkeley: University of California Press, 1983.

Markakis, John. *National and Class Conflict in the Horn of Africa*. Cambridge: Cambridge University Press, 1987.

"The Nationalist Revolution in Eritrea," *Journal of Modern African Studies*,

26:1, March 1988.

Markakis, John and Ayele, Nega. *Class and Revolution in Ethiopia*. Trenton, NJ: Red Sea Press Inc., 1986.

Mayall, James. *Nationalism and International Society*. Cambridge: Cambridge University Press, 1990.

"Self-Determination and the OAU," in I. M. Lewis (ed.), *Nationalism and Self-determination in the Horn of Africa*. London: Ithaca Press, 1983.

Mazrui, Ali A. and Tidy, Michael. *Nationalism and New States in Africa*. Nairobi: Heinemann Educational Books, 1984.

McCaan, James. *From Poverty to Famine in Northeastern Ethiopia: A Rural History, 1900–1935*. Philadelphia: University of Pennsylvania Press, 1987.

Medhanie, Tesfatsion. *Eritrea: Dynamics of a National Question*. Amsterdam: B. R. Gruner, 1986.

Morgenthau, Hans J. "International Organization and Foreign Policy," in *Foundations of World Organization: A Political and Cultural Appraisal*. New York: Harper & Brothers, 1952.

Nadel, S. F. "Land Tenure on the Eritrean Plateau." *Journal of the International African Institute*, 16, January 1946.

Races and Tribes of Eritrea. Asmara: British Military Administration, Eritrea, January 1944.

Nagati, Mahmoud. "Red Sea Oil Shows Attract Attention to Miocene Salt, Post-Salt Sequence," *Oil and Gas Journal*, December 7, 1992.

Naldi, Gino. *The Organisation of African Unity: An Analysis of its Role*. London: Mansell Publishing Ltd., 1989.

Negash, Tekeste. *No Medicine for the Bite of a White Snake: Notes on Nationalism and Resistance in Eritrea, 1890–1940*. Uppsala: Reprocentralen HSC, 1986.

Niblock, Tim. *Class and Power in the Sudan: The Dynamics of Sudanese Politics, 1898–1985*. New York: State University of New York Press, 1987.

Nzongola-Ntalaja, Georges. "The National Question and the Crisis of Instability in Africa," in Emmanuel Hansen (ed.), *Africa: Perspectives on Peace and Development*. London: The United Nations University, 1987.

Oded, Arye. *Africa and the Middle East Conflict*. Boulder: Lynne Rienner Publishers, 1987.

Oliver, Paula. *Sahara: Drama de una Decolonizacion, 1960–1987*. Mallorca, Spain: Miquel Font Editor, 1987.

Padmore, George. *Pan-Africanism or Communism*. New York: Doubleday & Co., Inc., 1971.

Pankhurst, E. Sylvia. *Eritrea on the Eve: The Past and the Future of Italy's "First-Born" Colony, Ethiopia's Ancient Sea Province*. Essex: Lalibela House, 1952.

Pankhurst, E. Sylvia and Pankhurst, Richard K. P. *Ethiopia and Eritrea: The Last Phase of the Reunion Struggle, 1941–1952*. Essex: Lalibela House, 1953.

Pateman, Roy. *Eritrea: Even the Stones Are Burning*. Trenton, NJ: Red Sea Press Inc., 1990.

"The Eritrean War," *Armed Forces and Society*, 17:1, Transaction Periodicals Consortium, Fall 1990.

Patman, Robert. *The Soviet Union and the Horn*. Cambridge: Cambridge University Press, 1990.

Payne, Richard J. *Opportunities and Dangers of Soviet–Cuban Expansion: Toward a Pragmatic US Policy*. New York: State University of New York, 1988.

Perham, Margery. *The Colonial Reckoning: The End of Imperial Rule in Africa in the Light of British Experience.* New York: Alfred Knopf, 1962.

Pettersen, Donald. "US Policy in the Horn of Africa, Ethiopia Abandoned? An American Perspective," *International Affairs,* 62:4, Autumn 1986.

Poscia, Stefano. *Eritrea: Colonia Tradita. (Eritrea: A Colony Betrayed.)* Rome: Edizioni Associate, 1989.

Puglisi, Giuseppe. *Chi'e dell'Eritrea? Dizionario Biografico. (Who is Who in Eritrea?)* Asmara: Agenzia Regina, 1952.

Rossini, C. Conti. *Proverbi Tradizionali e Canzoni Tigrini (Traditional Tigrigna Proverbs and Songs).* Italia: Amboglio Airoldi, 1942.

Sabbe, Osman Saleh. *The History of Eritrea.* Trans. Muhammad Fawaz Al Azein. Beirut: Dar Al-Masirah, 1974.

Said, Edward. "Figures, Configurations and Transfigurations," *Race & Class,* 32:1, July–September 1990.

Salen, Heba. "Now that the War is Over," *BBC Focus on Africa,* 3:3, July–September 1992.

Sandbrook, Richard. *The Politics of Africa's Economic Stagnation.* Cambridge: Cambridge University Press, 1985.

Schechterman, Bernard. "Horn of Africa Liberation Movements," *Middle East Review,* 19:1, Fall 1986.

Schwab, Peter. *Haile Selassie I: Ethiopia's Lion of Judah.* Chicago: Nelson-Hall Inc., 1979.

Seton-Watson, Hugh. *Nations and States: An Enquiry into the Origins of Nations and the Politics of Nationalism.* London: Methuen & Co., 1977.

Shepherd jun., George. *The Trampled Grass: Tributary States and Self-Reliance in the Indian Ocean Zone of Peace.* New York: Praeger Publisher, 1987.

Shepherd, Jack. *The Politics of Starvation.* New York: Carnegie Endowment for International Peace, 1975.

Sherman, Richard. *Eritrea: The Unfinished Revolution.* New York: Praeger Publishers, 1980.

Shoemaker, Christopher C. and Spanier, John. *Patron–Client State Relationships: Multilateral Crises in the Nuclear Age.* New York: Praeger Publishers, 1984.

Sklar, Richard S. "Democracy in Africa," in Patrick Chabal (ed.), *Political Domination in Africa: Reflections on the Limits of Power.* Cambridge: Cambridge University Press, 1986.

Smart, Barry. *Michel Foucault.* London: Tavistock Publications, 1985.

Spencer, Dayle, Spencer, William J., and Yang, Honggang. "Closing the Mediation Gap: The Ethiopia/Eritrea Experience," *Security Dialogue,* 3:23, 1992.

Spencer, John H. *Ethiopia at Bay: A Personal Account of the Haile Selassie Years.* Algonac, Michigan: Reference Publications Inc., 1987.

"Haile Selassie: Triumph and Tragedy." *Orbis,* 18:4, Winter 1975.

Tesfagiorgis, Gebre Hiwet. *Eritrea: A Case of Self-Determination.* Washington, DC: Eritreans for Peace and Democracy, Working Paper no. 1, January 1990.

Trevaskis, G. K. N. *Eritrea: A Colony in Transition, 1941–52.* London: Oxford University Press, 1960.

Triska, Jan F. (ed.). *Dominant States and Subordinate States: The United States in Latin America and the Soviet Union in Eastern Europe.* Durham: Duke University Press, 1986.

Von Glahn, Gerhard. *Law Among Nations.* New York: Macmillan Press, 1986.

Wallerstein, Immanuel. *The Politics of the World-Economy: The States, the Movements and the Civilizations.* Cambridge: Cambridge University Press, 1984.

"Voluntary Associations," in James S. Coleman and Carl Rosberg jun. (eds.), *Political Parties and National Integration in Tropical Africa.* Berkeley: University of California Press, 1964.

Welch, jun., Claude E. "The OAU and International Recognition: Lessons From Uganda," in Yassin El-Ayouti and I. M. Zartman (eds.), *The Organization of African Unity after Ten Years: Comparative Perspectives.* New York: Praeger Publishers, 1975.

White, N. D. *The United Nations and the Maintenance of International Peace and Security.* Manchester: Manchester University Press, 1990.

Wilson, Amrit. *Women and the Eritrean Revolution: The Challenge Road.* Trenton, NJ: Red Sea Press Inc., 1991.

Wolde Giorgis, Dawit. *Red Tears: War, Famine and Revolution in Ethiopia.* Trenton, NJ: Red Sea Press Inc., 1989.

Woldemariam, Mesfin. *Rural Vulnerability to Famine in Ethiopia, 1958–1977.* London: Intermediate Technology Publications, 1986.

Woronoff, Jon. *Organizing African Unity.* Metuchen, NJ: Scarecrow Press Inc., 1970.

Yohannes, Okbazghi. *Eritrea: A Pawn in World Politics.* Gainesville: University of Florida Press, 1991.

Young, Crawford. *Ideology and Development in Africa.* New Haven: Yale University Press, 1982.

"Self-Determination Revisited: Has Decolonization Closed the Question?" International Conference on the Conflict in the Horn of Africa. Madrid, Spain, September 12–14, 1989.

ORGANIZATIONAL SOURCES

EDM. *Political Statement of the Provisional Central Committee (PCC), Eritrean Democratic Movement (EDM) on the Presentation of Our Revolution.* Kassala, Sudan, October 1, 1983.

EDMLE. *Democraciawi Men'kis'kas Harnet Ertra: Temekuro DMHaE* (The Democratic Movement for the Liberation of Eritrea: The Experiences of the EDMLE). July 1989.

EFLNA. *Liberation* 2:3, March 1973.

ELF. *Eritrea: The National Democratic Revolution versus Ethiopian Expansionism.* Beirut, Lebanon: ELF Foreign Information Center, 1979.

"We Are Part and Parcel of the International Workers' Movement." *Eritrean Revolution,* 1:6 (October 1976–April 1977), Beirut, Lebanon: ELF Foreign Information Center, 1977.

ELF–PLF. *Eritrea: A Victim of UN Decision and of Ethiopian Aggression. Appeal of the Eritrean People to the 26th Session of the General Assembly.* New York, December 3, 1971.

First Organizational Congress 1977: The Resolution and the Constitution. ELF–PLF Information Office, 1977.

Misery of Progressiveness in the Arab World. Information Department, 1978.

"OAU Must Do Something to Stop Ethiopian Crimes in Eritrea: Eritrean Liberation Front Demands Formation of an African Commission of Inquiry on Eritrea," *The Eritrean Review*, 26, July 1975.

United Nations Documents on Eritrea. Tripoli, Arab Libyan Republic: ELF–PLF Foreign Mission, 1971.

EPLF. *"Abnetawi Hadnet"* (A Commendable Unity). *Fitzametat*, 120, September 1987.

Adulis, 8:5, May 1990.

A'enawi Minkiskas nai 1973 (The Destructive Movement of 1973). Eritrea, 1973.

"Africa Ketek'lebelu Zigba'e Amaratzi Fetah" (Resolutions that Africa should Pay Attention To). *Dimtzi Hafash*, EPLF radio broadcasts, July 14–20, 1990.

Democraciawi Baa'tatat Hegi Enda'Ba (Democratic Traditions of Customary Laws). July 7, 1992.

Dictionary: English-Tigrigna-Arabic. Rome: RICE, 1985.

"EDM m's EPLF Tetzenbiru" (EDM United with EPLF). *Sagem*, 2:11, November 1990.

Eritrea Challenge, 4, July 1989; 9, October 1990.

Ertra'n Kalsan'n: Kab Tinti Ksab 1941 (The Eritrean Struggle from Antiquity to 1941). January 1987.

Fitzame'tat, 120, 1987.

Hafeshawi Politicawi Temherti: 1 Kifli, Tikimiti 1978 (General Political Education, Part I, October 1978). Reprinted Boston: Asmara Printing Company, 1980.

Hafeshawi Politicawi T'mherti N'Tegadelti (General Political Education for Fighters). Eritrea, 1975.

"Hamed D'bae Nadew Keme'i Nei'ru?" (How was the "Nadew" garrison destroyed?) *Sagem*, 11, April 1988.

"Issaias Afeworki's Speech Delivered At Chatham House." *Adulis*, November 1988.

"Kalsi Ab Meda Diplomacy" (The Diplomatic Struggle). *Sagem*, 1, July 1987.

Kedamay Wudbawi Guba'e nai Hizbawi Hailtat Harnet Ertra (First EPLF Organizational Congress). January 31, 1977.

Memorandum to the 42nd Regular Sessions of the United Nations General Assembly. New York, October 1987.

Neh'naan Elamaa'nan (Our Struggle and its Goals). Eritrea, *Hizbawi Hailtat Harnet Ertra*, November 1971.

Objectives of the National Democratic Programme: First Organizational Congress. Eritrea, January 31, 1977.

Political Report and National Democratic Programme, Adopted at the Second and Unity Congress of the Eritrean People's Liberation Front and the Eritrean Liberation Front (Central Committee). Eritrea, March 19, 1987.

"Press Conference of Ato Issaias Afeworki," *Hadas Ertra* no. 78, May 29, 1993.

"Proclamation on the Structure, Powers and Tasks of the Government of Eritrea," *Hadas Ertra* no. 76, May 22, 1993.

"Referendum: Enko Agebab n' Nebari Fetah" (Referendum: The Only Path to a Lasting Solution.) *Sagem*, 2:6, June 1990.

"Statement Calling On The United Nations To Supervise A Referendum in Eritrea." Washington, DC: EPLF Office, May 8, 1990.

"*Ze'yelo Degef Hagerat Arab n'Sowra Ertra*" (Non-Existent Arab Support for the Eritrean Revolution). *Sagem* 2:8, August 1990.

ETEL. *Mae'bel Shekalay*. 1:1, September 1990.

TPLF. *Gemgam:Kh'alsi Hizbi Ertra: Kabei Na'bei* (An Assessment of the Struggle of the Eritrean People). April 1986.

INTERVIEWS

Interview with Abdu Abdellah, member of the ELF–RC, Head of the Public Information and Culture Bureau, August 11, 1990, Rome, Italy.

Interview with Andeab Gebremeskel, former EDM leader, Los Angeles, California, USA, May 4, 1991.

Interview with Ato Arefaine Berhe, Minister Counselor and Deputy Head of Mission, Embassy of Eritrea. Washington, DC, USA, August 9, 1993.

Interview with Ato Woldeab Woldemariam, Rome, Italy, August 3, 1990.

Interview with Dr. Bereket Habteselassie, EPLF representative to the UN. Telephone interview, Washington, DC, USA, September 6, 1991,

Interview with Blatta Omer and Kegnezmatch Gebreyesus, Adi Keih, Eritrea, August 1990.

Interview with Kesete Habtezion, New York, USA, August 14, 1990.

OTHER

Issaias Afeworki, "Address on Independence Day." Asmara, Eritrea, May 24, 1993.

Video cassette of the 1987 Bologna Congress. Eritrean People's Liberation Front. Bologna, Italy 1987.

ABC News Video, "War in Eritrea," MPI Home Video Presentation, ABC News Production, no. 052990.

Index

Abay, Haregot, 70
Abdelkerim, Ahmed, 111
Abdulla, Mohammed, 74
Adem, Idris, M., 57, 89, 103, 104, 109, 111, 115
Adem, Taha, 70
administration, 4, 146
Afeworki, Issaias, 114, 115, 129, 141–2, 144–5
Africa
  Ethiopia as symbol of, 25, 42–3
  post-WWII order, 35–8
  and the UN, 31
  unity of, 40–1, 47–51, 127–8
African National Congress, see ANC
aid, 44, 143
Ali, Blatta Mohamed Abdella, 73
Amharization, 90, 101, 102
ANC (African National Congress), 52
Andom, Aman, 118–19
annexation of Eritrea, 2, 88–91, 94
Arab states
  influence on armed struggle, 13, 15
  and liberation movements, 52
  support for Eritrea, 47–8, 54–5, 57, 108, 110, 124, 126, 127–8
Arabization, 25, 48, 52, 55, 108, 124, 126–7
armed struggle, 2, 5, 13, 15, 104–5 *see also* political violence, protest
artists, and nationalism, 102–3
Asberom, Tesemma, 70
Assembly, Eritrea, 87, 90, 93, 113
Association of Seven (*Mahber Shew'ate*), 101 *see also* ELM
Awate, Hamid Idris, 92, 104–5

Babu, A. M., on Eritrea, 16–17
Baduri, Omar Mohammed, 73
Bairu, Tedla, 69, 70, 72, 74, 87, 89, 113
balkanization, 25, 48, 51–2, 55, 124, 127
Beraki, Beyene, 70

Bevin–Sforza plan, 73–5, 77
Black Zionism, 27, 41, 50, 55
Blake, Robert, 93
BMA (British Military Administration), 61, 62, 67–8, 74–5, 78–9
borders, sanctity of, 56
Brazzaville group, 40
Britain, and the Horn of Africa, 62–4 *see also* BMA
British Military Administration, *see* BMA
Bull, Hedley, on hegemony, 20

Casablanca group, 40, 43
CFM (Council of Foreign Ministers), 62
Chege, Michael, on Eritrea, 19
citizenship, 138
Clapham, Christopher
  on Eritrea, 12–13, 15
  on Ethiopian revolution, 117
class division, 100
Cliffe, Lionel, on Eritrea, 17–18
colonialism, 1–2, 15–18, 30–2, 47
  and Ethiopia, 27, 54, 134
  Italian, 4, 61–2, 64
  and Pan-Africanism, 49–51
  and self-determination, 36–7, 53
  see also decolonization
Commandos, 113
communism, 58
conditional union, 68–9 *see also* federation
conflict resolution, and OAU, 39–41
Constitution of Eritrea, 83–8
  violations of, 88–9, 90–1, 102
Coptic Church, and politics, 66–7, 70–1, 72–3, 84 *see also* religion
cost of living, 88, 144 *see also* economy
Council of Foreign Ministers *see* CFM

De Rossi, Guido, 73
decolonization, 51, 61, 62–3 *see also* colonialism

demonstrations, 92–3, 102
Dergue, 3, 58
  legitimacy, 125, 134
  rise to power, 117–19
Dimetros, Keshi (Melaake Selaam), 91, 92, 105
diplomacy, Ethiopia, 44–5, 120
Drew, F. G., on Eritrean politics, 74

economy
  Eritrea, 13–14, 65, 79–80, 88–9, 129, 141, 143–5
  Ethiopia, 13–14, 44
  see also socio-economic system
EDF (Eritrean Democratic Front), 83–6
EDM (Eritrean Democratic Movement), 120–1
EDMLE (Eritrean Democratic Movement for the Liberation of Eritrea), 121
education, 102, 127, 129
Egypt, and Eritrea, 63–4, 110
El Rabita El Islamiya see ML
ELA (Eritrean Liberation Army), 112
elections, 84–7, 91
ELF (Eritrean Liberation Front), 52, 54, 98, 103–7, 108–9
  and Arab support, 57, 126
  Central Committee, 121
  challenges to, 116–17
  and ELM, 112
  and EPLF, 120–2, 131, 132
  and Ethiopia, 113
  fragmentation, 114–16, 120–2, 128
  ideology, 110
  and international recognition, 125–6
  organization, 109–114
  recruitment, 112, 113
ELF–PLF, 54, 114–16, 127–8
ELF–Ubel, 114–16
ELM (Eritrean Liberation Movement), 98, 99–107, 112
enfranchisment, 33 *see also* voting eligibility
EPLA (Eritrean People's Liberation Army), 133, 136
EPLF (Eritrean People's Liberation Front), 45, 52, 54, 108–9
  challenges to, 116–17
  development of, 123–5, 129–32
  and ELF, 120–2, 131, 132
  and government, 140
  ideology, 57–8, 131
  and independence, 141–3
  and international recognition, 126–7, 135
  legitimacy of, 124–5, 132–5
  manifesto, 126–7
  military power, 132, 133–4

objectives, 129
organization, 119, 129–32
political discourse, 133, 135
EPRDF (Ethiopian People's Revolutionary Democratic Front), 45, 131, 134
Eritrea
  and Egypt, 63–4, 110
  and Ethiopia, 118–20, 137–8, 143
  Ethiopian claims, 4–5, 63–4, 85, 93–5
  Ethiopian control, 102
  and Ethiopian unity, 47
  image, 11, 52–3, 108, 113
  independence, 11, 136–8, 143
  international recognition, 52–3, 125–8, 133, 135
  and Italy, 4, 47, 61–2, 64, 74
  and the OAU, 5, 45, 53, 128
  resistance to Ethiopia, 91–4
  and the Soviet Union, 121, 131
  and the UN, 45, 64, 73–4, 77–83, 139
  and the US, 45, 62, 92–3, 133
Eritrea for Eritreans (*Ertra n'Ertrawian*), 56–7, 66–7 *see also* LPP
Eritrean Democratic Front, *see* EDF
Eritrean Democratic Movement, *see* EDM
Eritrean Democratic Movement for the Liberation of Eritrea, *see* EDMLE
Eritrean Liberation Army, *see* ELA
Eritrean Liberation Front, *see* ELF
Eritrean Liberation Movement, *see* ELM
Eritrean People's Liberation Army, *see* EPLA
Eritrean People's Liberation Front, *see* EPLF
Eritrean War Veterans Association, *see* EWVA
Erlich, Haggai, on Eritrea, 12, 15, 120
Ertra n'Ertrawian, see Eritrea for Eritreans
Ethiopia
  aid, 44
  claims on Eritrea, 4–5, 63–4, 85, 93–5
  colonization of Eritrea, 27, 54, 134
  control of Eritrea, 102
  defeat, 136–8
  diplomacy, 44–5, 120
  economy, 13–14, 44
  and ELF, 113
  and Eritrea, 118–20, 137–8, 143
  Eritrean resistance to, 91–4
  famine, 44
  hegemony, 26–8, 41, 44–5
  historical development, 11–14
  influence of, 41–4, 52–3
  international recognition, 20
  military power, 43–4, 132, 133–4
  and OAU, 27, 43

portrayal of Eritrean struggle, 11, 52–3,
    108, 113
revolution, 117–20
and the Soviet Union, 44, 119
and liberation movements, 52–3
as symbol of Africa, 25, 42–3
unity of, 27–8, 47–8, 50, 120
and the US, 44
    see also Black Zionism, Ethiopianization,
    Greater Ethiopia, Pan-Ethiopianism
Ethiopia First (*Ityopia Tikdem*), 117
Ethiopian People's Revolutionary
    Democratic Front, *see* EPRDF
Ethiopianization, 90
ethnic divisions, 111–12, 113, 116–17
EWVA (Eritrean War Veterans
    Association), 73, 75, 83

factionalism, 72
famine, 44, 131
federation, 2, 78–9, 125–6
and annexation, 88–91
creation of, 82–8
termination of, 89–90, 94–7
    see also conditional union
First Panel of Legal Consultants, *see* FPLC
flag of Eritrea, 85, 87–8
Flames (*Nebelbal*), 119
Foucault, Michel, on the 'regime of truth',
    26
Four Powers Commission, *see* FPC
FPC (Four Powers Commission), 62–3, 73
FPLC (First Panel of Legal Consultants),
    85
France, Horn of Africa interests, 62–4

el-Gade, Yasin, 99, 101
Gebrekidan, Berhe, 71, 78
Ghebremeskel, Kidanemariam, 70
Glawdewos, Idris O., 109, 111
government of Eritrea, 138, 140–3
Gramsci, Antonio, on hegemony, 21–2
Greater Ethiopia, 11–15, 25–6, 28, 94 *see*
    also Ethiopia

Habteselassie, Bereket, on Eritrea, 15–16
Habtewold, Aklilu, 83
Hailemariam, Menghistu, 119, 136
Hailu, Ghebremedhin, 92
Hamid, Sheikh Hamid Ferej, 91
Harekat Tahrir Eritrea, *see* ELM
el-Hassan, Mohammed, 99
hegemony
    definitions, 20–6
    Ethiopian, 26–8, 41, 44–5
    regional, 22–5, 29

Henze, Paul B., on Eritrea, 13–14, 15
Hezbi-al-Watani (National Party of
    Massawa), *see* NPM
HGHE (*Hizbawi Genbar Harnet Ertra*), 116
    see also EPLF
HHHaE (*Hizbawi Hailtat Harnet Ertra*),
    116 *see also* EPLF
Hibret Sebawinet, 117–18
Hizbawi Genbar Harnet Ertra, *see* HGHE
Hizbawi Hailtat Harnet Ertra, *see* HHHaE
Hizbawi Haltat Harnet Ertra, *see* PLF
Horn of Africa, foreign interests, 62–4

IAE (Intellectual Association of Eritreans),
    73, 75, 93
Idris, Abdalla, 115
IEA (Italo-Eritrean Association), 74, 75,
    77, 83, 86
IEP (Independent Eritrea Party), 76, 83
IEUP (Independent Eritrea United with
    Ethiopia Party), 77, 83, 84
IML (Independent Moslem League), 77, 83,
    84 *see also* ML
independence, 11, 53–4, 140–3, 145
    as colonial struggle, 15–18
    and discourse, 53–4
    as "internal affair", 11–15
    as social development, 18–20
Independence Bloc, 75–8 *see also* EDF
Independence and Development Party of
    Eritrea: Eritrea for Eritreans, *see*
    LPP–Seraie
Independence and Progress Party: Eritrea
    for Eritreans, *see* LPP
Independent Eritrea Party, *see* IEP
Independent Eritrea United with Ethiopia
    Party, *see* IEUP
Independent Moslem League, *see* IML
Intellectual Association of Eritreans, *see*
    IAE
international order, and the UN, 32–5
Italo-Eritrean Association, *see* IEA
Italy, and Eritrea, 4, 47, 61–2, 64, 74
Ityopia Tikdem (Ethiopia First), 117
Iyay, Saleh Ahmed, 99, 100

Kadi, Omar, 89, 90–1
Kahsai, Woldai, 111
Kassa, Asrate, 113
Kebire, Abdel Kadir, 71, 73
Kekiya, Saleh Ahmed, 70
Keller, Edmond J.
    on Eritrea, 17
    on Ethiopia, 117–18
Kenya, 56

land reform, 130
languages, 85, 87, 102
legal reform, 138
Lemarchand, René, on hegemony, 22,
    24–5
Leonard, Richard, on Eritrea, 19
Liberal Progressive Party, see LPP
Liberal Unionist Party, see LUP
liberation movements, 17–19, 39, 51, 52 see
    also name of movement
Love of Country Association of Eritrea:
    Eritrea with Ethiopia, see MFHE
LPP (Liberal Progressive Party), 56, 70–1,
    75, 83 see also Eritrea for Eritreans
LPP–Seraie, 71
LUP (Liberal Unionist Party), 77, 83, 84

Maascio, Seyoum, 70, 77
Mahber Andinet, 69, 74
Mahber Fikri Hager Ertra: Ertra m's
    Ethiopia (Love of Country Association
    of Eritrea: Eritrea for Eritreans), see
    MFHE
Mahber Jeganu Wetahader (Eritrean War
    Veterans Association), see EWVA
Mahber M'huran Eritrawian (Intellectual
    Association of Eritreans), see IAE
Mahber Netzanet Ebyet Ertra: Ertra
    n'Ertrawian (Independence and
    Progress Party: Eritrea for Eritreans),
    see LPP Mahber Netzanet'n Limaa'tn
    Ertra: Ertra n'Ertrawain
    (Independence and Development Party
    of Eritrea: Eritrea for Eritreans), see
    LPP–Seraie
Mahber Shew'ate (Association of Seven),
    101 see also ELM
Mahber Teatre Asmara, see MTA
Makonnen, T. R., and Ethiopia, 50
Markakis, John, on Eritrea, 19, 129
Markos, Abune, 68–9, 70
Matienzo, Anze, 82–3, 87
Mayall, James, on self-determination, 55
Menkaa'e, 116–17
MFHE (Mahber Fikri Hager Ertra), 65–70
military power, 43–4, 132, 133–4
al Mirgani, Said Bubaker bin Osman, 70
ML (Moslem League), 56, 57, 70, 75, 83 see
    also IML, MLWP, NMPM
MLWP (Moslem League of Western
    Province), 77, 83, 84 see also ML
Monrovia group, 40, 43
Moslem League, see ML
Moslem League of Western Province, see
    MLWP
MTA (Mahber Teatre Asmara), 102–3

National Democratic Program, see NDP
national identity, emergence of, 1, 3–4, 11,
    56, 95–7, 123–4, 129, 143
National Moslem Party of Massawa, see
    NMPM
National Party of Massawa, see NPM
nationalism, 65–9, 96, 123–4
    and Arab support, 54–5
    and artists, 102–3
    fragmentation of, 73–81
    objectives, 98
    and religion, 57, 66
nationality, 138
natural resources, 144
Nawud, Mohamed, 99, 104, 105
NDP (National Democratic Program), 129,
    132
Nebelbal (Flames), 119
Neh'nan Elamaa'nan (Our Struggle and its
    Goals/We and Our Objectives), 115,
    126
NEP (New Eritrea Party), 75, 83 see also
    NEPIP
NEPIP (New Eritrea Pro-Italia Party), 73
    see also NEP
New Eritrea Party, see NEP
New Eritrea Pro-Italia Party, see NEPIP
NMPM (National Moslem Party of
    Massawa), 75 see also ML
NPM (National Party of Massawa), 73, 84
Nur, Ramadan Mohamed, 114, 129
Nzongola-Ntalaja, Georges, on Eritrea,
    19

OAU (Organization of African Unity), 29,
    36, 38, 43, 51
    Charter, 35–8, 51
    and conflict resolution, 39–41
    and Eritrea, 5, 45, 53, 128
    and Ethiopia, 27, 43
oil, 144
OLF (Oromo Liberation Front), 132
Oromo Liberation Front, see OLF
Our Struggle and its Goals (Neh'nan
    Elamaa'nan), 115, 126

PAFMECA (Pan-African Freedom
    Movement of East and Central
    Africa), 55–6
Pan-African Freedom Movement of East
    and Central Africa, see PAFMECA
Pan-Africanism, 38, 43, 47, 48–54, 55, 56
Pan-Ethiopianism, 41–6, 48, 55
Pateman, Roy, on Eritrea, 16
PGE (Provisional Government of Eritrea),
    138

PLF (*Hizbawi Haltat Harnet Ertra*), 114–16, 127–8
political coalitions, *see* EDF, Independence Bloc
political education, 127
political violence, 72, 74, 77, 83 *see also* armed struggle, protest
politics, 69–73, 99, 100–1
Proclamations
 no. 37/1993, 140
 no. 40/1993, 144
 no. 41/1993, 144
 no. 130, 88
protest, 99, 100–1 *see also* armed struggle, political violence
Provisional Government of Eritrea, *see* PGE

Radai, Sheikh Ali, 77, 87
referendum, 45, 131, 135, 137, 138–40, 145
regime of truth, 26–8, 41–6
religion, 71, 100, 106–7
 and ideology, 110
 and nationalism, 57, 66
 and unity, 56, 84–5, 99, 100, 103
 see also Coptic Church
religious division, 111–13
resistance, perceptions of, 52–3
res'kha me'khaal (self-reliance), 119
Resolutions, *see* UN Resolutions
revolution, Ethiopia, 117–20

Sabbe, Osman, S., 57, 104, 105, 109, 111, 115, 116, 127, 128
Sabr, Said, 99
Said, Nasser El-Din, 78
Saleh, Adem, 115
SCP (Sudanese Communist Party), 99–100
secession, 12–14, 51–2
Second Panel of Legal Consultants, *see* SPLC
Selaam, Melaake, *see* Dimetros, Keshi
Selassie, Haile, 3, 42, 93–4, 125
self-determination, 14, 32–5, 53–4
 and colonialism, 36–7, 53
 definitions, 37, 55
 limitation of, 35–7
 and territorial integrity, 37–8
self-reliance (*res'kha me'khaal*), 119
Selfi Natznet, *see* Independence Bloc
shifta activities, 72, 74, 78, 83, 92
slavery, and Pan-Africanism, 49–51
SNM (Somali National Movement), 52
social renewal, 136–7
socio-economic system, 4, 65, 144–8 *see also* economy
Somali National Movement, *see* SNM

Somali Salvation Front, *see* SSF
songs of nationalism, 91, 92, 101, 103, 136
South-West Africa People's Organization, *see* SWAPO
sovereignty, 39, 85
Soviet Union
 and Eritrea, 121, 131
 and Ethiopia, 44, 119
 Horn of Africa interests, 62–4
Spencer, John H., on Eritrea, 13, 14–15
SPLC (Second Panel of Legal Consultants), 85–6
SSF (Somali Salvation Front), 52
strikes, 91, 105–6
students, 91, 92–3, 102, 105–6
Sudanese Communist Party, *see* SCP
Sultan, Ibrahim, 65, 70, 71, 74, 75, 89, 101–2
SWAPO (South-West Africa People's Organization), 52

Tanzania, 56
Tedla, Heruy, 115, 121
territorial integrity, 18, 31–8, 43
Tesemma, Abraha, 70–1, 77
Tewolde, Abrha, 114
Tigrai, 67
Tigrai-Tigrigni, 67
Tigrayan People's Liberation Front, *see* TPLF
TPLF (Tigrayan People's Liberation Front), 132, 134
Trevaskis, G. K. N., on federation, 82

Ukbit, Tedla, 102
Umaro, Mohamed Ali, 111
UN (United Nations), 29, 30–1
 Charter, 32–3, 35
 Commission to Eritrea, 64, 77–83
 and constitutional violations, 90–1
 and Eritrea, 64, 73–4, 139
 inaction of, 5, 53, 126
 and international order, 32–5
 Security Council, 45
 see also UNOVER
UN (United Nations) Resolutions
 47/114, 137
 289 A(IV), 64, 74
 390 A(V), 82–3, 95
 1514(XV), 32–3
 2625(XXV), 34
Unionist Party, *see* UP
United States
 and Eritrea, 45, 62, 92–3, 133
 and Ethiopia, 44
 Horn of Africa interests, 62–4

UNOVER (United Nations Observer
    Mission to Verify the Referendum in
    Eritrea), 137
UP (Unionist Party), 56, 72–3, 83–4, 113
    and the Independence Bloc, 76–7

voting eligibility, 86, 138–9 *see also*
    enfranchisement

Wallerstein, Immaneul, on hegemony, 20–1
We and Our Objectives (*Neh'nan
    Elamaa'nan*), 115, 126
Woldeghiorghis, Asberom, 71
Woldemariam, Gheregziher, 73
Woldemariam, Solomon, 116

Woldemariam, Woldeab, 65, 66–7, 68–9,
    72, 76, 78, 101–2, 104–5, 116
Woldemichael, Asfha, 89, 91
Woldu, Gebremeskel, 65, 68, 69, 72
women's rights, 86, 129, 130

Yihdego, Tekie, 101
Yohannes, Sebhatu, 71

ZANU (Zimbabwe African National
    Union), 52
Zewelde, Maascio, 70
Zimbabwe African National Union, *see*
    ZANU

Other books in the series

64 Bankole-Bright and Politics in Colonial Sierra Leone: The Passing of the "Krio Era", 1919–1958 Akintola Wyse

65 Contemporary West African States Donal Cruise O'Brien, John Dunn and Richard Rathbone

66 The Oromo of Ethiopia: A History, 1570–1860 Mohammed Hassen

67 Slavery and African Life: Occidental, Oriental and African Slave Trades Patrick Manning

68 Abraham Esau's War: A Black South African War in the Cape, 1899–1902 Bill Nasson

69 The Politics of Harmony: Land Dispute Strategies in Swaziland Laurel Rose

70 Zimbabwe's Guerrilla War: Peasant Voices Norma Kriger

71 Ethiopia: Power and Protest: Peasant Revolts in the Twentieth Century Gebru Tareke

72 White Supremacy and Black Resistance in Pre-Industrial South Africa: The Making of the Colonial Order in the Eastern Cape, 1770–1865 Clifton C. Crais

73 The Elusive Granary: Herder, Farmer, and State in Northern Kenya Peter D. Little

74 The Kanyok of Zaire: An Institutional and Ideological History to 1895 John C. Yoder

75 Pragmatism in the Age of Jihad: The Precolonial State of Bundu Michael A. Gomez

76 Slow Death for Slavery: The Course of Abolition in Northern Nigeria, 1897–1936 Paul E. Lovejoy and Jan S. Hogendorn

77 West African Slavery and Atlantic Commerce: The Senegal River Valley, 1700–1860 James Searing

78 A South African Kingdom: The Pursuit of Security in Nineteenth-Century Lesotho Elizabeth A. Eldredge

79 State and Society in Pre-Colonial Asante T. C. McCaskie

80 Islamic Society and State Power in Senegal: Disciples and Citizens of Fatick Leonardo A. Villalon

81 Ethnic Pride and Racial Prejudice in Victorian Cape Town: Group Identity and Social Practice Vivian Bickford-Smith